ALSO BY TOBY WILKINSON

Early Dynastic Egypt
Royal Annals of Ancient Egypt
Genesis of the Pharaohs
Dictionary of Ancient Egypt
Lives of the Ancient Egyptians
The Egyptian World (editor)
The Rise and Fall of Ancient Egypt

The Nile

The Nile

A Journey Downriver Through Egypt's Past and Present

TOBY WILKINSON

ALFRED A. KNOPF   NEW YORK

2014

Chapter illustrations are from
The Nile; or, Glimpses of the Land of Egypt by W. H. Bartlett (1849).
Other images are from the author's own collection unless credited otherwise.

Library of Congress Cataloging-in-Publication Data
Wilkinson, Toby A. H.
The Nile : a journey downriver through Egypt's past and present /
by Toby Wilkinson.—First American edition.
pages cm
"Originally published by Bloomsbury, London, in 2014."
Includes bibliographical references and index.
ISBN 978-0-385-35155-3 (hardcover)   ISBN 978-0-385-35156-0 (eBook)
1. Wilkinson, Toby A. H.—Travel—Nile River.   2. Nile River Valley—
Description and travel.   3. Nile River Valley—History.
4. Egypt—Civilization.   I. Title.
DT116.W55 2014
962—dc23   2013045874

Jacket photograph: The Cheops pyramid at Giza, Egypt,
during a flood of the Nile, ca. 1875, by Antonio Beato.
Adoc-photos / Art Resource, N.Y.
Jacket design by Isabel Urbina Peña
Maps by John Gilkes

Manufactured in the United States of America
First American Edition

For Umm Toby

Egypt . . . is an acquired country—the gift of the river.
—HERODOTUS

Egypt is always herself, at all stages in her history.
—JEAN-FRANÇOIS CHAMPOLLION

Contents

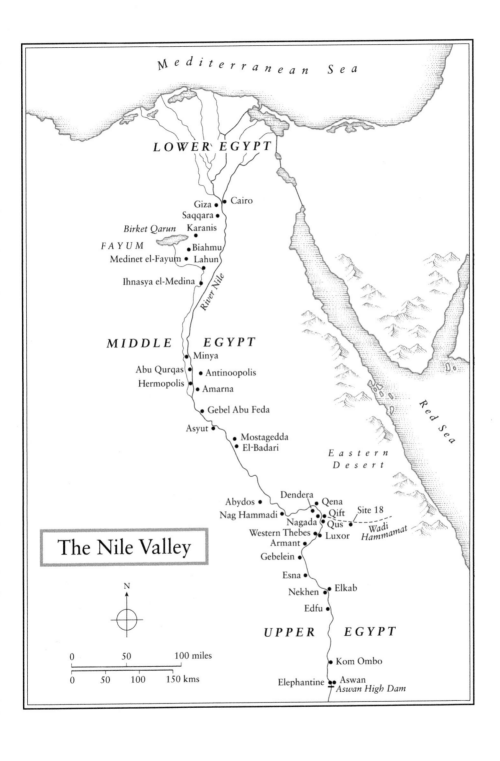

Mediterranean Sea

LOWER EGYPT

Giza • • Cairo
Saqqara •
Birket Qarun Karanis •
FAYUM • Biahmu
Medinet el-Fayum • Lahun
Ihnasya el-Medina •

River Nile

MIDDLE EGYPT
• Minya
Abu Qurqas •
Hermopolis • • Antinoopolis
• Amarna
• Gebel Abu Feda
Asyut •
• Mostagedda
• El-Badari

Eastern Desert

Red Sea

Dendera
Abydos • • Qena
Nag Hammadi • • Qift
Nagada • Site 18
Western Thebes • • Qus
Armant • Luxor *Wadi Hammamat*
Gebelein •
Esna •
Nekhen • • Elkab
Edfu •

UPPER EGYPT

The Nile Valley

N

0   50   100 miles
0   50   100   150 kms

• Kom Ombo
Elephantine • • Aswan
Aswan High Dam

Preface

The country is a palimpsest in which the Bible is written
over Herodotus, and the Koran over that.[1]

—LUCIE DUFF GORDON

Egypt is the most populous country in the world's most unstable region. It is the key to Middle East peace, the voice of the Arab world, and the crossroads between Europe and Africa. Its historical and strategic importance is unparalleled. In short, Egypt matters. Understanding the country and its people is as vital today as it has ever been.

The key to Egypt—its colourful past, chaotic present and uncertain future—is the Nile. More than two thousand years ago, the ancient Greek historian Herodotus famously remarked that Egypt is "the gift of the river,"[2] and so it is. Egypt is the Nile, the Nile Egypt. The river is the unifying thread that runs throughout Egyptian history, culture and politics. It has shaped Egypt's geography, controlled its economy, moulded its civilisation, and determined its destiny. From Egypt's earliest art (prehistoric images of fish-traps, carved into cliffs overlooking the river) to the Arab Spring (fought over on the bridges of Cairo), the Nile has been central to Egypt's story. Throughout the country, the connections between past and present are many and deep. Travelling down the Nile, past villages, towns and cities, dazzling ancient monuments and ambitious modern developments, is the best way to feel the pulse and understand the unique character of this chaotic, vital, conservative and rapidly changing land.

As I write this, in a boat on the Nile, Egypt stands at the most critical juncture of its recent history. With a past longer than most countries, its future has never looked less certain. Its first democratically elected leader—in five thousand years—has assumed dictatorial powers. Parliament and the courts are at loggerheads. Islamists and secularists are fighting (and dying) over radically different visions of Egypt's future. The balance of power in the Middle East and the entire trajectory of the Arab world rest on the outcome. The world holds its breath.

Yet with the sunlight sparkling on the water, waves lapping gently at the sides of the boat, herons wading in the shallows and fishermen casting their nets in mid-stream, there is a timelessness to life on the river that belies the momentous events sweeping the country. Political Egypt seems a world away, a distant sideshow. Rural life continues much as it has for millennia—sowing and harvesting in the fields, fishing on the Nile. The river and its rhythms, not the pronouncements of politicians, are the measure of people's lives. As one Victorian traveller to Egypt remarked, "There is a sense that transcends the passage of years or the stirring events of history. The visitor to the Nile can smell the same smells as the Ancient Egyptians, of hot dust and damp reeds, of the river itself as it flows smoothly toward the north."[3]

In a country heavy with history, the continuities and interconnections of Egypt's past and present are particularly visible along the Nile. The same stretch of water along which I am now passing has conveyed pharaonic battleships sailing south to crush rebellions in Nubia and returning laden with the spoils of battle; barges carrying great obelisks from the granite quarries of Aswan to the temples of Thebes; Ptolemaic grain-ships and Roman troop-carriers; papyrus skiffs and Cook's Nile steamers. On the banks, satellite dishes sprout from the roofs of mud-brick houses, churches and mosques jostle for space with the ruins of pagan temples, and men in galabeyas ride donkeys while talking on mobile phones.

Egyptians are acutely aware of their rich inheritance. They could not fail to be, with physical manifestations of their past all around. A common complaint about the Muslim Brothers is that they are ignoring Egypt's long history of diversity and accommodation. As an Egyptian friend put it, "They think we forgot the last seven thousand years; we didn't."[4] In an attempt to comprehend the enduring influence of those seven thousand years, this book sets out to tell the story of Egypt from the vantage point of its great river. Down the millennia, disparate periods, places and people have been united by the common experience of the Nile. Together, their stories weave the history of an entire country— a country in flux, a country that demands to be understood.

By the time this book is published, Egypt may have resolved its current crisis and charted a new course—or it may still be in limbo. It may have embraced democracy or it may have reverted to its more accustomed tradition of autocratic rule. For the vast majority of its long-suffering and resilient people, life will continue as before, a daily struggle to make ends meet, put food on the table, nurture the next generation. Amidst all the uncertainties, the Egyptians know they can count, as they always have, on the Nile. Its steady flow is the heartbeat of a nation, and its life-giving waters offer the eternal promise of a better future.

Since I finished the first draft of this book in December 2012, events in Egypt have unfolded rapidly and violently. Everything has changed and nothing has changed. In the postscript, I reflect briefly on the situation at the time of going to press.

—TOBY WILKINSON
The Nile, Egypt
December 2012

The Nile

ONE

The Nile

Egypt's Eternal River

Egypt is the Nile . . . The Nile has created its
limits and gifted it with opulence.[1]

—SAMUEL COX

Egypt covers an area of over 380,000 square miles. Ninety-five per
cent of it is barren desert. The climate across most of the country is
extremely dry, and nowhere receives sufficient rainfall to support agriculture. Without the Nile, there would be no Egypt. The narrow strip of
green—the floodplain of the Nile—that runs through Egypt from south
to north constitutes less than one-twentieth of the country by area, yet
supports more than 96 per cent of its population. As the Roman geog-

rapher Strabo put it, "Egypt consists of only the river-land";[2] and that sentiment remains as true today as it was two thousand years ago.

We now know that the Egyptian Nile is born of the confluence of two great rivers, the Blue Nile which rises in the highlands of Ethiopia, and the White Nile which is fed by Lake Victoria. Just downstream of the Sudanese capital, Khartoum, they join to form a single mighty watercourse, a river that runs northwards for a thousand miles until it reaches the sea. In the southern half of its course, barriers of hard, igneous rock intrude across the Nile Valley at various points. Each barrier causes the river to divide into narrow streams and rivulets as it surges around the natural obstacles in its path. These are the Cataracts of the Nile, conventionally numbered from north to south (even though the river flows from south to north). They are not the massive waterfalls found on other African or American rivers, but regions of rocks and rapids no less hazardous to shipping.

Only when the Nile has broken through the last such barrier—the granite outcrops of the First Cataract at Aswan—can it continue its journey, uninterrupted, to the Mediterranean. Flowing gently between cliffs of sandstone, its floodplain is at its narrowest, the strip of green on either bank no more than a few feet wide in places. Beyond the towering quarries of Gebel el-Silsila, the sandstone gives way to limestone, creating a softer landscape of age-eroded bluffs, and a broader valley. North of Luxor, the Nile swings sharply to the east in a great bend that brings it closer to the Red Sea than at any other point in its course. But it soon returns to its northwards flow, its floodplain broadening out still further in the remote backwaters of Middle Egypt. Some 625 miles from the First Cataract, the power of the Nile begins to abate and it divides into smaller channels as it makes its increasingly sluggish way to the sea, its alluvial plain fanning out to produce the Delta. (The ancient Egyptians conceptualised their land as a papyrus plant, the narrow valley forming the stalk and the broad delta the flower-head.) Finally, the river meets the sea in a series of brackish coastal lagoons before disgorging its last remaining sediment into the Mediterranean—the sea known to the ancient Egyptians as "the great green."

By way of counterpoint to this south–north direction of flow, there is the east–west dynamic of the Valley. Over the aeons, the river has shifted within its floodplain, creating and destroying alluvial land as it goes. The meandering of the river's channel means that the broader expanse of fertile alluvium is sometimes to be found on the east bank, sometimes on the west. At some points in its course, the river runs close up against the western escarpment, with barely a strip of green between; at other places, it is the eastern cliffs that approach the river's edge, while the western hills are hazy in the distance beyond the fields. It is this east–west rhythm of the river as much as its south–north flow that has determined the human geography of the Nile Valley. Between the First Cataract and the Delta, the major settlements alternate between the east and west banks, depending on the local topography: Aswan on the east, Edfu and Esna on the west; Luxor, Qift and Qena on the east; Abydos, Asyut and the towns of Middle Egypt on the west; and, finally, Cairo back on the east bank.

As well as the alluvial land that makes agriculture and human settlement possible, the Nile has also created some of the most striking and memorable scenery anywhere in the world. The landscape, with its patterns of blue, green and yellow-brown, has remained largely unchanged since the days of the pharaohs and imparts a timelessness to the Valley that somehow manages to blur the intrusions of modern life. While the Nile's green thread is most strikingly apparent from the air, the scenery along its banks is best appreciated from the water itself,

> the level bank shelving down steeply to the river; the strip of cultivated soil, green with maize or tawny with dura; the frequent mud-village and palm-grove; the deserted sugar factory with its ungainly chimney and shattered windows; the water-wheel slowly revolving with its necklace of pots; the shadûf worked by two brown athletes; the file of laden camels; the desert, all sand-hills and sand-plains, with its background of mountains; the long reach, and the gleaming sail ahead.[3]

Indeed, "the traveller on the Nile really sees the whole land of Egypt . . . through which the Nile has been scooping its way for uncounted cycles . . ."[4]

The Egyptians have always been acutely aware of their unique environment; its harmonies and contrasts have shaped their society and world view. The sharp divide between the green strip of floodplain and the yellow-brown desert on either side only emphasises the precariousness of existence and the delicate balance between feast and famine, life and death. In such a world, Egyptians of all periods have revered their river and the life it makes possible.

Since the dawn of time, Egyptians have speculated about the creation of the world; they have invented various stories, but the most powerful of the ancient myths tells how a small island emerged from the waters of chaos, like a sandbank from the Nile, bringing the possibility of life to the world. Christian and Muslim theologians came up with different accounts, but the importance of the Nile remained strong. Writing around AD 1000, the Arab scholar al-Muqaddasi praised Egypt with the following words: "God has mentioned this region repeatedly in the Qur'an, and has shown its pre-eminence to mankind. It is one of the two wings of the world . . . its river the most splendid of rivers."[5]

Belief in the Nile's creative power has continued down to modern times. After Europeans discovered the Nile, they attributed to it quasi-magical properties. Nile water was believed to encourage the birth of twins, or even sextuplets, and was exported in sealed jars for purchase by wealthy—and gullible—clients. Even as great a polymath and scholar as Jean-François Champollion, the man who deciphered hieroglyphics, took Nile water as a curative. In 1825, an Irish doctor named Dr. Richard Madden opined, "In its wholesome properties, I believe the water of the Nile exceeds that of any other river in the world . . . by its gentle action as an aperient, it benefits health"—even though his close examination of the said water under a microscope had revealed it to be "alive with animal-culae"[6] (parasites, algae and bacteria).

While the Nile's water has always been more likely to kill than cure, it does, however, have miraculous properties, properties upon which Egyptian civilisation itself was built. Until 1964 and the completion of the High Dam at Aswan, the river's unique gift was made manifest in its peculiar annual regime. Each summer, the rains falling over the Ethiopian highlands surged downhill, swelling the Blue Nile and causing it to breach its banks in a great inundation. In Egypt, the flood first became apparent in mid-July at the First Cataract—as much by the noise of the crashing torrent as by the increased volume of water. Over the course of just a few days, the flow at the Cataract rose fifteen-fold; as the flood spread northwards, the entire floodplain was inundated to a depth of six feet, with only dikes and the towns and villages on higher ground remaining dry above an inland sea.

If too great, such an inundation could prove devastating—it was common practice for watchmen to be stationed along dikes at regular intervals at the start of the flood season, to monitor the rising water level and build emergency defences if the flood threatened to overwhelm settlements. But, in a good year, the flood brought twin blessings: water to the fields (even those some distance from the river) and a fresh deposit of fertile silt, carried downstream from the Horn of Africa. An average inundation carried 110 tons of sediment into Egypt, replenishing the soil and renewing its fertility on an annual basis. As Strabo noted, "The water stays more than forty days in summer and then goes down gradually just as it rose; and in sixty days the plain is completely bared and begins to dry out."[7] The after-effects of the flood—the magical combination of water and nutrients, under the warmth of the Egyptian sun—gave the Nile Valley an agricultural productivity that was the envy of other lands. (The introduction of perennial irrigation in the early twentieth century raised the number of crops that could be grown each year from one to three, increasing yields and profits still further. Another result, with unforeseen consequences in the long term, was a rapid rise in Egypt's population.) It was thanks to the annual inundation that Egypt was able not only to feed itself but to develop a sophisticated civilisation.

The flood was so vital a phenomenon that the ancient Egyptians set their calendar by it, the first day of the first month of the inundation season marking the start of the new year. The flood was worshipped as the corpulent fertility god Hapy, bringer of abundance, and hymns were composed to him. Classical authors likewise rhapsodised on the Nile flood, and the magnificent Palestrina mosaic was created to celebrate the river's bounty. The Arab poet Abd al-Latif al-Baghdadi praised the after-effects of the inundation, which meant that "all the earth is cultivable."[8]

The only problem with the Nile's annual miracle was its variability. The Roman historian Pliny explained that

An average rise is one of sixteen cubits [twenty-seven feet]. A smaller volume of water does not irrigate all localities, and a larger one by retiring too slowly retards agriculture . . . in a rise of twelve cubits [Egypt]

senses famine, and even at one of thirteen it begins to feel hungry, but fourteen cubits brings cheerfulness, fifteen complete confidence and sixteen delight.[9]

A flood measuring six feet below normal at Aswan could reduce agricultural yields by three-quarters, bringing famine. By contrast, a flood six feet above normal would breach dikes, overwhelm settlements, destroy granaries, encourage plagues of insects and delay sowing, causing the ripening crops to wither under the hot summer sun. (The year 1818 witnessed just such a flood; whole villages were washed away, several hundred people were drowned, and "Every available boat was engaged in carrying precious grain to higher ground."[10]) Thus, as well as bringing life and prosperity to Egypt, the Nile's waters also determined the country's fate—year after year. This explains the Egyptian preoccupation with measuring the height of the annual inundation, by means of Nilometers built at key locations in the Valley—notably the island of Elephantine at the foot of the First Cataract and the island of Roda on the outskirts of Cairo. The annual measurements of the inundation were pored over by priests and bureaucrats alike, for they gave an unerringly accurate prediction of the following year's harvest. It is telling that Egypt's earliest historical records—a set of annals, carved on a slab of basalt, noting the main events of each year of each reign starting at the beginning of the First Dynasty—give pride of place to the height of the annual Nile flood, measured in cubits, palms and fingers. For every man, woman and child in Egypt, not just the country but their very lives were the gift of the river.

THE NILE BRINGS WATER and fertility to the fields of Egypt, turning what would otherwise be barren desert into a picture of abundance. That is not its only gift. The river also connects every settlement in Egypt and has the added bonus of flowing from south to north, against the prevailing wind which blows from north to south. This means that travel both up- and downstream is practical and convenient—at least in theory. The river is not just the source of Egypt's agricultural wealth, it is also a great waterway whose cargoes—human and material—have built a civilisation.

Once the Nile has passed the First Cataract, for the rest of its course it flows at a gentle pace and can give the impression of being an easy river to navigate. Looks can be deceptive, however. The very sluggishness of the current lends itself to the accumulation of hidden sandbanks which are prone to shift position without warning. This makes navigation difficult by day and dangerous by night. Ancient Egyptian literature is full of metaphors about being marooned on sandbanks, and the same danger has persisted throughout history. In his observations of mid-nineteenth century life in rural Egypt, Edward Lane noted that

> In consequence of the continual changes which take in the bed of the Nile, the most experienced pilot is liable frequently to run his vessel aground; on such an occurrence, it is often necessary for the crew to descend into the water to shove off the boat with their backs and shoulders.[11]

Later in the century, when tourist trips down the Nile became popular, ship captains were issued with instructions, prominent among which was that "Captain and Pilot must know the exact draught of the boat on which they are working."[12] Even today, in an era of sonar and navigational aids, sailing on the Nile is impossible without an experienced *rayyis* (pilot) who can tell, simply by looking at the surface of the water, what lies beneath. The prevalence of sandbanks and sunken rocks in the bed of the Nile has influenced both navigation and the design of Nile craft, most of which draw very little water at the stern, allowing them to be freed more easily if they run aground. (In the Pyramid Age, boats were sometimes adorned with figureheads in the form of hedgehogs, looking backwards—though exactly how this was believed to help navigation remains one of the more esoteric riddles of Egyptology.)

Another challenge for Nile shipping is the unpredictability of the wind. Although the prevailing direction is northerly, winds from the south are not uncommon; in such conditions, faring upstream—against both current and wind—becomes impossible and boats are easily becalmed. This must have been a frequent occurrence in earlier times, and a major impediment to the free movement of people and materials. It was just as well that, for most of pharaonic history, the major pyramids and temples were located downstream of the quarries that supplied them, so that the transport of heavy building stone could rely entirely on the Nile current.

Lack of wind is one problem; in the narrowest parts of the Nile Valley, where the river flows between steep cliffs, sudden whirlwinds and squalls present another danger. An abrupt bend in the course of the river at Gebel Abu Feda in Middle Egypt has always been particularly notorious for sudden gusts of wind, with dangerous consequences for lightweight craft. A visitor to Egypt in the late nineteenth century recounted a memorable incident:

> On our way to Cairo we gave shelter to Edwin Arnold and his wife and daughter who had just been shipwrecked under the cliffs of the Gebel Abu-Fôda. They were ascending the Nile in a small dahabia [a flat-bottomed house-boat] and a sudden gust of wind in the early morning had capsized the boat. The ladies were still in bed, and had been obliged to crawl through the windows of their cabins in their nightdresses; Edwin Arnold and his son had managed to put on a few clothes. No one was drowned except the cook, but, so far as I could judge, the Arnolds seemed to consider the loss of their water-colour sketches a more serious calamity than that of their cook. They had to sit for several hours on the upturned bottom of the dahabia, like "sea-gulls in a row" . . . and when at last they landed, cold, hungry and half-clothed, it was the eastern shore, which in those days was barren and uncivilised. Eventually, however, a dahabia came to their rescue, in which young Arnold continued his voyage up the Nile; the rest of the family had had quite enough of it.[13]

(Edwin Arnold was undaunted by this mishap; he went on to pursue a successful career as a journalist, poet and interpreter of Buddhism to the West; among other accomplishments he arranged Stanley's journey to discover the course of the Congo, and was awarded the Order of the White Elephant by the King of Siam.)

Besides geological and meteorological hazards, travellers on the Nile faced dangers from wildlife. Ancient Egyptian art and literature are full of references to the crocodile and hippopotamus, two species which presented daily hazards to communities along the river. Crocodiles were a major threat at the water's edge; the reptiles are well known for observing and learning the daily patterns of behaviour of their prey, and there must have been numerous incidents where people or animals coming down to the Nile to drink or wash were seized by a crocodile and dragged down into the depths. Hippos, on the other hand, presented more of a danger to those crossing the Nile, especially in flimsy or unstable craft. (Even today, more people in Africa are killed by hippos than by crocodiles.) It is no accident that a small statuette of a hippo was a favourite item of tomb equipment in ancient Egypt: since the beast posed a threat to Nile navigation, there was a strong belief that the winding waterways of the underworld would be similarly infested, and magical protection was thus deemed essential.

Despite such dangers, shipping of all kinds and for all purposes has plied the waters of the Nile since the earliest days of human habitation in the Valley. Because all settlements in Egypt (until very recently) were located within easy reach of the river, the Nile has traditionally offered the fastest communication within Egypt. Boats were the main engines of trade and warfare, and the principal means of moving men and materials. In ancient times, travel anywhere in Egypt meant travel by boat, to the extent that the word for "travel north" was written with the sign of a rowing boat, while "travel south" was written with a sailing boat. The terms for "port" and "starboard" entered the language to denote "left" and "right" even on land, and the language was replete with nautical metaphors. Hatshepsut, the female pharaoh of the Eighteenth Dynasty, was lauded as "the bow-rope of Upper Egypt, the mooring-post of the Southerners, the effective stern-rope of Lower Egypt."[14] In their autobiographies, courtiers boasted of giving "a boat to the boatless" alongside feeding the hungry and clothing the naked. Commoners and kings alike regarded a boat as essential for the afterlife journey.

The simplest Nile craft were lightweight skiffs constructed from bundles of papyrus reeds. Paddled like a canoe or propelled with a long pole, like a punt, they offered an inexpensive and easy solution for short journeys. If the tomb scenes are to be believed, high-ranking members of ancient Egyptian society used them for leisure pursuits, notably fishing or fowling in the reed marshes along the banks of the river. Such skiffs (though made from sedge or sugar cane rather than papyrus, which is now extinct in the wild in Egypt) can still occasionally be seen today in the more rural parts of Upper Egypt, where they are particularly well suited for travelling along shallow irrigation canals.

For longer journeys and the transport of cargo, wooden boats were the preferred option and remain a common sight on the Nile today. Different boat types were developed for different purposes. At one end of the spectrum, small rowing boats were—and are—perfect for criss-crossing the Nile and for fishing midstream. (It is curious that, although the oars surviving from ancient boats have well-defined blades, their modern counterparts are generally no more than planks of wood. This makes the act of rowing heavy work.)

Rowing may be fine for crossing from one side of the river to the other, but for journeys along the river, especially upstream, sailing offers a more practical solution. In ancient times, sailing boats were steered by one or more long steering-oars at the stern; today, a rudder is used, albeit a very broad one necessitated by the shallow draught of most Nile craft. As for the different types of sailing boat, form has always been determined by function. For royal and religious use, barques and ships of state were among the most spectacular boats to be seen on the ancient Nile. A "Director of the Royal Boat" is first attested at the dawn of Egyptian history, and from the beginning of the First Dynasty Egypt's kings embarked on regular royal progresses the length of the Nile Valley to see and be seen, to adjudicate on important matters of state, and to reinforce their authority.[15] Down the millennia Egyptian rulers have rec-ognised the symbolic power as well as the convenience of boats. Perhaps the most impressive of all such craft—and the oldest complete boat in the world—is the solar boat buried next to the Great Pyramid and lov-ingly reconstructed in the 1950s to sit in its own museum at Giza. Built from planks of costly cedar wood, imported from the hills of Lebanon, it measures 143 feet long by nearly twenty feet in the beam and has a displacement of forty-five tons. With its slender, curved form, roofed cabin and high stern, it is a stunning example of the ancient shipwright's craft, built "frame-first," its planks lashed together with such skill that no caulking would have been required to make the boat watertight.

Barques of similar design were employed in the most important reli-gious festivals of ancient Egypt. For example, during the annual Festival of the Sanctuary, inaugurated in the Eighteenth Dynasty, the sacred image of the god Amun-Ra was carried in procession by boat from his cult centre at the temple of Karnak to the temple of Luxor and back again amid scenes of great rejoicing. The god's special boat was called the *Userhat*, "powerful of prow"; its bow and stern finials were carved in the shape of rams' heads (an animal sacred to Amun-Ra); and its central cabin (which held the god's shrine) was fashioned with gold, silver and precious stones.

In more recent times, the royal yacht belonging to the last king of Egypt, Farouk, was an equally sumptuous craft. Yet the statement it made about royal power turned out to be rather hollow: the *Kassed Kheir*, as it was called, was the boat that bore Farouk into exile, following the military coup of 1952.

Ancient Egyptian boats, with their non-existent keels, flat bottoms and enormous sails, could not have sailed light for fear of capsizing; they must have been weighted with ballast, stowed under the deck. Indeed, where river transport really came into its own was in the carriage of freight. During the inundation, heavy boats with a deep draught could navigate the main Nile channel in safety, while boats with shallower draughts could travel across the flooded fields to the very edge of the cultivation. From the stone-barges of the Pyramid Age to the grain-ships of the Roman and Arab periods, Egyptian civilisation has been built on the extraordinary capacity of the Nile to transport materials.

In the causeway of the pyramid of Unas at Saqqara, dating from the Fifth Dynasty (circa 2325 BC), panels of relief decoration show massive barges transporting columns and door-jambs of granite from the First Cataract all the way north to Saqqara to adorn the king's pyramid complex. The accompanying inscription describes the scenes as "coming from Elephantine bringing granite columns/door-jambs for the pyramid."[16] Nearly a thousand years later, barges of a similar design were used to transport the twin obelisks of Hatshepsut from the quarries at Aswan to her mortuary temple at Thebes. Throughout pharaonic history the river must have been busy with cargo boats carrying blocks of granite and basalt, sandstone and limestone for the construction of pyramids and temples. Even today, barges carrying building materials (stone and sand) are a common sight on the Nile. Less harmless cargo was also transported by river, as witnessed by a nineteenth-century traveller to Egypt who observed "a government tug towing three or four great barges closely packed with wretched-looking, half-naked fellâheen bound for forced labour on some new railway or canal."[17]

In the mind's eye it is not the barges, ships of state or rowing-boats that have come to epitomise life on the Nile, however, but three other distinctive types of vessel. The first, and most characteristic of all, is the *felucca*. With its broad beam, shallow draught, curved mast and single triangular sail, this is the quintessential Nile boat. Typically crewed by two or three men (although it can be sailed solo), and accommodating up to ten passengers, the felucca remains a stalwart of Nile travel. There can be no more quintessential image of Egypt than a flotilla of feluccas at Aswan, their white sails standing out against the blue water, or circling on the Nile in front of the temple of Luxor as the sun sets over the west bank.

More elaborate than the felucca is the *dahabiya*, a flat-bottomed, two-masted house-boat whose Arabic name, "golden one," recalls the gilded state barges of Egypt's medieval Muslim rulers. The basic design of the dahabiya goes back even further, to ancient times, and "reproduces in all essential features the painted galleys represented in the tombs of the kings."[18] With its shallow draught, easily poled off moorings and sandbanks, the dahabiya is ideally designed for Nile travel, and became firmly established as the transport of choice for well-heeled visitors to Egypt during the nineteenth and early twentieth centuries. Most dahabiyas had at least two or three bedrooms and a bathroom, perfect for a party of four or five, while the crew typically comprised a rayyis, eight sailors, a steersman and a kitchen boy. The largest boats had a main cabin large enough to seat eight for dinner. The lower deck, covered by a canvas awning, doubled as a seating area for the guests during the day and a sleeping area for the crew at night; while an upper deck was typically "furnished with lounge-chairs, table and foreign rugs, like a drawing-room in the open air."[19]

In the last quarter of the nineteenth century, feluccas and dahabiyas were joined by double-decker steamers, modelled on Mississippi river boats. They had multiple bedrooms and lounges that were glazed from floor to ceiling to take advantage of the Nile scenery. Despite the protestations of the more romantically inclined—who argued that "the choice between dahabeeyah and steamer is like the choice between travelling with post-horses and travelling by rail. The one is expensive, leisurely, delightful; the other is cheap, swift, and comparatively comfortless"[20]—the steamers caught on and became the most common form of cruise ship on the Nile. In due course, they were superseded by even larger craft with many more bedrooms, swimming pools and all the other paraphernalia expected by present-day holiday-makers.

In the last fifty years, the Nile has been replaced as Egypt's principal means of transport by road and rail. Most freight is carried by land, leaving the river as the preserve of fishermen, village ferries and trippers. (Ironically, the roads are so bad, the railways so run-down, that a boat remains by far the most pleasant and reliable form of transport.) At the height of the season, from December to March—assuming a stable political situation and a functioning economy—the Nile is crowded with cruise ships: along the corniche at Luxor, they moor up ten abreast; they form long queues at the Esna barrage; and they fill the river between Luxor and Aswan, their bright lights and pounding music disturbing the peace and tranquillity. Egypt may be the gift of the river, but the river itself has largely been gifted to tourists.

EVER SINCE Herodotus travelled to Egypt and wrote his memorable descriptions of the country in the fifth century BC, the Nile Valley, with its picturesque scenery, enchanting tableaux and ancient civilisation, has intrigued and captivated the Western imagination. Herodotus' account, compiled from personal observation and information provided by Egyptian priests, opened the eyes of the classical world to the mysteries of pharaonic Egypt and spawned an interest in the history and geography of the Nile Valley that has never abated. Subsequent classical authors, notably Diodorus Siculus (circa 70–20 BC) in the middle of the first century BC and Strabo (64 BC–AD 25) a generation later, followed in Herodotus' footsteps, literally and literarily, explaining to eager readers the land of the pharaohs.

After Julius Caesar sailed up the Nile with his lover Cleopatra in 47 BC, Egypt became firmly established as a favourite destination for the wealthy and curious. The dozens of Greek and Latin graffiti carved into the façade of the great temple of Abu Simbel in Lower Nubia and on the legs of the Colossi of Memnon at Thebes record the names, motives and impressions of tourists who visited the Nile Valley in classical times.

Mostly, they came to marvel at the ancient ruins—Pliny the Elder was one of the first authors to describe the Sphinx at Giza, while Homer had written of the fabled "Hundred-gated Thebes"—or to hear the "singing of Memnon" (the eerie sound emitted from one of the Colossi of Memnon) at dawn, an experience that became especially fashionable in the reign of Hadrian. Many visitors were soldiers in the Roman army who took advantage of a tour of duty in Egypt to see some of the sights.

With the coming of Christianity to the Roman Empire, the "pagan" temples and tombs of the ancient Egyptians rather lost their appeal, and it was Egypt's deserts that drew new visitors, in the form of hermits seeking a life of prayerful asceticism and solitude. The Islamic conquest of the Nile Valley in the mid seventh century AD changed all that. While Christian monasteries in the wilderness continued to flourish, Arab scholars showed renewed interest in Egypt's ancient past, and a particular fascination for the River Nile upon which the country's prosperity depended—and which was so different from anything to be found in the Arab homelands. The wonders of the Nile inspired writers based in Egypt, many of them teachers at Cairo's al-Azhar mosque, as well as visitors from further afield, such as the Persian traveller Naser-e Khosraw who visited Cairo in the eleventh century and the German monk Rudolph von Suchem who saw the pyramids in 1336. In 1589, an anonymous Venetian reached as far upstream as Luxor, becoming one of the first Europeans since Roman times to comment on the ruins of ancient Thebes.

It was not until the eighteenth century, however, that Egypt really started to impinge on European consciousness. In the wake of the Enlightenment, many of the early visitors were devout Christians in search of concrete proof of the Old Testament stories. Hence the first Englishman to travel up the Nile much beyond Cairo was an Anglican clergyman, Richard Pococke, who came to Egypt in the winter of 1737–8. After visiting the pyramid of Meidum and the low-lying Fayum depression, both accessible by donkey from Cairo, Pococke hired a dahabiya to take him upstream all the way to Aswan and beyond. The published account of his travels, *A Description of the East and Some Other Countries* (1743), contained the first drawings and descriptions of many of Egypt's major monuments, including the temples of Karnak and Luxor, Esna and Edfu, Kom Ombo and Dendera, stimulating further interest in pharaonic civilisation. At the same time, a Danish naval captain named Frederik Norden travelled to Egypt at the command of King Christian VI to make a full and detailed account of the country; Norden reached as far south as Wadi Halfa (at the foot of the Second Nile Cataract, now in Sudan) and published the first description by a European of the temples of Nubia. By the middle of the eighteenth century, European explorers had opened up the entire Nile Valley, from Cairo to the First Cataract, and brought its ancient monuments to a wider audience than ever before. Popular interest in Egypt had begun in earnest.

The Napoleonic expedition to Egypt in 1798 and the resulting publication of the monumental *Description de l'Egypte*, together with Nelson's famous victory at the Battle of the Nile and the decipherment of hieroglyphics by Jean-François Champollion, all fed a growing fascination with the Nile and its ancient civilisation. A steady flow of European travellers made their way to Egypt, often as part of a wider "grand tour" of the Holy Land. Most tourists (such as Florence Nightingale in 1849) chose to hire a dahabiya to sail up the Nile, and at the start of the season some two or three hundred craft could be found moored up at Bulaq, the main river port of Cairo, awaiting hire. Tourists in the know would employ a local guide to choose a suitable boat and make all the arrangements for them. It was important to select the right craft, for, with no hotels south of Cairo, a dahabiya would need to serve as a floating home for at least two months, the typical journey time up the Nile to Aswan and back again.

On hiring a boat, the first thing to be done was to scuttle it in the river, to rid it of rats, snakes and other infestations of vermin. Those who failed to take this precautionary measure were invariably afflicted by all sorts of biting insects throughout their trip up the Nile. After immersion in the river for a few hours, the dahabiya would be brought out to dry, and then the provisions could be taken aboard. The standard list of requisites recommended for any journey up the Nile included basics such as tea and coffee, sugar and flour, rice and potatoes. Baedeker suggested, in addition, sixty bottles of Médoc supérieur, thirty-five further bottles of red and twenty-five of white wine, a bottle each of brandy, cognac, whisky and vermouth, plus champagne for festival days and entertaining guests. The daughter of the British financier Ernest Cassel insisted on taking a cow on board her dahabiya, to provide her with fresh milk daily. Other wealthy patrons took a piano for evening entertainment.

By the second half of the nineteenth century Egypt had carved out a distinctive niche for itself as a fashionable winter resort for the wealthy. From late November to the end of March, consumptive aristocrats and arthritic financiers abandoned their cold, damp, foggy homes in London or New York for the clear blue skies and warm dry air of the Nile Valley. The Prince of Wales (the future Edward VII) took a trip up the Nile in 1862 and liked it so much he returned six years later, giving the country a royal seal of approval. The grand opening of the Suez Canal in 1869 put Egypt in the international spotlight as never before and increased demand for Nile travel yet further. Suddenly, there was an opportunity to make money from mass tourism. One enterprising man from Leicester seized it, changing the face of Nile travel—and of Egypt—for ever.

Three extracts from his travel company's 1887 programme tell the story:

> The events of the last four or five years have created a greater desire than ever in the minds of those who can afford the necessary time and money to visit Egypt and the Nile;[21]

> Prior to 1869 the only mode of travelling on the Nile was by the luxurious and expensive dahabeah, or by small steamers, worked at irregular dates and at considerable inconvenience to travellers, by what was termed the Azizeeh Company;[22]

> This was the position when . . . the founder of our business, engaged, in February, 1869, two of the small steamers for the first publicly-advertised party to the First Cataract and back.[23]

The Leicester entrepreneur was none other than Thomas Cook. Together with his equally business-minded son John Mason Cook, they revolutionised tourism to Egypt, in terms of price, speed and reliability. In January 1870, J. M. Cook hired from the Khedivial administration (for the princely sum of £1,848, payable before departure in English and French gold) a new, large steamer called *Beherah*, with beds for forty-four guests (ten times the number usually accommodated on a dahabiya), and thus "personally conducted to the First Cataract and back the largest party of English and American tourists that had to that date ascended the river as one party."[24] The trip was a great success, and gave Cook & Son "the idea that the traffic of the Nile might be considerably developed, and that through its development the fellaheen might be considerably benefited."[25] Thus was Victorian entrepreneurship dressed up as philanthropy, and by the autumn of the same year Cook's had been granted the sole agency for a passenger service by Nile steamer.

With their monopoly and their Victorian efficiency, Cook's were able to announce the first regular, reliable fortnightly service from Cairo to Wadi Halfa and back, calling at points of interest at fixed dates—and all for a fixed price (inclusive of all travel expenses and guides). What had previously taken two or three months by dahabiya could now be accomplished by steamer in three weeks (departure from Cairo on day one, arrival in Luxor on day seven, Aswan on day twelve, and back in Cairo on the evening of day twenty). The cost, too, had come down dramatically, from £90–120 per month for a dahabiya to £44 for the whole holiday by steamer. A trip up the Nile was suddenly both affordable and safe. That first season of 1870, three hundred American tourists registered at the U.S. consulate in Cairo before embarking on an Egyptian cruise.

To cater for this growing number of visitors, further developments were undertaken both inside and outside Egypt. A new steamship service cut the journey time from Italy to Alexandria to just three-and-a-half days; a train from Alexandria to Cairo obviated the need for a hazardous boat-trip or overland journey; carriages were laid on in Cairo for the excursion to the pyramids, sparing patrons the discomfort of a donkey-ride; and official guides were provided at all the major sites throughout the Nile Valley. Tourism as we know it today had arrived.

Some travellers bemoaned such panderings to convenience and lamented the rapid development of the country that followed in its wake: within just a few years of the steamers' arrival, the once sleepy village of Luxor could boast post and telegraph offices, tennis courts and sporting clubs, a bar, a barber and an English church complete with its own chaplain. Those with the time and money could still opt for the romance of travelling by dahabiya, but for the thousands who patronised Cook's offices in London (Ludgate Circus), New York (261 Broadway) and Cairo (at Shepheard's Hotel), the convenience and price of a Nile steamer were a winning combination. Throughout the 1870s and 1880s, Cook's was in buoyant mood and expansionary mode. Just six years after launching its first steamer service from Cairo to Aswan, the company inaugurated a connecting service between the First and Second Nile Cataracts. The following year, 1877, Cook's opened the first hotel in Luxor, to accommodate visitors who wanted to stay longer amidst the glories of ancient Thebes. Cook's also had offices in all the principal towns along the Nile Valley, where tourists could send and receive mail and make onwards travel arrangements. (For example, steamer passengers could telegraph ahead before reaching Cairo to ensure their hotel carriages were waiting at the quay to meet them.) At Saqqara, Cook's even paid to have the pyramid of Unas opened and cleaned, to provide customers with another monument to visit.

For the winter season of 1886–7, Cook's brought into service a new fleet of first-class steamers "fitted with every modern improvement"[26] to cater to the same wealthy patrons that used to hire dahabiyas. According to the promotional literature,

> Each steamer has a piano, a small library, containing a few of the most interesting books upon Egypt, facilities for amusement in the saloon and on deck at night, a European doctor, and medicine chest fitted with all the drugs and appliances we consider most likely to be required on a Nile voyage . . . Each steamer is under the control of a competent European manager, in addition to the dragoman who acts as guide and interpreter on shore. The waiters and servants of every description are the best we can obtain in Egypt.[27]

The first-class fare of £70 from Cairo to Wadi Halfa and back included accommodation for ladies' maids. The ships were named after Egyptian royalty, ancient and modern—*Tewfik, Prince Abbas, Prince Mohammed Ali* and *Ramesses*—and attracted a corresponding clientele. A list of the VIPs who travelled up the Nile with Cook's in its first two decades of business reads like a who's who of Victorian high society:

TRH the Duke & Duchess of Edinburgh
HRH the Duke of Connaught
the Emperor & Empress of Brazil

HM the Queen of Denmark
HRH Prince Alexander of Hesse
Prince Jerome Napoleon
HH the Maharajah of Baroda
HH the Rao of Kutch
HH the Thakore of Morvee
four sons of the King of Siam
His Grace the Late Archbishop of Canterbury
Rt. Hon. W. E. Gladstone M.P.

From first-class steamers and luxurious steam dahabiyas to cheaper express steamers and mail boats, Thomas Cook & Son had Nile travel effectively sewn up. In the company's own modest opinion, "It will thus be seen that all who wish to travel on the Nile . . . need not hesitate to place their arrangements in our hands."[28]

Not all visitors to Egypt, however, fell under Cook's spell. The company enjoyed an effective monopoly, but catered mainly for customers interested in "doing the sights" in as short a time as possible and having a relaxing holiday against an exotic backdrop (*plus ça change*). Individuals of a more romantic disposition, or with a genuine interest in Egyptian civilisation, still preferred—if time and money were no object—to travel the old-fashioned way, by dahabiya. And it is the dahabiya set who have provided the most evocative and enduring accounts of sailing on the Nile during the golden age of travel. Two such writers stand out—very different in character and disposition, but equally influential in the history of Egyptology.

Amelia Edwards (1831–92) was a journalist and author whose literary career began at the tender age of seven, when one of her childhood poems was published in a weekly journal. In adulthood, as well as writing for various Victorian periodicals such as the *Morning Post* and the *Saturday Review*, Edwards edited popular books on history and art, and wrote novels of her own with titles such as *Miss Carew*, *Monsieur Maurice* and *Half a Million of Money*. But it was Egypt that became her abiding passion, sparked by an early introduction to John Gardner Wilkinson's best-selling *Manners and Customs of the Ancient Egyptians* and confirmed during a trip up the Nile by dahabiya in the winter of 1873–4. Edwards observed Egypt with a journalist's eye—noting the "poverty, sickness and squalor"[29] of the towns—and described it with the flair of a popular novelist. (Her evocation of life on the Nile, where "the skies are always cloudless, the days warm, the evenings exquisite,"[30] is characteristic.) The resulting book, *A Thousand Miles up the Nile* (first published in 1877), remains a classic of travel writing. Her accounts of the ancient monuments are as memorable as her observations of nineteenth-century Egyptian life. Behind every pen-portrait there is a sensibility combined with a sharp wit that together make Edwards' prose irresistible—and eminently quotable. Yet Edwards was no dilettante or mere observer. Appalled at the widespread destruction and mutilation of monuments she witnessed throughout the Nile Valley, on her return she founded the Egypt Exploration Fund (later Society) of London, with the express purpose of conducting scientific recording and publication of Egypt's heritage before it was too late. In the work of the EES, and of the successive holders of the chair in Egyptology established by Edwards at University College London, her legacy lives on.

In her noble aims for Egyptology, Amelia Edwards would have found a kindred spirit in another, near-contemporary writer on Egypt. The Reverend Archibald Sayce (1845–1933) would have concurred wholeheartedly with Edwards' waspish observation that "the people in dahabeeyas despise Cook's tourists; those who are bound for the Second Cataract look down with lofty compassion upon those whose ambition extends only to the First."[31] Unlike Edwards, Sayce was an academic and intellectual. He held the professorship of Assyriology at Oxford for nearly three decades and made pioneering contributions to the decipherment of the ancient Carian and Hittite scripts. But it was Egypt, rather than Assyria, which held a special place in Sayce's affections, beginning with his first trip up the Nile in the early 1880s:

> Every day was a fresh revelation to me, the cloudless skies and warm air . . . gave me a sensation of life such as I had never felt before, and for the first time since I was born I found it a pleasure to live for the mere sake of living. The fellahin were still simple and unsophisticated, and the European was still to them a sort of prince who had dropped for a moment from another world. The Nile, with its myriad sails, was still the great highway of the country, untramelled by barrages and railway bridges.[32]

Sayce was no romantic, however, and acknowledged the very real privations and dangers of rural Egyptian life:

> Two of the provinces still bore the marks of the famine of the preceding year, and in the more out-of-the-way places the peasantry and their children still held out their hands with the plaintive cry: *loqmet êsh*, "a crumb of bread." Here and there the eastern bank was infested with bandits.[33]

Sayce laid much of the blame for Egypt's parlous state at the feet of the British imperial authorities, accusing Gladstone's government of "making desperate efforts to escape from its responsibilities in Egypt,"[34] with the consequence that "Upper Egypt that winter was in a state of anarchy . . . The Beduin on the outskirts of the desert . . . were plundering and murdering the fellahin."[35] In the absence of an effective government, "there were scarcely any tourists" and the infrastructure in Upper Egypt "had practically ceased."[36] (A visitor to Egypt over a century later, at the end of 2012, could easily have formed the same impression. In the wake of the Arab Spring, continuing political unrest was keeping the tourists away and dealing a hammer-blow to the already beleaguered Egyptian economy. In Aswan and Luxor, all government projects had ceased, new roads and bridges had been abandoned half-built and there were mile-long queues outside every petrol station. Tourists were few and far between, and hotel occupancy in Luxor, even in high season, was a dismal 5 per cent.)

Despite such difficulties, Sayce fell in love with the Nile Valley. He resigned his chair at Oxford and his teaching duties, moved to Egypt and bought a dahabiya: "On the 3rd of January 1891 I went on board my new home and entered upon a new life."[37] His boat was one of the largest of its type on the Nile and required a crew of nineteen, plus two servants. For the next eighteen years, Sayce spent his winters on the Nile, copying inscriptions, meeting Egyptologists, and entertaining various aristocratic visitors: "The Marquess of Northampton, then Lord Compton, with his wife and daughter, hired a dahabia and accompanied us up and down the river. At Assuan we found Lord and Lady Amherst of Hackney on board another dahabia . . ."[38]

But the march of modernity could not be stopped, and the time of

the Nile dahabiya was coming to an end, just as surely as the age of aristocracy. By the winter of 1907–8, Sayce felt that

> Life on the Nile had ceased to be the ideal existence it once was. Mod-
> ern conditions had made the sailing dahabia an impossibility. Instead of
> sailing beside the banks and watching the ever-changing scenes on the
> shore it was now necessary to remain always in the middle of the stream
> and to substitute the smoke of the steamer for the sights and scents of
> the fields . . . The race of dahabia sailors was becoming extinct; they
> found it more profitable to serve on the steamers, where wages were
> higher and work less.[39]

That same season—which also saw the Duke and Duchess of Devon-
shire take a dahabiya up the Nile from Cairo to Wadi Halfa, a journey
memorably documented in the letters of the Duke's personal physician, A.F.R. Platt—was to be Sayce's last in Egypt. The introduction of
the wagon-lit service from Cairo to Luxor had made the winter resorts
of Upper Egypt easily accessible by rail, and a lengthy Nile voyage to
reach them redundant. Shortly thereafter, two world wars and the Great
Depression curtailed the Western appetite for exotic holidays. And by
the time tourism to Egypt once again became popular and affordable in
the era of the jet-engine, what had once been called "the classic Nile" had
become "the great water-way for a large number of travellers."[40] Smaller
passenger boats all but disappeared, to be replaced by the multi-decked
gin palaces that ply the Nile today (some of them still operating under
the name Thomas Cook).

Yet, for the well-heeled visitor to Egypt in search of something quieter, slower, more romantic, there are still a few dahabiyas to be found
on the Nile, modern replicas that faithfully recreate the atmosphere
of nineteenth-century travel—albeit with an Internet connection and
a plasma TV in the state room. From such a craft, seated under the
shaded awning on the top deck, it is still possible, with no other boats
in sight, to lose yourself in the river's special aura, and to observe along
its banks scenes unchanged since the days of the pharaohs. Travelling
no faster than the current itself, you can witness every era of Egypt's
long history—pharaonic, Greek, Roman, Byzantine, Islamic, colonial

and contemporary—unfold before your eyes like the petals of a water lily. For the river is the green thread that runs all the way from the dawn of history to modern times. Sailing gently on its waters is the best way to appreciate Egypt and the truth of Herodotus' timeless observation, that the country is indeed the gift of the Nile.

TWO

Aswan

Source of the Nile

The Nile rose from between two sharp peaks . . . which lay
between Elephantine and Syene. Half flowed toward Egypt
and the other half toward Ethiopia.[1]

—HERODOTUS

In the whole corpus of ancient Egyptian literature, the word for "cloud"
occurs just twice—once in the Book of the Dead, and once in the
Pyramid Texts in an obscure verse describing celestial portents. Clouds,
let alone rain-bearing ones, are a rarity in Egypt, and especially so in
the far south of the country. On a recent visit to Aswan, a few spots of
precipitation (which, in England, would not even be classed as a passing
shower) were a cause for celebration among the locals—not least, one

suspects, because it gave car-drivers a rare opportunity to try out their windscreen wipers.

But, while rain brings a welcome drop in temperature, a brief respite from the searing heat, the Egyptians have no real need of it. For, as the pharaoh Akhenaten put it in his hymn to the sun god in the fourteenth century BC, while foreign peoples rely on water falling from the heavens, Egypt is nourished by the waters of the inundation, welling up from below ground:

> *An inundation from the sky for foreigners . . .*
> *For Egypt the inundation that comes from the underworld.*[2]

For the ancients, this inundation had its source in underground caverns beneath an island in the Nile. For today's Egyptians, reliable, perennial irrigation is made possible by a High Dam. In both cases, it is the city and region of Aswan that are the source of Egypt's water. And hence the source of all its life.

As in all Egyptian towns, so in Aswan, every period of history has left its traces. The attentive visitor can observe a palimpsest, with remains from pharaonic, Ptolemaic, Roman, Christian, Islamic, colonial and post-colonial times to be found side by side or one upon another. And, like everywhere in Egypt, Aswan is both timeless and ever-changing. The geographical setting is as spectacular as ever—especially the view over the Nile from the cliffs of the west bank—but where once there was desert, now there are whole suburbs of houses, each with its own satellite dish, crowding the slopes of the eastern escarpment, and multi-storey apartment blocks lining the crest of the hill. The one constant is the river itself, winding its way through the heart of the city, still the life-bringer and the source of Egypt's prosperity.

Aswan presents the story of Egypt in microcosm—constancy and change, decay and rebirth—and, as the ancient and modern source of the Nile's life-giving waters, it is a fitting place to start any journey down Egypt's great river.

ON A HOT, HUMID AUGUST DAY in 1858, after a year's punishing trek across desert, marsh and mountain, an officer in the Indian Army, John Hanning Speke, climbed to the summit of Isamiro Hill in present-day

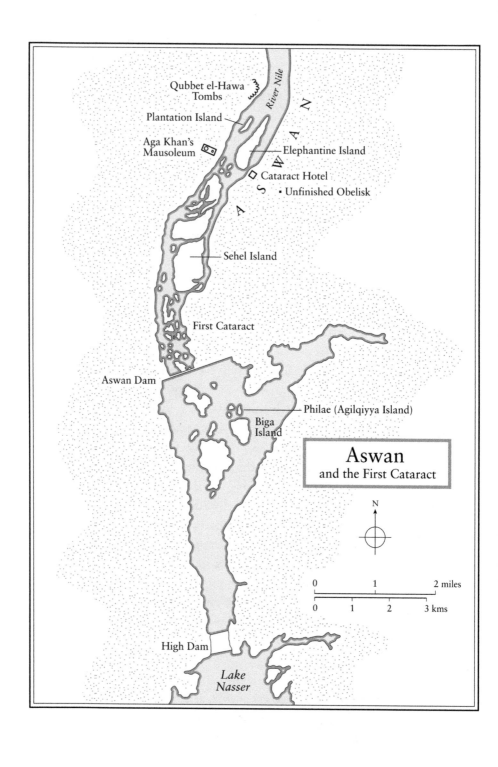

Qubbet el-Hawa
Tombs

River Nile

Plantation Island

Aga Khan's
Mausoleum

Elephantine Island

A S W A N

Cataract Hotel

• Unfinished Obelisk

Sehel Island

First Cataract

Aswan Dam

Philae (Agilqiyya Island)

Biga
Island

Aswan
and the First Cataract

N

0   1   2 miles

0   1   2   3 kms

High Dam

*Lake
Nasser*

Tanzania and took in the view. Here, laid out before him, in the heart of Africa, was a great lake whose still waters stretched to the horizon and beyond. Speke was the first white man to set eyes on this massive body of water. With characteristically imperialist chutzpah, he immediately named it Lake Victoria, in honour of his sovereign. Elated at his discovery, Speke wrote, "I no longer felt any doubt that the lake at my feet gave birth to that interesting river, the source of which has been the subject of much speculation."[3] For Speke was certain that he, and he alone, had discovered the source of the Nile.

Today, we may question Speke's nineteenth-century confidence—Lake Victoria is itself fed by the Kagera River, which flows from the Burundi highlands, while a secondary tributary of the Nile, the Semliki River that feeds Lake Albert, rises in the fabled Mountains of the Moon. But at the time, the British officer appeared to have solved a mystery that had intrigued countless scholars and explorers for over two thousand years.

The Greek historian Herodotus—a man ahead of his time in so many ways—seems to have been the first to speculate in writing on the source of Egypt's great river. In his extensive commentary on Egyptian geography and history, he conveyed the general ignorance and confusion which surrounded the question in ancient times. At one point, he admitted, "Of the sources of the Nile no one can give any account . . . it enters Egypt from beyond," before hazarding a guess, in line with local folklore, that "the Nile rose from between two sharp peaks . . . which lay between Elephantine and Syene [Aswan]. Half flowed toward Egypt and the other half toward Ethiopia."[4]

For the ancient Egyptians, the source of the Nile was indeed to be located in the vicinity of Aswan, where the river entered Egypt and where its annual floodwaters first made their presence noisily felt as they rushed between the boulders and granite outcrops of the First Cataract. More precisely, the ancients believed the Cataract to be the source, not of the river itself, but of its inundation, whose fecundity and bounty they personified as the god Hapy. Depicted as a prodigiously corpulent man with pendulous breasts (what we today would call "moobs"), Hapy cuts an unmistakeable figure. The island of Elephantine, at the foot of the rapids, was venerated as a dwelling-place of Hapy; and a cavern deep below the island was identified as the place where the waters welled up at the start of each flood season.

Travellers who are accustomed to the Nile as broad, tranquil and slow-flowing find the First Cataract a shock and a challenge. As the river breaks through a barrier of hard granite to the south of Aswan, its channel is forced into numerous branches, with torrents flowing swiftly around outcrops and piles of boulders worn smooth by millennia of abrasion. The resulting rapids and shoals, sunken rocks and abraded channel, which extend over a distance of about four miles, present a considerable hazard to shipping, as countless generations of travellers have discovered—sometimes to their cost.

Just six months after Speke had gazed upon Lake Victoria, another giant of Victorian England, the engineer Isambard Kingdom Brunel (1806–59), was experiencing the Nile for himself. Like many of his time and class, Brunel had travelled to Egypt because of ill health, to escape the foggy, raw and dull climate of an English winter for the sun and warmth of a Nile cruise. From Cairo, he sailed southwards in an iron boat called the *Florence*. But this was too heavy to negotiate the Cataract safely, so he purchased and converted an old wooden date-barge for the journey to Nubia. In a letter to his sister dated 12 February 1859, Brunel described his boat being hauled up rapids at Aswan. For a man used to overcoming immense practical challenges, it was a fascinating experience:

> . . . they really do drag the boats up rushes of water which, until I had seen it, and had then calculated the power required, I should impru-dently have said could not be effected.[5]

Brunel's description of the operation as being accomplished with "an immense expenditure of noise and apparent confusion and want of plan, yet on the whole properly and successfully"[6] is a fine summary of the Egyptian modus operandi, then and now.

A yet more vivid description of navigating the Cataract flowed from the pen of Amelia Edwards during her trip of 1873–4. This was the era of travel (for the monied classes) by stately dahabiya, and the local big-wig of Aswan knew a money-making opportunity when he saw one. The sheikh of the Cataract exercised a monopoly on shipping through the rapids, and charged travellers the princely sum of £12 for the return trip, up- and downstream, as a succession of dahabiyas made their way to Wadi Halfa and back again during the high season. The actual work of hauling ships up the rapids was left to local Arabs. It took two hundred men four days to haul a single dahabiya through the Cataract, "by sheer stress of rope and muscle."[7] This feat was repeated forty to fifty times each year between November and March. The result was an unforgettable experience for tourists, and a small fortune for the sheikh.

The return journey, running with the current downstream, took a mere half-hour. For Victorian trippers, as for countless travellers down the centuries, navigating northwards through the First Cataract announced their arrival in Egypt, and their entry into another world: "We left behind us a dreamy river, a silent shore, an ever-present desert. Returning, we plunged back at once into the midst of a fertile and populous region."[8]

The main centre of population in the Cataract region has always been on the east bank of the Nile, where a broad plain runs back from the river's edge at the northern end of the rapids. By contrast, the islands in the channel further south, though more easily defensible from marauding desert tribes, have been settled only rarely and sparsely. Since earliest times, these lonely and desolate places have been the haunt of wild animals and the abode of gods.

As a boat heading downstream towards Egypt rounds the first bend in the Nile at the southern end of the Cataract, the island of Biga looms into view. In the golden age of the pharaohs, during the New Kingdom, this was a distribution centre for Nubian imports; but its practical function soon gave way to a more sacred status when it was identified as the location of the grave of Osiris, god of the dead and of resurrection. What more fitting place for the epicentre of rebirth than the island marking the beginning of Egypt! Because of Osiris' connection with the life-giving waters of the inundation, Biga also came—through the web of associations so characteristic of ancient Egyptian religion—to be regarded as the source of the Nile. The island's rocky surface thus hid two miracles. Not for nothing was Biga called iat-wabet, "holy island."

If Biga, way-station to Egypt, belonged to the national god Osiris, then the island of Sehel, at the mid-point of the Cataract, was sacred to the local goddess Anuket. Her name, "embracer," has a deliberate double meaning: like the Cataract itself, Anuket could both protect and crush. In common with the rapids she embodied, she defended Egypt's southern frontier but also demanded to be appeased. A shrine to Anuket in the centre of Sehel island and a huge number of dedicatory inscriptions bear witness to the Egyptians' devotion. In ancient times, expedition leaders, before departing for Nubia, made a pilgrimage to Sehel to pray to Anuket for their safe return. Once arrived back in Egypt, they carved further inscriptions of thanks to the goddess. Sehel was the island of prayers, both offered and heard.

Anuket's vice-like grip on shipping through the Cataract has remained hard to dislodge. In the nineteenth century BC, under King Khakaura Senusret III, scourge of Nubia, a canal was dug to bypass the Cataract and speed the way for the royal warships as they headed south to conquer and exploit the gold-rich land of Kush. Although the canal, named "Beautiful are the ways of Khakaura," remained in use for some five hundred years, it regularly silted up under the weight of sediment brought down in the annual floodwaters. Eventually, when pharaohs no longer had the means or the will to dredge it, it disappeared for good and its exact location has never been established. Not until the twentieth century AD, and the construction of the Aswan Dam, was shipping able to navigate the rapids safely. And, even today, the locals who sail their feluccas and fishing-boats through the winding channels and submerged rocks have cause to respect the sacred powers of the Cataract.

The rocks of the Aswan region have proved a considerable blessing as well as a curse. One of the most extensive inscriptions on Sehel lists seven different kinds of rock and three times as many types of precious stone, metal and pigment, all of which could be obtained from quarries in the immediate vicinity. The mineral wealth of the First Cataract was legendary. Throughout pharaonic history, granite for pyramids and temples was quarried on both sides of the river, and on the smaller islands in the Nile. As recently as the early twentieth century, the local rock has been used for major building projects.

The sheer labour involved in extracting large blocks of granite from the bedrock, especially in an era before modern tools, is daunting. Nowhere are the determination and persistence of Egyptian quarrymen more impressively attested than in one of the granite quarries just south of the modern city of Aswan. Here lies one of the unfinished wonders of the world: an abandoned obelisk of truly gigantic proportions. Measuring nearly 140 feet in length and weighing nearly 1,200 tons, the obelisk is the largest known from ancient Egypt. Still lying in its trench, it reveals the secrets of stone-quarrying in the heyday of the pharaohs. Despite the abundance of granite close to Aswan, few quarries would have been suitable for the excavation of so massive a monument. Great experience would have been needed to identify a seam of rock strong and flawless enough. Once the experts had chosen the precise spot, the quarrymen could start their work. First, the dull, outer, weathered layers of rock had to be removed. This was accomplished, laboriously, by lighting fires on the surface and suddenly dousing them with water to shatter the rock, then pounding away with stone hammers until the richly coloured rock underneath was reached. Next, the masons hollowed out vertical test-pits around the perimeter of the quarry site to test for weaknesses or faults in the stone. Only after successful testing did the excavation begin in earnest. The ancient Egyptians' copper tools were useless against the hardness of granite; only hammers made from dark grey-green igneous dolerite were strong enough. Using such primitive tools, the quarrymen carefully dug trenches to separate the shaft of the emerging obelisk from its parent rock. Pairs of workers, one man squatting facing the shaft of rock, his partner backed up against it, hammered away together, all around the quarry site—perhaps as many as a hundred men at a time. Lines drawn in red ochre on the trench walls showed them where to dig.

The final stage in the process, detaching the obelisk from the bedrock, was especially difficult. Undercutting was nigh-on impossible in such a confined space, and the natural bedding planes seldom ran as desired. Only by inserting stout wooden levers into the vertical shafts, and leaning on them with every ounce of muscle and sinew they could muster, could the quarrymen begin to prise the obelisk free. It seems an almost impossible task, but achieve it they did, and on numerous occasions. Some twenty-nine ancient Egyptian obelisks still survive today, in temples along the Nile Valley itself and in public places from New York to Istanbul.

At last, as the great shaft began to loosen, the front wall of the hole was quarried away to enable the obelisk to be slid out of its trench to a waiting barge for transport to its final destination. But, in the Aswan quarry, for the workers on Egypt's greatest ever obelisk, that moment never came. For, at an unbelievably late stage in the process of extraction, the great granite shaft developed a fault. Realising it would never stand erect and intact, the masons had to turn their backs on months, perhaps years, of back-breaking work, and abandon the obelisk in its stony grave. There it still lies, witness to the wealth and toil bound up in the Cataract's rocky landscape.

IF THE ROCKS AND RAPIDS of the Cataract were the place where the Nile's life-giving force began, then the surrounding region was considered the starting-point of Egypt. From earliest prehistoric times, the Cataract region was a cultural and ethnic frontier zone, a borderland where Egyptian and Nubian peoples and their distinctive ways of life mixed and mingled. Prehistoric Nubian pottery has been found several miles north of the Cataract, Egyptian pottery a considerable distance to the south. This intermingling of cultural traditions no doubt reflects a mixed community of Egyptians and Nubians, a feature that characterises Aswan to this day. While the foaming waters of the Cataract formed a natural, geographical and symbolic boundary, it was always a permeable frontier as far as people were concerned.

Where people come together, so do goods and produce for trade and exchange. At the northern end of the Cataract, where the Nile takes on its peaceable Egyptian character and where the portage road circumventing the rapids comes to an end, there is a broad plain on the river's east bank where people and their goods have congregated since time immemorial. Here, around a thriving marketplace (ancient Egyptian *sunu*), a burgeoning settlement grew up, named after its most distinctive feature. Sunu, classical Syene, is better known today by the Arabic form of its name, Aswan. The first city of Egypt—the first major settlement north of the Nubian frontier—is still dominated by a bustling souk. In the latter part of the nineteenth century, Egyptians rubbed shoulders with Turks, Abyssinians, Nubians, Sudanese tribespeople, and the Ababdeh and Bishariyah bedouin of the Eastern Desert. The goods on sale at Aswan included lion- and leopard-skins and elephant tusks from sub-Saharan Africa and basketry from Nubia of an ancient design. As Amelia Edwards remarked, "The basket-makers have neither changed their fashion nor the buyers their taste since the days of Ramesses the

Great."[9] Today, the market stalls of Aswan are laden with fruit and vegetables, herbs and spices—especially the dried hibiscus flowers used to make the infusion known as *karkadeh*, a favourite drink in these parts.

Aswan, with its two strategic roles as entrepôt and frontier, has been of particular interest to Egypt's national authorities down the centuries. In Ptolemaic times, a fortified wall over thirty feet high, fifteen feet thick at the base, and nearly five miles long was built behind Syene, running south from the city harbour to the plain of Shellal at the southern end of the Cataract, to protect the portage road against raids by bedouin tribes. To reinforce this physical security, soldiers were garrisoned at Aswan throughout the Ptolemaic and Roman periods, their other important role being to collect government taxes on the lucrative trade that passed through the Cataract region. For the most part, the troops saw little military action beyond repelling occasional border raids. They were, however, involved in one armed encounter which, in retrospect, has a special place in Egyptian history. It was at Aswan, on 27 August 186 BC, that the very last native Egyptian to proclaim himself pharaoh made his final stand. Ankhwennefer was a native of the southern Nile Valley, the heartland of Egyptian nationalism, and at his father's death in 199 BC he found himself leader of a long-running rebellion against Ptolemaic rule. In a decade-long campaign against the Greek-speaking authorities, Ankhwennefer showed impressive strategic ability, rallying much of southern Egypt to his cause and harrying Ptolemaic troops along a considerable stretch of the Nile Valley. But he met his match in the troops stationed at Aswan. In a decisive final battle, his army was defeated, his son killed, and Ankhwennefer himself was taken prisoner. His rebellion was extinguished and the Egyptians resigned themselves to a long period of foreign domination. Not for another 2,138 years and the generals' coup of AD 1952 would Egypt be ruled by one of its own countrymen.

As I stand on the riverbank on a chilly December morning, with the city of Aswan behind me, and look westwards to the towering cliffs on the opposite shore, the long, low outline of Elephantine dominates the view. Perhaps nowhere else in Egypt has such a rich and layered history as this little island in the Nile's stream. At every period, Elephantine has been at the heart of events on Egypt's southern border. Its places, its people and its stories evoke the frontier mentality which imbues the

Cataract region. The island's very name indicates its importance, from earliest times, as an emporium for the ivory trade; and Elephantine's position has always made it the perfect place from which to control the movement of goods and people between Nubia and Egypt.

Once I have crossed over to the island in one of the small, brightly painted boats that line the quayside at Aswan, I climb up the steps to the old museum, then turn left towards the archaeological zone. Hurrying through a thicket of mimosa, past blocks of decorated stonework and mud-brick walls, I am keen to see the spot that gave Elephantine its special status. After a ten-minute walk, I arrive on the south-eastern edge of the island, atop the towering granite boulders that resemble a herd of slumbering elephants. From here, I have an unparalleled view of the deep water channel through which all north- and southbound river traffic must pass. People have been coming here, for just this view, for millennia. In 3000 BC, one of the very first acts of the newly formed Egyptian state was the construction of a large fortress on the highest point of the island. A rectangular structure with semi-circular bastions for extra protection, the fort combined the functions of border post, customs house and government storage facility. Its construction and subsequent enlargement created a building that dominated the island, towered over the neighbouring hovels and interrupted access to the local community shrine. It was an early, and stark, indication that a government's priorities (revenue collection and national security) do not always coincide with the best interests of its people.

Elephantine is today full of archaeology, but rarely visited by tourists. On the day I visit, both its museums—one built by the English a century ago, the other a new display of finds from the ongoing German and Swiss excavations—are deserted. For not only is Elephantine a little off the beaten track, it has also had its fair share of problems in recent decades. The Nubian village adjoining the archaeological zone is a notorious flashpoint, and the villagers have a reputation for violence. So despite the presence of valuable ancient remains beneath the houses and streets, the archaeologists and authorities steer well clear. A chain-link fence keeps the two rival groups—Nubians and archaeologists—apart. Despite these tensions, there is significant activity at the northern tip of the island, in the form of a new hotel. Following the conclusion of a fifteen-year court case which had stopped all construction, the empty concrete shell, for so long a blot on the landscape, is at last being clothed and finished, to become an annexe of the Mövenpick next door. The ground between the two buildings is being levelled to accommodate a huge swimming pool. There must be antiquities aplenty here, but, as a local guide explains, the first reaction of an Egyptian to finding antiquities on a building site is "to cover it with concrete."[10] Otherwise, the land would risk being compulsorily seized by the Antiquities Department. And, of course, the whole of Egypt is potentially an archaeological site.

Throughout the pharaonic period, troops were stationed on Elephantine to escort caravans of goods travelling from Nubia to Egypt, before the main garrison was moved across the Nile to Syene under Ptolemaic and Roman rule. The life of one particular and rather special military community has been brought to light by the discovery of a remarkable collection of papyrus documents. Found amongst the ruins of mud-brick houses in the south-eastern corner of Elephantine, the papyri, written in Aramaic, date from the fifth century BC. They comprise twenty-four legal documents, eleven letters and a list; and they chronicle the lives of a community of Jewish mercenaries and their families who guarded Egypt's southern frontier over a period of ten generations.

The contribution of Jews to the history of the Nile Valley is largely forgotten because of today's geopolitics, yet it is a story of long and significant engagement. Jews had been living in the Cataract region for at least two hundred years when a Persian army conquered Egypt in 525 BC. The Persian policy of deploying mercenaries from one corner of the empire to keep control in another (a policy still used today by governments from Syria to China) bolstered the numbers of foreigners stationed in Egypt. So, besides the Jewish mercenaries garrisoned on Elephantine, there were other peoples from western and central Asia, including Arameans (stationed at Aswan), Babylonians, Caspians and Persians themselves. The Jewish archives from Elephantine come from the households of three men called Mibtahiah, Ananiah and Jedaniah— all named in honour of their god Iahu (Yahweh). Together, the documents provide the earliest testimony of the life of a Jewish community anywhere in the world—here on Egypt's southern border and the Persian empire's farthest frontier.

As soldiers, the Jews of Elephantine received a standard monthly ration of grain and lentils, which they supplemented with locally grown fruit and vegetables. As mercenaries in the employ of the Persian government, they also received a monthly payment in silver from the royal treasury. This made them somewhat wealthier than most of their Egyptian neighbours, and ownership of a house was within reach of most mercenary families. The Jews lived in distinctive houses with long, narrow rooms and barrel-vaulted ceilings, quite different from the wooden-beamed roofs of their Egyptian neighbours. Despite close personal links between the island's two ethnicities, Egyptian and Jewish, the combination of cultural difference and economic disparity did not always make for stable community relations.

Ananiah ben Azariah was a leading member of the Jewish community on Elephantine. His wife, Tamut, was an Egyptian woman who had been a slave girl. Even after her marriage she remained bound to her master, and later to his son. Ananiah and Tamut lived together in a large house on King Street. Its location was especially convenient, for it lay directly opposite the temple of Yahweh where Ananiah worked as a priest. A literate man among largely illiterate neighbours, Ananiah was likely called upon to write messages on behalf of others. Long-distance letters were written on lengths of papyrus, rolled, tied and sealed, while communications destined for Syene, just across the river, typically used cheaper material such as flakes of pottery or stone. Aware of the importance of writing as a permanent record, Ananiah certainly made sure that important legal transactions affecting him and his family were committed to papyrus. One such contract was the gift of half his house to his wife, probably when she bore him a son. Like all his Jewish compatriots, Ananiah wrote in Aramaic, the lingua franca of the Persian empire; but his name, and those of his Jewish relatives, is Hebrew, reflecting their particular cultural heritage.

Ananiah's workplace, the temple of Yahweh, had been built before the Persian invasion. It was a magnificent building by local standards, sixty cubits (101 feet) long with stone pillars, five stone gates with bronze hinges and a cedarwood roof. In accordance with Jewish custom, the temple faced towards Jerusalem. Yet, despite worshipping Yahweh, Ananiah and his fellow Jews were not particularly devout. They sometimes broke the Sabbath. They happily absorbed gentiles (like Ananiah's own wife) into their community. And they were quite happy to swear legal oaths by other deities, including Elephantine's Egyptian goddess Satet.

But this acceptance of other customs and cultures extended only so far. At the important Jewish festival of Passover, Ananiah and his people were determined to honour their own religious tradition by sacrificing a lamb—to the evident disgust and outrage of the local priests of Khnum, god of the Cataract, whose sacred animal was the ram. As revenge for what they saw as an act of supreme sacrilege (or, perhaps, to get even with a community that was markedly better off than the local Egyptians and in cahoots with the Persian oppressors), the Khnum priesthood instigated a riot that destroyed the temple of Yahweh. The Jewish community went into mourning for three years; and when their Persian protectors were ousted from Egypt in 399 BC, the Jews of Elephantine left swiftly afterwards, bringing to an end centuries of coexistence on this small island in the Nile.

While we have tantalising glimpses of the lives of Ananiah and his fellow Jews, it is in death that the native Egyptian inhabitants of Elephantine are best known to us. High above the river, hewn into the cliffs of the west bank below a promontory known as Qubbet el-Hawa, the "dome of the winds," there is a series of rock-cut tombs, many of them still vibrant with colour and detail. They are the funerary monuments of Elephantine's pharaonic elite. Here, on the porous frontier between Egypt and Nubia, one particular category of official was especially esteemed: the desert scout. In the Sixth Dynasty (2325–2175 BC), towards the end of the Pyramid Age, when the Egyptian government was feeling its way to an accommodation with the nascent kingdoms of Nubia, men who knew the terrain beyond the Cataract and who could lead an expedition into Nubia (and safely home again) commanded both huge respect and considerable wealth. The status of individuals like Sabni—who led a secret expedition to Nubia to repatriate the body of an Egyptian government agent killed by hostile tribes—is written all over his richly decorated tomb. His neighbour in death, Harkhuf, led not one but four expeditions deep into the interior of foreign territory, bringing home a king's ransom in exotica ("300 donkeys laden with incense, ebony, precious oil, grain, panther-skins, elephant tusks, throw-sticks: all good tribute"[11]) and winning royal recognition for his exploits. A detailed account of his remarkable journeys can still be read, as fresh as the day it was carved, over four thousand years ago, on the façade of his rock-cut tomb above the Nile.

Sabni and Harkhuf achieved fame and fortune in their day as masters of the Cataract region. But for another of this elite group of desert scouts, one Pepinakht, the prize of bravery and derring-do was nothing less than immortality. At the very end of the Pyramid Age, in the reign of King Pepi II (2260–2175 BC), the loyal Pepinakht (whose very name means "Pepi is victorious") was entrusted with a mission of great political sensitivity. The kingdoms of Nubia were in the ascendant, and Egypt felt its national interests increasingly threatened. In this febrile atmosphere, an Egyptian caravan leader had been killed while on government business in Nubia—building a ship for a trading expedition to the fabled land of Punt, on the Red Sea coast of modern Sudan. Bringing back his body for burial in Egypt was thus not just a matter of national pride, but also of national security.

To Pepinakht fell the responsibility of accomplishing this covert task. The details do not survive (perhaps they were subject to an ancient Official Secrets Act), but we can be sure that Pepinakht was successful. For not only was he granted a rock-cut tomb at the Dome of the Winds, but, as a national hero, he also achieved celebrity status throughout the Cataract region, where he was given the nickname Heqaib, loosely translated "heart-throb." After his death, a shrine in his honour was built on Elephantine, and for generations afterwards Egyptians came to pay their respects and offer their prayers to the great man, hoping no doubt that some of his worldly success would rub off. Today, thanks to the painstaking efforts of archaeologists, the sanctuary of Heqaib, the heart-throb of the Cataract region, has emerged from the rubble of centuries to provide a window on the distant past.

JUST A STONE'S THROW from the sanctuary of Heqaib is one of the least impressive but most important monuments in all of Egypt. On the eastern bank of Elephantine, an inconspicuous flight of rock-cut steps descends from ground level down to the water's edge, and the walls of this stone staircase are scored with horizontal lines at regular intervals. Easily overlooked, this is the Nilometer, the key to Egypt's fabled wealth. As we have seen, the height of the annual Nile flood was a direct predictor of the following season's agricultural yield. Measuring the Nile allowed the government, quite literally, to set the budget for the year ahead. And because the floodwaters first manifested themselves at the Cataract, the calculation made at the Nilometer on Elephantine determined the parameters for the entire Egyptian economy. This humble monument—carved under the pharaohs, rebuilt under the Roman emperors, used until modern times—measured the heartbeat of Egypt.

For as long as people have farmed by the banks of the Nile, they have had an interest in measuring the river's flood. Another ancient Nilometer once stood on the island of Philae at the southern end of the Cataract, before it was quarried away to build a palace. Elsewhere in Egypt, simple measuring sticks would have done the same job. Along with determining the height of the Nile's flood, controlling its waters has been crucial to Egypt's prosperity. From ancient times, the paraphernalia of irrigation—dykes and ditches, shadufs and water-wheels, pumps and sluices—have dotted the Egyptian landscape. By a variety of methods, simple and ingenious, the Nile's water has been channelled, raised, diverted and retained to produce food for people and their animals. Not, however, until the twentieth century was an attempt made to contain and harness the river's full force. That epic endeavour is one of the most remarkable in Egypt's long history, and its ramifications continue to be felt, not only at Aswan, but throughout the country.

In the second half of the nineteenth century, the ruler of Egypt, Muhammad Ali, was engaged in an ambitious programme of national renewal. To carry out this enterprise he hired large numbers of European advisors, while he also set about enlarging Egypt's army to project the country's new-found authority. Both actions required substantial finance; the easiest way of generating the necessary revenue was through the export of cash crops; the most lucrative crop was cotton; and cotton needed perennial irrigation. So the equation was simple: Muhammad Ali's modernisation meant controlling the Nile. Without the latter, the former would be impossible. Moreover, since the cotton-growing lands of the Delta belonged to the Egyptian royal family and its wealthy supporters, the introduction of perennial irrigation promised a rapid rise in the fortunes of Muhammad Ali and his inner circle.

The question was how best to harness the power of the Nile in order to even out the effects of the annual inundation and permit year-round watering of the fields. The man chosen for the task was a 31-year-old English engineer by the name of William Willcocks (1852–1932). He duly set off for Egypt in 1883 and, seven years later, as Director-General of Reservoir Studies for the Egyptian government, published his formal study of Egypt's irrigation potential. Willcocks had little doubt that the solution to Muhammad Ali's challenge lay in the construction of a dam: "By the winter of 1890," he wrote, "I had made up my mind that the best reservoir for Egypt would be formed by a dam built across the Nile at some suitable rocky barrier, provided a sufficient number of openings were made in the work to allow the flood to pass through."[12] Having studied the geology and hydrology of the southern Nile Valley, Willcocks identified three possible sites: from south to north, Kalabsha, Aswan and Gebel el-Silsila. To adjudicate on the preferred location, and the best form for a dam, the Anglo-Egyptian government appointed an International Commission. Despite their very different characters, the Commission's three members—the ascetic British engineer Benjamin Baker, builder of the Forth Bridge; the Frenchman Auguste Boulé, a connoisseur of fine food; and the Italian Giacomo Torricelli—came to an agreement and issued their opinion accordingly: "The Commission recommends a single dam pierced by numerous sluices as the best and safest solution. It accepts the Aswan Cataract as the best site."[13] Words were simple; putting them into practice would prove a major challenge.

The engineers proposed to build the dam at the southern end of the Cataract, but this would inevitably mean the submersion of Philae, regarded by many as "the most beautiful spot on the Nile."[14] Boulé was so horrified by this likely consequence of the project that he insisted on issuing a minority report, vehemently opposing the scheme while supporting the engineering assessments that had led to its recommendation. Others, too, were appalled; archaeologists in particular issued a storm of protest. But more influential voices in London remained unmoved. Winston Churchill, then a precocious teenager, ridiculed the academic objections and urged that Philae should be sacrificed for the economic and political benefits a dam would bring. Moreover he looked forward to a day when dams along the entire length of the Nile Valley would harness the full power of the river and when "the Nile itself, flowing for three thousand miles through smiling countries, shall perish gloriously and never reach the sea."[15] Then, as later, a powerful and persuasive orator, Churchill's argument won the day. The decision was taken to proceed.

By 1895 a design for the dam had been agreed (Willcocks had proposed a curved solution, but had been outvoted, so the dam would be straight), but construction was delayed by the Anglo-Sudanese war—waged, not coincidentally, for control of the Blue and White Niles. Only after the Battle of Omdurman on 2 September 1898 effectively brought the conflict to an end could the building of the Aswan Dam begin. Construction commenced that December, and on 12 February 1899, Queen Victoria's son the Duke of Connaught laid the foundation stone of the greatest engineering project to be undertaken in Egypt since the building of the Great Pyramid four thousand years before.

If the engineering challenge was immense, so was the cost. The contract, awarded to the firm of Sir John Aird & Co., was worth the enormous sum of £2 million. It was agreed that the Egyptian government would pay in half-yearly instalments of £78,613 over a period of thirty years, and would issue government bonds to finance the deal. The financier Ernest Cassel took over the bonds and paid cash to the contractors by means of monthly certificates. At its peak, the workforce reached nearly fifteen thousand men: the British supplied specialist blacksmiths, machine fitters, locomotive and crane drivers, carpenters and masons; the Italians sent expert stonecutters; while the Egyptians provided the unskilled labour. Work was carried on for ten hours a day, and on rest days all nationalities came together for football matches. An entire village, complete with its own water supply, was built to accommodate the workers at the building site, a remote and inhospitable spot some four miles south of Aswan. Two railways, serviced by up to sixty trains a day, were constructed to transport building materials to the site. The dam was built of granite rubble masonry bound together by Portland cement. In total, 75,000 tons of cement mortar and 28,000 tons of coal, all imported from England, went into the project. To allow construction of the main dam, five separate coffer dams had to be built to regulate the Nile's flow through the Cataract.

The Aswan granite proved not as strong in places as had been hoped, and had to be dug out with pickaxes to locate firm foundations for the dam. This unexpected complication added a staggering £1 million to the overall cost of the project. But, notwithstanding such challenges, the Aswan Dam was completed in June 1902, a year ahead of contract. In a nice symmetrical touch, the finishing stone was laid by Louise of Prussia, the wife of the Duke of Connaught, on 10 December 1902, just four years after construction had begun. Almost immediately, bitter disagreement about the dam's pros and cons started.

The advantages were clear to see and swift to be felt. The dam, together with a barrage at Asyut built in parallel (to supply an irrigation canal in Middle Egypt), brought immediate benefits to Egyptian agriculture. Thanks to perennial irrigation, cotton production increased fourfold from 1877 to 1907, making Egypt the third largest producer in the world. Sugar cane also became a major export crop for the first time. Bigger agricultural yields led to a rapidly burgeoning population: Egypt's 6.8 million people in 1882 had grown to 11.3 million in 1907. The British Consul-General in Cairo, Lord Cromer, confidently declared that "the foundations on which the well-being and material prosperity of a civilised community should rest have been laid,"[16] and the Aswan Dam was a great source of British national pride—despite the fact that it had been built by the sweat of thousands of Egyptian brows. Finally, on the plus side, the dam generated electric power and facilitated safe navigation through the Cataract—via a system of four locks—for the first time in history.

On the down side, as feared, the dam had caused fields and villages upstream to be submerged and the government was forced to pay out over half a million pounds in compensation to those affected. Indeed, local scepticism about the dam's benefits had been deep-seated from the start. The early years of construction had been marked by a series of low Niles, and "it was no wonder that the fellahin ascribed the disaster to the building of the barrage. The spirit of the Nile, they believed, was wrathful at the attempt to curb and confine his waters."[17] Monuments as well as communities were drowned as the dam rose in height, the start of a sorry process of cultural despoliation in the name of progress that continues to this day. And the very character of Egypt was changed for ever. As Archibald Sayce commented wistfully, by 1907 "the quietude of Upper Egypt was also gone. The population had multiplied and the waste-places of the desert were waste-places no more. The railway was now running to Assuan, the river was full of steam-craft, and it was difficult to escape from the postman or telegraph boy. Prices had risen accordingly . . ."[18] As Muhammad Ali had intended, the construction of the Aswan Dam marked Egypt's emergence into the modern world . . . for good and ill.

One of the dam's individual casualties was William Willcocks himself. Disgruntled and disillusioned, he had left the project in 1897, even before building began. He launched a hate campaign against his many critics and ended up in a Cairo courthouse in 1921, convicted of defamatory libel and sedition, bringing an illustrious career to an inglorious end.

Despite all the drawbacks, pressure soon mounted for the Aswan Dam to be raised in height, to permit yet more irrigation and a further increase in agricultural production. The wily Ernest Cassel, scenting an opportunity to augment his already considerable fortune, had bought a huge tract of low-lying desert north of Aswan, and he used his influence in Whitehall to lobby successfully for the raising of the dam. No matter that "this meant the disappearance of most of the temples of the Nubian Nile and of all the villages adjoining them."[19] Desert was turned into farmland and Sir Ernest netted a tidy profit from cotton and sugar cane. A second raising of the height of the dam followed between 1929 and 1933, so that eventually the reservoir upstream held five times the volume of water it had done in 1902. In 1945, a plan was discussed to raise the height still further, but it was not to be. The old Aswan Dam was a symbol of Egypt's colonial past, a past that was fast disappearing in the aftermath of war. Egypt's new nationalism demanded an entirely new structure, one that looked resolutely to the future.

In 1959, seven years after the military coup that toppled Egypt's last king, General Nasser announced to the Egyptian people a project to build a vast new dam that would harness the full power of the Nile. Al-Sadd al-Ali, the High Dam, would be an awesome structure indeed: two-and-a-quarter miles long, rising 366 feet above the river bed; over half a mile wide at its base and broad enough at its top to support a dual carriageway; and incorporating a hydroelectric plant with six turbines capable of producing 2.1 gigawatts of electricity. Fearing the further rise of Egyptian nationalism in the aftermath of the Suez Crisis, Western nations refused to help Nasser realise his ambitious plans. The Soviet Union, by contrast, had no such scruples. So, when the High Dam was opened on 15 January 1971, after eleven years of construction, its sum-

mit would be crowned by a monument to Soviet–Egyptian friendship—
cocking a snook at the old colonial dam a few miles downstream.

Even more effectively than its predecessor, the High Dam has regu-
lated the flow of the Nile, consigning the annual inundation—the natural phenomenon that built Egypt—to the history books. There are no
more high or low Niles, no more drought-induced famines. As well as
benefiting irrigation agriculture, the reservoir created by the High Dam,
Lake Nasser, also supports a huge fish population, providing lucrative
catches for commercial fisheries. But the ill effects, too, have been mag-
nified. While the original plans of the first Aswan Dam allowed silt
to pass through its sluices during the inundation, the High Dam traps
all sediment behind it. The fertility of Egypt's soil has been rapidly
depleted, forcing farmers to use chemical fertilisers which, in turn, are
blamed for a rise in cancers and other illnesses. With less fresh water to
flush salts out of the soil, salinity has increased throughout Egypt, turning fields into unproductive wastelands and causing immense damage to
ancient monuments. Lake Nasser has permanently changed the climate,
causing rain to be more frequent in southern Egypt than before, and has
provided a perfect breeding-ground for snails and mosquitoes, leading to
an increase in schistosomiasis and malaria. The confident assertions of
the High Dam's cheerleaders, back in the late 1950s, now have a hollow
ring. As one son of Aswan laconically put it, the High Dam "is slowly
killing Egypt."[20]

While the long-term effects of controlling the Nile are still being
felt in towns and villages the length of Egypt, the impact of the first
Aswan Dam and the High Dam on the landscape of the Cataract region
has been profound and irreversible. Lake Nasser extends for over three
hundred miles behind Aswan, deep into Nubia. Its creation led to the
permanent submersion and loss of countless ancient monuments. An
international Nubian Rescue Campaign, led by UNESCO, managed to
move thirty-five major temples; uprooted from their original locations,
they now find themselves marooned in the shadow of the High Dam
or in Western museums. Only the great temples of Ramesses II at Abu
Simbel remain in situ—or, rather, cut up and reassembled a couple of
hundred feet higher up, above the lake's shore, in an operation which
took four years and cost forty million dollars.

The threats posed by the High Dam to Egypt's cultural heritage prompted international action, but the drowning of countless Nubian villages went almost unnoticed. Whole communities were forcibly relocated to shanty towns in and around Aswan, with little or no compensation. (On this point, Nasser's revolutionary government proved less obliging than Egypt's erstwhile colonial authorities.) As a result, the demography of the Cataract region is once again a vibrant mixture of Egyptian and Nubian, just as it was before the time of the pharaohs. The Nile has been tamed and history has come full circle.

OVER THE MILLENNIA, the Cataract region has welcomed expeditions and armies, quarrymen and dam-builders. Today, it is tourists who come in their hundreds of thousands to marvel, not just at the natural beauty, but at the monuments. Ever since the first dahabiyas of well-heeled trippers sailed up the Nile in the 1820s, one place above all has drawn them to the Cataract region: a place synonymous with the beauty and majesty of Egypt, a place whose stone walls tell of a long history as pharaonic shrine, Roman frontier and Christian refuge. That place is Philae, jewel of the Nile. As an early European visitor put it, "There are four recollections of a traveller, which might tempt him to wish to live for ever: the sea view of Constantinople, the sight of the Colliseum by moonlight, the prospect from the summit of Vesuvius at the dawn, and the first glimpse of Philae at sunset."[21]

Philae has always been a place of pilgrimage. In Ptolemaic times, it was linked in the Egyptian imagination with the neighbouring island of Biga, burial place of Osiris. Philae and Biga were within hailing distance of each other but Biga, with its looming bulk and rounded granite outcrops, hiding the interior of the island from view, had the greater air of mystery.

Because Biga was hallowed ground, off limits to all but a few priests, worshippers descended instead on Philae to petition Osiris' sister-wife Isis for a touch of the Nile's resurrective powers. Just as Isis had helped to resurrect her dead husband, so, it was hoped, she would pour out equally revivifying blessings on her devout followers. Isis grew rapidly in popularity, eclipsing the traditional Cataract deities of Anuket, Khnum and Satet. By the time the Roman writer Diodorus Siculus visited Philae, in the first century BC, the cult of Isis was the most powerful in Egypt and her island sanctuary was regarded as the holiest place in the whole country.

Every ten days, the goddess's image was ferried across to Biga to unite her with her husband, a splendid piece of theatre watched from Philae's western colonnade by hundreds of pilgrims. Once a year, from 8 to 26 December, the time of sowing new seed, an even more impressive spectacle celebrated the death and rebirth of Osiris during the Festival of Choiak. The culmination of the festivities was the ferrying of Isis from Philae to Biga on 18 December for the ceremonial burial of Osiris. Eight days later, Osiris' victory over death and the revival of his powers were marked by the erection of a great maypole-like pillar, again to much rejoicing by onlookers. As a visitor to Philae from distant Alexandria noted, "Whoever prays to Isis at Philae becomes happy, rich, and long-lived."[22]

The stones of Philae are carved with numerous inscriptions, ranging from pilgrims' graffiti to priestly incantations. Among them is the very last text ever written in Egyptian hieroglyphics, a simple prayer carved by a priest of Isis on 24 August AD 394. Over the following sixty years, a poignant collection of inscriptions left by members of a single family charts the last gasps of pagan religion and the end of pharaonic culture. On 2 December AD 452, on the eve of the Festival of Choiak, two brothers, Smet the Elder and Smet the Younger, carved the last inscription in Egypt's native language, written in the demotic script. Four years later, the brothers, whose name means "staff of Isis," carved their final testaments, but this time in Greek. Thereafter the priests fell silent and their prayers ceased to echo around the stones of Philae. The reason is found in another inscription a short distance away: it reads, "The cross has conquered. It always conquers."[23] Christianity had come to Philae, displacing millennia of pharaonic religious observance.

In practice, it was not quite so clear-cut. As the stronghold of a powerful priesthood, Philae remained a cult centre of Isis-worship even after Egypt was forcibly Christianised under the Edict of Theodosius in AD 379. Philae had a bishop from the early fourth century onwards, and for a time the priests of the old and new religions lived side by side. The transformation from pagan sanctuary to Christian shrine was a gradual process, and it took some two hundred years for Christianity to become the dominant faith in the Cataract region. During this time, Philae's ancient cults were sustained by pagan tribes from the south, the Blemmyes and Noubades, who came to the island as late as AD 567 (thirty years after the temples had been officially closed) for an act of traditional worship. Eventually, with the final extinction of Egyptian religion, Philae was reborn as a Christian stronghold from which monks led missions to convert the heathen Nubians.

The last bastion of pharaonic religion, the Cataract region was also the last area of Egypt to be conquered by the Arabs. Because of its contacts with Christian tribes to the south, Philae remained a thorn in the Arab side. The area as a whole was only fully converted to Islam under Saladin (in the late twelfth century AD). But its ancient sanctity proved impossible to dislodge. When Napoleon's army arrived in 1799, Philae's atmosphere of holiness was not lost on the French troops. Seventy-five years later, Amelia Edwards was at her most poetic when describing Philae's special, antique charm:

> The approach by water is quite the most beautiful. Seen from the level of a small boat, the island, with its palms, its colonnades, its pylons [gate-towers], seems to rise out of the river like a mirage. Piled rocks frame it on either side, and purple mountains close up the distance. As the boat glides nearer between glistening boulders, those sculptured towers rise higher and even higher against the sky. They show no sign of ruin or of age. All looks solid, stately, perfect. One forgets for the moment that anything has changed. If a sound of antique chanting were to be borne along the quiet air—if a procession of white-robed priests bearing aloft the veiled ark of the God were to come sweeping round between the palms and the pylons—we should not think it strange.[24]

Given Philae's particular appeal, it is not surprising that the threat to the island posed by plans for the first Aswan Dam created an outcry. As Sir William Garstin had made clear in 1894, "the dam, if made, can only be made at Aswan. If the dam be made at Aswan, the Temple must either be raised, removed or submerged."[25] His own recommendation was the removal of Philae's ancient monuments to the neighbouring island of Biga. Others involved in the dam project soon weighed in with their own suggestions. Sir Benjamin Baker advocated leaving the temple on Philae but raising it to a height above the highest floodwater. The Egyptologist Somers Clarke, unable to countenance such interference with an ancient monument, recommended leaving Philae alone, to be submerged. Willcocks, as contrary as ever, seriously suggested that submergence for six months of the year would be good for Philae, citing "the really preserving effect of the freshly flowing Nile water."[26]

In the end, it was decided to leave Philae where it was. Archaeologists grudgingly agreed on three conditions: first, that the entire site be subject to a thorough scientific investigation; second, that a water-tight coffer dam be built around Philae island, to protect the temple; and third, that the Aswan Dam should not be above a certain height. Eager to press on with the dam project, the Anglo-Egyptian government assented to all three demands. But Philae was far from safe.

The subsequent raising of the height of the Aswan Dam, not once but twice, drove a coach and horses through the agreement, and by 1933 all but the cornices of the temple were submerged. The temple had to have underpinning work to save it from collapse. Flinders Petrie, the father of Egyptian archaeology, wrote bitterly that economic interests—turning "barren acres into land worth millions"[27]—had caused the temple's ruin. Rose Macaulay went further, lamenting, "We should have kept it as it was: to drown it was one of the more sordid enterprises of utilitarian greed."[28] With such influential backers, the question of Philae would simply not go away, and the debate over the temple's fate resumed.

The removal of the monuments to a different, higher location had been rejected in 1901, and there were still those who thought it was a bad idea, not only because "Philae will be deprived of its fascination and glamour by separating its temples from their enchanting natural setting"[29] but also because of "the enormous cost to carry out this futile work."[30] Building a series of coffer dams around the entire island was an alternative suggestion, but this was dismissed as impractical. Eventually, the decision was taken to transfer the monuments to the nearby island of Agilqiyya, in a project as bold in its own way as the construction of the Aswan Dam. In 1972, work commenced with the building of a huge but temporary steel coffer dam around the entire site. Once protected from the waters, the temple could be dismantled safely. Over two-and-a-half years, the structures were cut up into forty thousand blocks. These were then transferred by boat to Agilqiyya to be cleaned, measured and reconstructed like a giant Lego® model. In 1980, after the best part of a decade's work, the temple of Philae, in its new home, was reopened to tourists. So nearly consigned to death and oblivion, Philae has been reborn. Visitors remain enchanted; the ancient priests of Isis have been vindicated.

The Cataract region's close association with the life-giving waters of the Nile and the resurrective power of the inundation has remained a potent belief. Two of Aswan's most prominent modern monuments owe their origins to similar notions of cheating death. Standing proudly on the river's edge, overlooking the island of Elephantine, the long, low, brown-painted buildings of the Cataract Hotel are every bit as much an Aswan landmark as the city's ancient remains. Set amongst luxuriant sub-tropical gardens, the hotel conjures up images of a bygone age, of wealthy guests sipping cocktails on the terrace at sunset, of colonial administrators and exiled royalty, of panama hats and pith helmets. Agatha Christie stayed here, and it was the natural point of assembly for her fictional guests in *Death on the Nile*. Hercule Poirot's remarks on the view from the hotel grounds remain true today: "The black rocks of Elephantine, and the sun, and the little boats on the river. Yes, it is good to be alive."[31] It is a sentiment that would have been shared by many of the hotel's early guests, for the Cataract Hotel was actually built as a sanatorium, a place where wealthy Europeans and Americans suffering from tuberculosis, gout or any of the other conditions of early twentieth-century urban living, could escape the cold, damp, unhealthy air of a Western winter for the warm, dry, health-giving climate of Aswan. A description of the hotel in 1899, a year before its official opening, focussed on its benefits as a health resort:

> In the construction of this Hotel, great attention has been given to the requirements of invalids—most of the rooms have verandahs, and a warm, sunny aspect; many are fitted with fireplaces, and the position and form of the building has been chosen to provide shelter from the prevailing winds. The sanitary arrangements have been carefully studied, Moule's earth closet system being adopted . . . Every modern convenience is provided in the form of electric light, hot and cold water baths, &c., and a reference to the plan will show that there are a number of private sitting-rooms to meet the requirements of invalids. There

is an English physician and nurse in Assouan, and an English house-keeper is in charge of the domestic arrangements of the Hotel.[32]

The Cataract Hotel has recently reopened after a long and painstaking restoration, and it is no longer the haunt of invalids and consumptives. There are fewer places in the world more pleasant to spend December or January, especially knowing that it is cold and wet in London or New York. Sipping a cocktail on the terrace, you can watch the sun set over the western cliffs, while from the hotel's riverside balconies, a panorama of remarkable beauty opens up before you: to the left, the rocks and islands marking the northern end of the Cataract, interspersed with reed beds alive with snowy-white egrets; to the right, the smooth, rounded, grey granite boulders of Elephantine; behind it, the lush oasis of Gezirat el-Bustan (Plantation Island), presented to Lord Kitchener in 1898 after his successful campaign in Sudan, and planted with trees and shrubs from tropical Africa; and, on the far shore of the Nile, the steep desert cliffs, plunging down to the water's edge.

Below the crest of the western escarpment, on a low ridge, stands a lone, domed building, its sandstone walls blending into the sand dunes all around. In the best tradition of the First Cataract, it is a place of contem-plation, worship and pilgrimage—not for Christians or Isis-worshippers, but for Ismaili Muslims. Set alongside the tombs of Aswan's ancient princelings, this is the mausoleum of a modern prince, the third Aga Khan. How a descendant of the prophet Muhammad, a knight of the British Empire and one of the world's wealthiest men came to be bur-ied on a desert ridge opposite Aswan is a remarkable story of twentieth-century global politics and the abiding allure of Egypt.

Mohammed Shah was born in Karachi (then British India, now Pakistan) on 2 November 1877, a member of the ruling Kajar dynasty in Persia. On the death of his father, he succeeded as the third Aga Khan (a title bestowed on his grandfather by the British) and, more importantly, the forty-eighth head of the Ismaili sect of Shiite Muslims. Hence, at the age of just sixteen, the Aga Khan found himself the spiritual leader of twelve million followers spread across the Islamic world from North Africa to the Bay of Bengal. A liberal and a moderate, he urged his fol-lowers to integrate themselves into their host societies—a stance that won him considerable favour with the British imperial authorities. Received at Windsor Castle in 1898 by Queen Victoria, who personally invested him as a Knight Commander of the Most Eminent Order of the Indian Empire, the Aga Khan was subsequently recognised as the leader and spokesman for all Indian Muslims and was elected the first president of the All-India Muslim League. It was in this capacity, as a prominent Muslim leader and a trusted friend of the British, that the Aga Khan was sent by Lord Kitchener to Egypt in 1915 following the outbreak of World War I. His sensitive mission was to secure the country's internal stability and pro-British allegiance, despite the Khedive's pro-German leanings. Egypt, after all, was of great strategic importance to the British, with all shipping between Britain and India passing through the Suez Canal.

The Aga Khan already knew Egypt well. It was home to a substantial number of his Ismaili followers, and during an earlier visit in 1908 he had met, fallen in love with and married an Italian dancer. Now, seven years later, he used his connections to promote the British cause. On arrival in Cairo, he went directly to al-Azhar University to speak to its professors, who were (and remain) some of Egypt's most influential Muslim leaders. Lambasting the Germans' autocractic and illiberal attitude, the Aga Khan portrayed them (unfairly) as a threat to education. His arguments proved persuasive, just as Kitchener had hoped. The professors of the al-Azhar backed the British, the Khedive was deposed and Egypt was declared a British protectorate for the duration of the war. The Aga Khan was lauded in the British press as a national hero.

He now devoted himself to his growing passion, horse-breeding and racing. Just four years after coming to the English turf, the Aga Khan won the Queen Mary Stakes at Ascot. This was followed by the Triple Crown in 1935, and no fewer than four Derby wins. When he received the Knight Grand Cross of the Order of St. Michael and St. George from Queen Elizabeth II in 1955, one may suspect it was as much for his prowess with horses as for his career as a statesman and philanthropist. Indeed, his political influence had waned following the partition and independence of India. But his interest in Egypt remained strong. In the 1930s, he had made several trips to Cairo to visit the Egyptian king. On one of these visits, in 1937, the Aga Khan met a former Miss France, Yvette Labrousse, who was living as the mistress of a rich Egyptian.

Richer, and more dashing, the Aga Khan won her heart and stole her away. She returned with him to Europe, and they married in 1944 in Switzerland, where she was to care for him in his old age.

When the Aga Khan died at his home near Geneva in 1957, Yvette, known as the Begum, announced to the world that this most international of men had chosen Aswan for his burial: a place where he might lie, like the pharaohs, undisturbed for eternity. There were undoubtedly other, more personal reasons for the choice. Egypt was where the Begum and her husband had met and fallen in love. The couple had recently built a villa, called Noor el-Salaam ("light of peace"), on the banks of the Nile at Aswan. It was on the hill above the villa that the Begum planned to build an airtight mausoleum where her husband might lie for all eternity. In the meantime, the Aga Khan would be laid to rest temporarily in a vault sunk into the villa's inner courtyard. The funeral and interment blended ancient and modern symbolism in characteristically chaotic Egyptian fashion. The Aga Khan's body was flown from Cairo, but before the plane could land at Aswan, in the fierce sun, sand had to be swept from the runway with brooms. From the runway, where it had been received by the Governor of Tanganyika (as the representative of Queen Elizabeth II) and the Governor of Aswan, the coffin was carried and dragged to the banks of the Nile. With much heaving and after nearly falling into the river, the coffin was finally hauled aboard a large barge for the journey over to the west bank—the traditional Egyptian land of the dead. A flotilla of small boats, filled with journalists, mourners and sightseers, crowded round to catch a glimpse of this extraordinary pharaonic spectacle. Because of the low Nile, the barge had difficulty mooring at the villa's small landing-stage, but eventually the coffin was carried ashore and set down in the entrance of Noor el-Salaam.

The exertions of the day had already begun to tell on the Aga Khan's nearest and dearest: his son, Sadruddin, telegraphed his fiancée: "Aswan glowing heat—complete chaos—impatient to return to you."[33] But more tribulations lay ahead. The following morning, after a solemn service in Aswan's mosque, the heavy oak coffin was carried by the Aga Khan's four closest male relatives, with help from the Egyptian army, into the villa's inner court where it was lowered into the waiting vault. Unfortunately, the architects had miscalculated, and the door to the vault was too narrow to receive the coffin. The mourners had to wait in the boiling sun while workmen were summoned to widen the door with hammers and chisels. It was late afternoon before the coffin was finally installed.

For over a year following the interment the Begum remained at Aswan, supervising the construction of the mausoleum that would be her late husband's final resting place. For his burial on 1 February 1959, five hundred guests were invited from around the world. The entire Cataract Hotel was taken over for the guests' exclusive use; but even its three hundred rooms were insufficient, so the Begum hired the (not yet finished) Grand Hotel, bringing in fixtures and fittings from Cairo. Three thousand Ismaili mourners, complete with one hundred barbers, descended on Aswan, and were accommodated in a great tent city erected on the outskirts. A temporary bridge was built over the Nile at Noor el-Salaam, since there was not enough space for a large flotilla of boats to dock nearby. When all the mourners were in place, the coffin was brought out of its vault and covered with a sheet of pure white silk. At three o'clock in the afternoon, the coffin was raised on to the shoulders of the Aga Khan's male heirs and fellow Ismaili leaders and carried up the hill to the mausoleum with its burial vault built of solid white marble at the staggering cost of £150,000. As the procession passed the women's tent, the Begum, together with her secretary and maid, all dressed in white, emerged and joined the mourners—in direct contravention of Muslim law and against the express instructions of the new Aga Khan. Just before sunset, when the men had left, the Begum led a large procession of women to the mausoleum, making sure that the world's press were there to take photographs. A love forged on the banks of the Nile proved stronger than bonds of custom.

THREE

The Deep South

Where Egypt Began

An ancient Egyptian town and village must have
presented much the same appearance as an Upper
Egyptian town and village of to-day.[1]

—WINIFRED BLACKMAN

I am standing on the upper deck of a dahabiya, moored a little north of Aswan, on the west bank of the river. It is late afternoon, but the heat is still intense. As I look towards the shore, a timeless scene unfolds: dark-skinned Nubian boys play in the shallows, water-buffalo wallow or graze on the lush green grass, donkeys wait patiently in the blistering sun, swishing away the flies, occasionally goaded by some of the naughtier boys but otherwise left unmolested. Two young men bring a camel calf down to the water's edge and, after much grunting and snorting, the beast is persuaded to immerse itself for a brisk wash. Clouds come over, the egrets fly off to roost and another day ends.

Until very recently, life in the villages and fields of Egypt's deep south had changed little in thousands of years. Yet, in the twenty-first century, under the pressure of a relentlessly rising population, modernity is fast encroaching. North of Aswan, a huge new bridge spanning the Nile seems to go from nowhere to nowhere. In fact, it has been built to serve a new city, springing up out of sight behind the hills of the west bank. "New Aswan" already has its building plots, roads and street lamps, its water towers and electricity wires. This is where Aswan's overflow population will be accommodated in the next decade, until New Aswan, like its parent, has nowhere left to expand.

But aside from the lines of electricity pylons which now march along both banks of the river, the scenery is otherwise unchanged. As the river flows between steep sandstone cliffs, its floodplain is a thin ribbon of green, impossibly narrow in places, yet able to support a series of thriving farming communities. The continuity of occupation here in the southern Nile Valley is remarkable. It was here, along a quiet, unassuming stretch of the river, that Egyptian civilisation began: here that Egypt's earliest art is carved into the rocks; here that Egypt's first city and first temple were built. The ancient Egyptians themselves acknowledged the primacy of the deep south as the cradle of their civilisation, recognising a local deity, the falcon-god Horus, as the very embodiment of their distinctive system of rule, divine kingship.

Over the millennia, religions and rulers have come and gone, all leaving their mark on Egypt. Some regions have prospered, others have declined, but the southern Nile Valley has remained relatively unchanged: self-sufficient but not prosperous, significant but seldom central to national affairs. Here, more than anywhere else in Egypt, past and present are constant bedfellows, and the threads of a long history weave an enchanting tapestry.

ABOUT AN HOUR'S GENTLE SAILING downstream from Aswan, the Nile rounds a wide bend and there, on the right-hand bank at the river's edge, stand the majestic ruins of Kom Ombo. After Philae, the temple of Kom Ombo has perhaps the most dramatic location of any in Upper Egypt. Its looming riverside presence has as much to do with the recent movement of the Nile as with the designs of its ancient architects. Indeed, the great gateway that now dominates the view from the river was once preceded by an entire courtyard and a further, forward gateway. These have been lost to the Nile, which, since the temple was completed in the early Roman period, has moved steadily eastwards, scouring out the bank and sending bankside buildings toppling into the river below. Only the construction of a stone embankment in the late nineteenth century prevented further collapse, and, for the time being, has saved the remaining temple buildings from their watery doom.

A stone plaque on the wall of the temple records how, in 1893, the Antiquities Service reconstructed and restored the entire building in just four months. In the early twenty-first century, the Egyptian government has invested once again in the tourist infrastructure. Docks have been built for cruise ships, allowing them to moor up as close as possible to the ruins; a paved esplanade with shops and cafés takes visitors straight to the temple; local businesses have been encouraged to set up along the corniche; and the effects of tourism are beginning to transform the local economy. But, as always in Egypt, official bureaucracy is as often an impediment as a stimulus. In late 2010, a museum built to display objects found at Kom Ombo stood shuttered and closed, despite the hordes of tourists; it could not open its doors until the Secretary-General of the Supreme Council of Antiquities found a window in his diary to perform the official opening. The museum finally opened on 31 January 2012, by which time the Secretary-General was on his way out of office, along with the rest of Mubarak's discredited regime.

Thanks to its riverside location, Kom Ombo is one of the more romantic Egyptian temples for today's visitor. Its situation reflects the Nile's abundant rewards and hidden risks. Kom Ombo—the ancient temple and the modern village—sits at the edge of a large, fertile basin. As the twentieth-century financier Sir Ernest Cassel appreciated when he bought land nearby in readiness for the raising of the Aswan Dam, this part of the Nile's east bank—given perennial irrigation—is bountiful in its productivity. Since the late nineteenth century, the region has been an important centre of sugar production. In Ptolemaic times, the abundant fodder grown in the surrounding fields proved an ideal source of food for African elephants, which were brought to Kom Ombo for training as war machines in the pharaoh's army. Earlier still, in the distant prehistory of the Upper Palaeolithic period (15,000–12,000 BC), some of Egypt's earliest inhabitants lived in this part of the Nile Valley, working local flints for their tools and living off the river's riches.

A place of such abundance was a natural location for a pharaonic temple, where the king could give thanks to the gods for their generosity and receive their blessings for his continued rule. The earliest temple at Kom Ombo was founded during the golden age of the New Kingdom, but today's ruins date to the time of the Ptolemies and the first Roman emperors. In fact, Kom Ombo is not one temple but two, cleverly conjoined in a single edifice, but preserving twin axes, twin offering chapels and twin sanctuaries. The western half is dedicated to the sky-god Horus; his sacred animal was the falcon which still inhabits this stretch of the Nile Valley, soaring high up on the thermals that rise from the western cliffs. The eastern half, by contrast, is dedicated to a deity far more down-to-earth, and far less beneficent than the celestial falcon. His image is to be found on almost every wall: a man with a monstrous reptilian head, cold, unblinking eyes, and a fierce, toothy grin. He is Sobek the crocodile, bringer of doom to the unwary.

Venerated from early times, Sobek's prominence at Kom Ombo is no accident. Where the river bends around, there is a large island in the Nile and an associated series of sandbanks, hazardous enough to shipping even today, but more dangerous still in centuries gone by when they were a favourite basking place for crocodiles. As one of Africa's most dangerous wild animals, the crocodile was to be feared, worshipped and appeased. Ancient Egyptian literature is full of references to this calculating Nile predator, for it loomed large in the imaginations of people who lived and worked by the water's edge, always at risk from the unseen attacker lurking beneath the waves. An ancient literary work called the *Admonitions of Ipuwer*, which imagines Egypt in a state of utter chaos, includes the chilling lines, "Lo, crocodiles gorge on their catch, People go to them of their own will."[2] In another text of the same period, a man's wife and children are lost when their boat founders; he is particularly distraught to think of his children "who have seen the face of the

Crocodile before they have lived."[3] An earlier series of magical tales ends abruptly when a maidservant goes down to the river to draw water and is snatched by a crocodile.

The inhabitants of Kom Ombo knew, more than most, what it meant to mingle with crocodiles, and they were eager to do whatever they could to appease this fearsome creature—even to the lengths of building a great temple in its honour. Where once there were pools in the temple precincts, filled with sacred crocodiles, now there is—inevitably— a "Crocodile Museum," home to a few mummified specimens. These are the only crocodiles left at Kom Ombo. The creature's demise in Egypt was the result of Western tourism. By 1845, crocodiles were confined to Upper Egypt, and the chance to hunt them was highly prized by wealthy visitors. Forty years later, only a handful of beasts survived in the Egyptian Nile. The Reverend Archibald Sayce, in his reminiscences of a trip to Upper Egypt in the winter of 1885, chronicled the last days of the Egyptian crocodile:

> Our landing-place on the western bank was usually a strip of sand immediately opposite the island of Elephantine, where our boats were moored . . . I had been in the habit of bathing there, but one morning when we landed one of the Sirdar's aide-de-camps . . . observed the recent footprints of a large crocodile. After that there was no more bathing. It was one of the last few crocodiles left north of the First Cataract. A few weeks afterwards I saw another crocodile which was killed by the natives at Gebel el-Silsila . . . When they cut it open the four hoofs of a donkey and the two ear-rings of a donkey-boy were discovered inside it. For a few years longer another crocodile survived in a back-water near Qina, distinguishing itself by occasionally surprising and eating a woman who was drawing water, and successfully resisting all attempts to capture or kill it. But in time it too passed away, and before 1890 the Egyptian Nile had ceased to be the home of its ancient symbol.[4]

After the construction of the Aswan Dam, crocodiles were forcibly confined to Nubia, unable to pass through the sluices and into the Egyptian Nile. In Nubia, too, tourism took its toll: "the nervous creature could not stand the noise of the paddle-wheels of the steamers and retired before them into the Sudân."[5] In recent years, crocodiles have returned to Lake Nasser, where hundreds congregate in certain sheltered bays. But along the Egyptian Nile, even the song of the *shadûf*-men, sung in days of old to scare the crocodiles away, is only a memory.

While the images of Sobek on the walls of Kom Ombo recall the creatures of the Nile two, three and four millennia ago, even older rock carvings a few miles downstream tell a tale of Nilotic life from the very dawn of human settlement. North of the Kom Ombo plain, the line of cliffs on either side of the Nile swing back towards the river, confining its floodplain within steep-sided walls of Nubian sandstone. On the west bank, near the small village of el-Hosh, the boulders at the top of the cliff have taken on the chocolate-brown patina of age. Lightly pecked into these boulders, now faint and hard to discern, are strange drawings from remotest antiquity. They have been dated to the late Palaeolithic period between 10,000 and 5,000 BC, in other words some 7,500 to 2,500 years before the pyramids. The rock-drawings of el-Hosh are perhaps the oldest art to survive anywhere in the Nile Valley, echoes from the Stone Age.

The curious, curvilinear designs that form the bulk of these early images resemble nothing so much as mushrooms on long stalks. From parallels in other cultures and other periods, they have been plausibly interpreted as "labyrinth fish-traps," wicker-work constructions that the Nile Valley's earliest inhabitants would have placed in the river to catch fish. During the annual inundation, the prehistoric people of Upper Egypt would have waded on to the floodplain where the waters were less turbulent and where the fish schooled in abundance. Setting their traps in the slow-flowing current, they would have beaten the water's surface (as Nile fishermen do to this day) to scare the fish towards the mouth of the wicker-work nets. The result of a few hours' work would have been nature's bounty: a short-term feast, and, with air-drying, a valuable source of protein to sustain a small community for months. Little wonder that these early fisherfolk adorned the boulders above their catching-grounds with images of the miraculous technology that brought them so great a harvest. Egypt's earliest art, carved with care at occasions of thanksgiving, records the river's abundance and its annual regime by which Egyptians throughout the ages have measured their lives. Today, below the cliffs of el-Hosh, fishermen still cast their lines and nets in the shallows, while dragonflies dart over the surface. Thickets of lush green reeds at the water's edge are reflected in the mirror-like surface of the Nile, while in midstream clumps of water hyacinth slow the river's flow. Egrets and herons wade along the shoreline, and a hawk soars overhead.

The cliffs beyond el-Hosh mark a major transition in the geology of the Nile Valley, from rose-red Nubian sandstone to pale gold Egyptian limestone. But before the hard southern rock gives way to its softer northern cousin, it has one final spectacle to afford the traveller. As the Nile rounds a left-hand bend, immense slab-sided cliffs rise up on either side, dotted with rock-cut stelae and chapels. On the west bank, a large boulder, balanced precariously atop a great pinnacle of sandstone, acts both as a navigational aid—there are sunken rocks in the bed of the river here, which present a major hazard to shipping—and as a beacon of welcome. For we have arrived at Gebel el-Silsila, gateway to the north, terminus of desert routes, and the place that literally gave birth to all of ancient Egypt's most magnificent temples.

The Nile Valley is at its narrowest at Gebel el-Silsila. The river here once ran through rapids, and the area was generally avoided by ancient travellers who preferred to circumnavigate the site to avoid its hazards. Because of the dangers of navigation, the site was a cult centre for water deities: Hapy, god of the inundation; Heqat, the frog-goddess; and Sobek, the crocodile. Shrines and stelae dot the cliffs on both sides of the Nile, and the isolation of the site imparts a holy feel. It is a special place. Yet, for somewhere so significant to Egyptian civilisation, Gebel el-Silsila is remarkably unknown to tourists. The authorities have invested in stone steps, flood defences, floodlights and interpretative signs, but few cruise ships stop here on their rushed journey north to Luxor. Those visitors who do disembark and stay awhile are rewarded with one of the most amazing ancient industrial landscapes anywhere in the world. For, in Amelia Edwards' memorable description, "the yellow cliffs have been sliced as neatly as the cheeses in a cheesemonger's window."[6] On both sides of the river, quarries were opened up in ancient times to supply construction projects the length and breadth of Egypt. Those on the east bank provided stone for the temples of Karnak and Luxor, the mortuary temples of western Thebes, and for Ptolemaic temples throughout Upper Egypt, including Kom Ombo and Edfu. From the quarry face, great blocks of stone were dragged down a causeway to the riverbank, to be loaded on to barges. On the west bank, where the cliffs are steeper, ships risked capsizing and sinking as they were loaded with tons of freshly cut stone blocks. To prevent this, eye-holes were cut through the walls flanking the main quarry entrance, and ropes passed through these so that the waiting boats could be tied up securely. The eye-holes are still there, together with the countless chisel marks left by the ancient quarrymen, who worked carefully and economically, leaving little debris. It is as if the last team of workers left only last week, and yet most of Gebel el-Silsila's stone was worked out by Roman times. Other than the extraction of some stone for the Nile barrages in the late nineteenth and early twentieth centuries, systematic quarrying activity at Gebel el-Silsila has not taken place for nearly two thousand years.

While ancient stone-cutting created this extraordinary landscape, modern extraction of a different kind is threatening to destroy it. At the edge of the cliff on the west bank, overlooking the Nile, an official chose to be buried in the fifteenth century BC, perhaps to remind him of quarrying expeditions successfully managed and completed. For centuries, he had lain in peace in this beautiful spot, until robbers came, cut away and removed the entire top half of his rock-cut tomb. In recent years, local villagers were caught using dynamite to extract other monuments for sale on the illicit antiquities market. Under Egyptian law, they were convicted, not for damaging antiquities, but for having explosives without a licence, and sentenced to just one year in prison. They will be back. Before long, without further protection, the monuments of Gebel el-Silsila will, like the cliffs behind them, have been quarried away to satisfy the cravings of wealthy patrons many hundreds of miles away.

THROUGHOUT EGYPTIAN HISTORY, stone has, by and large, been a building material reserved for the wealthiest in society. In ancient Egypt, quarrying was a royal monopoly: the logistics required to cut and transport blocks of stone were simply too great to be within reach of ordinary households. Even the state could baulk at the effort involved, which explains the frequent re-use of blocks from earlier buildings in later constructions. The gate-towers of the New Kingdom temple of Karnak were filled with blocks taken from Middle Kingdom shrines that had stood on the same site, just as the pyramids of the Middle Kingdom had cannibalised stone from their Old Kingdom predecessors. In medieval times, the pyramids of Giza offered a ready supply of pre-cut blocks for the builders of Cairo's city walls. In this way, almost every significant stone building in Egypt is a palimpsest, incorporating within its structure the toil of earlier generations.

While stone, with its strength and durability, has long been preferred for state building projects, Egypt's ordinary citizens have, down the centuries, made do with altogether humbler materials—materials that, like the people's very livelihoods, are gifts of the Nile. For nearly seven millennia, Egyptians have built their houses, byres, granaries and workshops using silt, timber and reeds from the riverbank. Even today, rural Egypt is largely a creation of mud, wood and straw.

Sun-dried mud brick is the quintessential Egyptian building material. It is easily manufactured by mixing together alluvial silt with a temper of chopped straw and dung. This unprepossessing material is pressed into an open, rectangular wooden mould, then slapped out like pats of butter to dry in the sun. After just a day or two of drying, the resulting brick is ready to use. The basic technique and the standard size of brick have not changed for thousands of years. Ever since Egyptians first started living in towns, some six thousand years ago, mud brick has been the defining characteristic of the urban environment. Its grey stain is ubiquitous on archaeological sites. In the modern era, vast quantities of decayed mud brick have been quarried away for use as a cheap, organic fertiliser (Arabic *sebakh*). But despite the efforts of centuries of *sebbakhin* (those who dig for sebakh), mud-brick buildings from every era of Egyptian history still litter the landscape, stubbornly resisting the ravages of sun, wind and sand. Nowhere in Egypt illustrates the versatility, strength and durability of mud brick better than a small stretch of the Nile Valley north of Gebel el-Silsila.

In ancient times, this particularly fertile part of Upper Egypt was home to twin towns, important hubs of manufacture and commerce that faced each other on opposite sides of the river. On the west bank stood the town of Nekhen, an early centre of pottery and beer production that stood at the Nile Valley terminus of Western Desert routes to the oases and beyond. On the east bank, its twin settlement of Nekheb guarded the entrance to the Wadi Hellal, which provides a route through the hills to the gold-bearing regions of the Eastern Desert and the Red Sea coast. Together, Nekhen and Nekheb were pioneers in the process of state formation and the foundations of pharaonic civilisation. In their heyday, they were amongst the most important towns in all Egypt, with burgeoning populations. While today they have reverted to small rural villages, traces of their past greatness survive.

To reach Nekheb (now known by its Arabic name, Elkab), my boat has to double back. Huge floating mats of reed and weed block access to the shoreline, so we drift along the west side of an island before carefully navigating a small patch of clear water and then sailing back down an inner channel to the village mooring. On the way, we narrowly avoid a small fishing-boat. An older man rows it with planks of wood while a young boy smacks the surface of the water with a long stick to bring the fish up from the depths. On the mounds of floating weed there are egrets, stilts and glossy ibis. Pied kingfishers hover overhead before plunging into the river for an easy catch.

Nile cruises between Aswan and Luxor generally restrict themselves to the major sites, such as the temple of Kom Ombo. Even Gebel el-Silsila is rarely visited, despite its impressive remains and modern facilities. Rural, isolated Elkab, it appears, has never seen a tourist boat before. Instead of bazaars and caleche drivers awaiting us, there is just an age-old scene of village life: little children in grubby galabeyas, boys riding donkeys, geese and ducks dabbling among the flotsam at the river's edge. The villagers are as fascinated by us as we are by them, and there is great excitement as our boat comes alongside. Young mothers venture from their ramshackle houses, semi-naked babies in their arms, to gawp at the unusual sight: strangely attired white men and women, cameras and binoculars in hand, arrived from out of nowhere.

I have come to visit the nearby rock-cut tombs of Elkab, with their famous scenes of rural life from 3,500 years ago. Exactly the same tableau, only alive and in three dimensions, is happening around me. Despite lengthy negotiations with the village elders, there is no motorised vehicle to take me to the tombs. I politely decline the offer of a donkey-ride and decide to walk. In the village square—an open stretch of bare ground between groups of houses, close to the riverbank—is the village brick-yard. Freshly moulded mud bricks are drying in the sun in neat rows, a scene repeated in rural communities throughout Egypt since time immemorial. What makes this example particularly poignant is its location, for just a few yards away stands a massive 2,400-year-old wall, made from identical mud bricks. This is the city wall of ancient Nekheb, and it remains perhaps the single largest ancient mud-brick construction in Egypt. Enclosing an area 622 by 600 yards, the wall measures over thirty-six feet thick at its base and stands as high in places. Inside these formidable defences once stood the city of Nekheb—a jumble of domestic and sacred buildings covering every era of pharaonic history from the First Dynasty to the Roman period. The temple to the local goddess Nekhbet was so revered as a shrine of national importance that it was rebuilt at least ten times.

Excavations within the city wall have also uncovered evidence for earlier human occupation at Elkab. Fragments of pottery show that people lived here in the predynastic period (5000–3000 BC), while small stone tools belong to an even earlier phase of activity, as far back as the seventh millennium BC. At this time, hunter-gatherers made seasonal camps each autumn on the east bank of the Nile, to take advantage of the lush new growth and the game it attracted. The particular groups who came to Elkab are called by archaeologists Elkabian, so distinctive are their flint implements. Yet even they were not the first people to live here: stone hand-axes found in the hills surrounding the Wadi Hellal date back as much as 300,000 years. In its own quiet way, the riverbank of Elkab has witnessed the entire history of human activity in the Nile Valley.

The town and tombs of Elkab were once linked by a stretch of low desert, but the construction of a railway, and later of the main Aswan to Luxor highway, divided the site in two. Although this has destroyed its integrity, it has been a blessing in disguise. The vast majority of visitors who come by road do not stray beyond the tombs. Popular with tourists since the late nineteenth century, the rock-cut sepulchres created for the New Kingdom mayors of Elkab remain a favourite stop-off for coach parties travelling between Aswan and Luxor. Today the site boasts a purpose-built coach park and ticket kiosk, and a small shelter by the roadside contains three large water jars on a stand, shaded from the fierce sun. It is a thoughtful pitstop for passing travellers, an Egyptian Welcome Break—and particularly welcome on days when, with the temperature reaching 47° C in the shade, the wind feels like a fan-assisted oven. By contrast, on the other side of the busy road and railway line (moments after I cross, and without warning, a train comes hurtling by), the ancient city wall offers no concessions to the visitor and thus remains largely off-limits. That is its best hope of survival.

From the tombs with their scenes of agricultural activity—sowing and reaping, harvesting and threshing—I return along the line of the great mud-brick wall to the Nile, rejoin my boat and we find a quiet mooring for the evening a short distance to the north of the village. On the riverbank, a bucolic scene plays out, bringing the ancient tomb paintings to life: big, brown-eyed cattle graze in the shade of a large tree; children sit watching the boat. A little girl in a colourful print dress collects herbs while a small boy chews on a stick of sugar cane, cut from the next-door field with a knife. An older boy arrives on a donkey-cart, dismounts and unhooks the cart. Fodder is brought for the donkey while the cart is loaded with freshly cut sugar cane. The children strip lengths of cane and pass them to our crew who have gone ashore. As the sun sets, the younger boy and girl ride back to their village on their donkey, and the cart is driven home by the farmer with the older boy sitting on top of the load. In the fading light, egrets fly up from the fields to roost on a reedy islet in the Nile.

If the city wall of Elkab demonstrates the strength of mud brick, its durability as a building material is exemplified by a monument on the opposite bank of the Nile, at the ancient site of Nekhen. Here, too, most of the traces of a once glorious past have vanished. The only testaments to the site's ancient significance are a few decorated rock-cut tombs in the escarpment and a huge mud-brick edifice on the plain. In the case of Nekhen, the edifice is not a city wall but a towering enclosure. It, too, is one of the great unsung wonders of the ancient world. Known colloquially as the "Fort," it measures 221 by 188 feet and its buttressed walls reach thirty feet high. Most remarkable of all is its early date: as much time separates its construction from the wall of Elkab as separates the wall of Elkab from today. The Fort was built circa 2700 BC in the reign of King Khasekhemwy, making it the oldest freestanding mud-brick building in the world. Its purpose remains mysterious. The best guess is that it was built for the celebration of the king's cult—some fragments of decorated stone from the Fort's entrance gateway show the king engaged in ceremonial activity—both during his lifetime and after his death. Its particular location acknowledged the fact that Nekhen had been one of the earliest centres of Egyptian kingship.

Some miles to the west of the Fort, down a remote desert wadi, lies a site of special significance in the development of Egyptian civilisation: the earliest royal burial ground in the Nile Valley. Site HK6, as archaeologists call it, was established around 3800 BC—over a thousand years before the Fort—as a cemetery for the rulers of Nekhen. Grave goods included statues of the rulers themselves (the beginning of a long tradition of royal sculpture), and wild beasts sacrificed to accompany the deceased into the next world (the earliest evidence for sacred animals). The tombs themselves were marked on the surface by pillared halls of timber and matting, enclosed within reed walls. It was a reminder, deep in the desert, that life and rebirth depended on the fruits of the Nile.

This connection between the afterlife and the river was made more explicit in a slightly later royal tomb, Tomb 100, dug into the low desert nearer the Fort. Now lost, but known from black-and-white photographs taken at the time of its discovery in the early twentieth century, Tomb 100 is better known as the "Painted Tomb." Dating from about 3400 BC, one of its inside walls was plastered and painted with scenes of a royal river pageant. Surrounding the main procession of boats are other references to royal power, including captive animals and the ruler smiting his enemies. This last motif was to endure as the defining image of kingship for the next three millennia. The Painted Tomb is the earliest decorated tomb ever discovered in Egypt; in its conception and its decoration it marks the beginning of one of the quintessential traditions of pharaonic civilisation. No wonder that the ancient Egyptians themselves, when considering their origins, considered the southern Nile Valley in general, and Nekhen in particular, as the crucible of civilisation, the place where Egypt began.

A postscript to the story of mud, straw and origins is prompted by the site of Adaima, just a few miles north of the Painted Tomb and the Fort. Unlike Elkab and Nekhen with their monumental mud-brick constructions, Adaima has absolutely nothing for the visitor to see. The remains here are entirely subterranean, revealed by the archaeologist's trowel and brush just a few centimetres under the desert surface. Spread over a vast area of nearly a hundred acres, the thinnest of deposits has yielded evidence for an extensive settlement and its associated cemetery, dating back to the middle of the fourth millennium BC. The dwellings were made of wood and straw, post-and-matting structures that gradually became larger and more sturdy over the passing centuries. But at no time did the inhabitants of Adaima turn to mud brick. In their burials, too, they showed a preference for plant materials, with a simple mat providing the only protection and the only equipment for many interments. A few children were buried in pots, a few adults in leather bags or unfired clay coffins, but wood and straw were the predominant materials, in life and in death.

So ancient was the tradition of using plant materials that it became a hallowed archetype, used in the construction of sacred buildings even after mud brick had become popular. The earliest temple in Egypt, which was built at Nekhen, just a few hundred yards away from the Painted Tomb, and at about the same time, was thus created from tree trunks, mats and wicker-work fences. According to modern reconstructions, it looked nothing like the classic Egyptian temple of later periods. Instead of a rectangular building with gateways and courts, it consisted instead of a rough oval enclosure with a smoothed mud floor, a wooden flagpole at one end and a crude post-and-matting building at the other. In this way it encapsulated in its very architecture connotations of antiquity and the river's bounty.

ELKAB, with its great city wall, and Nekhen, site of Egypt's first temple, declined in importance because of the rise of two other regional centres. Edfu to the south and Esna to the north, both founded in pharaonic times, became the dominant settlements of southern Upper Egypt in the Ptolemaic and Roman periods, a status which they retain to this day. Edfu and Esna are also, not coincidentally, famous for their great, late temples—the final flowerings of Egyptian religion at a time when the Nile Valley was already ruled by foreigners. For two thousand years, the stories of each town and its temple have been closely intertwined, and never more so than today.

Until about 1860, most of the temple of Horus at Edfu was buried under sand. Only the tops of the pylons were visible and there were sixty-four houses on the temple roof. Gustave Flaubert, a visitor to Egypt in 1849, accused the local inhabitants of using the temple as a public latrine. It fell to another Frenchman, Auguste Mariette, the first Director of the Egyptian Antiquities Service, to excavate Edfu from the accumulations of centuries and reveal the temple in its full glory. Its almost pristine state of preservation impressed Victorian visitors, just as it does today. As Amelia Edwards put it, "So perfect, so solid, so splendid is the whole structure; so simple in unity of plan; so complex in ornament; so majestic in completeness, that one feels as if it solved the whole problem of religious architecture."[7]

Construction of the temple began on 23 August 237 BC under Ptolemy III. The plan, to build one of the grandest edifices in the history of ancient Egyptian religion in the deep south of the Nile Valley, was no accident. Conscious of its renown as the birthplace of pharaonic civilisation, and proud of its long tradition of supplying kings to the Egyptian throne, Upper Egypt was a hotbed of nationalism during the reigns of the Greek-speaking Ptolemies. Nothing was better calculated to appease native Egyptian sentiment than a very public act of piety towards their old gods. Building and beautifying temples had been one of the primary duties of kingship since the dawn of Egyptian history, and the Ptolemies were at pains to be seen as legitimate pharaohs by their restive Egyptian subjects. The temple of Edfu, with its dedication to Horus—patron deity of ancient Nekhen and god of kingship—did not disappoint. When it was finally consecrated in 70 BC, a few months before the birth of Cleopatra, it was as spectacular as any monument erected by the pharaohs.

With its massive pylon gateways and expansive columned halls, it managed to combine Egyptian and Hellenistic forms in a unified whole, achieving the harmony of cultural traditions that successive generations of Greek pharaohs had struggled to create. In a nod to Greek learning, the temple included a "laboratory" inscribed with prescriptions for making sacred oils and unguents. Wholly Egyptian, however, was the "Nile chamber," where sacred water brought from the river was poured into a basin for use in religious rituals. Texts on the temple walls explained how the temple stood upon the very spot where the primeval mound had emerged from the waters of chaos at the time of creation. And thousands of ritual scenes showed the king—Greek in culture and background but attired as a pharaoh—presenting offerings to the traditional gods of Egypt.

The ecstatic crowds who witnessed the dedication of Edfu temple were not, however, included in its cult activities. As Amelia Edwards noted, "an Egyptian Temple was not a place for public worship. It was a treasure-house, a sacristy, a royal oratory, a place of preparation, of consecration, of sacerdotal privacy. To the rest of the community, all that took place within those massy walls was enveloped in mystery."[8] The exception to this rule, and perhaps the most interesting of the many festivals celebrated at Edfu, was the Sacred Marriage. Celebrated each year in the run-up to the inundation, this involved the ceremonial transport of a statue of Hathor by barge from Dendera to be reunited with her consort, Horus of Edfu. The whole festival lasted a month, beginning at the full moon when the cult image of Hathor left Dendera, bound for Edfu. En route, the barge called at Thebes and Nekhen so that Hathor could "visit" other important temples and their resident deities. The flotilla arrived at Edfu at the new moon, staying for two weeks until the following full moon when Hathor's statue was taken back to her boat—amid much rejoicing—for the journey home to Dendera.

Today, the river and its traffic remain central to the life and prosperity of Edfu. In place of religious barges come tourist cruisers. The destination remains the same: the temple of Horus. Following this well-sailed path, we moor up at the quayside of Edfu next to a two-masted felucca. It is laden with rocks, yet scarcely draws any water thanks to its exceptionally broad beam. Men are hoisting massive chunks of stone on to their shoulders and walking along a narrow plank from boat to shore, then up a steep rocky bank to dump the stone into a waiting lorry. It is backbreaking work, carried out barefoot, in the full glare of the sun, and a reminder of the way the temples of ancient Egypt were built, with human toil and sweat.

Alongside the stone-barge, the scene on the riverbank perfectly captures the juxtaposition of ancient and modern so characteristic of this part of Egypt: men in the river, washing themselves and their horses; waiting caleches; and a single motorised vehicle (the stone lorry). A fisherman comes alongside our boat, rowing with two planks of wood (functioning as bladeless oars), extracting his modest catch from his net. He holds up a grotesquely bloated puffer-fish as a trophy—poisonous to eat but often seen in Egyptian houses stuffed and hung on a wall as decoration. He hands over a few edible fish in exchange for a few pounds from one of the crew, before rowing off again. After this age-old exchange, modernity intrudes: an air-conditioned coach appears from nowhere to whisk us in comfort to the temple. As we drive through the city at high speed, scattering donkey-carts and caleches before us, we pass townspeople going about their business: young women in colourful scarves, older women swathed in black, walking in pairs; men sitting outside cafés, smoking; people queueing at the government bread stores; small stalls selling brightly coloured, embroidered dresses. When we return to our boat two-and-a-half hours later, the stone carriers are still hard at work. It will probably take the two men all day to unload the ship's cargo.

A subsequent visit to Edfu temple, at the end of 2012, requires a different method of approach. Following the Arab Spring and the precipitous decline in tourists to the Nile Valley, the caleche-drivers of Edfu have formed themselves into a militant trade union, determined and desperate to preserve their livelihoods in the face of dwindling customers. Their chosen technique is to insist that all tourists disembarking at the river quay should travel to the temple by caleche. Any bus or taxi that tries to follow the same route risks being pelted with stones and barred from entry into the temple compound. The tactic has certainly drawn attention to the drivers' plight (and that of their fellow workers in the tourist industry), but has largely failed to drum up business. Western insurance companies refuse to insure their clients for travel by caleche— so fierce is the drivers' reputation—so most tourists approach Edfu by road, breaking the ancient bond between Nile and temple. The same Upper Egyptian rebelliousness that Edfu was built to appease has come back to haunt town and temple more than two thousand years later.

The caleche-drivers of Edfu excepted, Upper Egyptians are generally content with their lot; but it was not always so. Under Roman rule, the Nile Valley was a sorry place for its native inhabitants. Treated as aliens in their own land, in the cities they were denied citizenship and in the countryside they suffered crippling levels of taxation. The tax on Egypt's agricultural produce supplied a third of Rome's annual grain consumption. To facilitate this economic exploitation, the Romans stationed a massive military force at key sites throughout the Nile Valley. The soldiers' duties included guarding the hated tax collectors, protecting the grain ships bound for Rome, and stamping out dissent among the native population—many of whom fled their villages to live as outlaws on the margins of society.

The place in Upper Egypt where the Roman presence was trumpeted most loudly was Esna. It was frequented by Roman soldiers on leave from their garrisons in the Eastern Desert, and its temple, though dedicated to the Egyptian creator-god Khnum, was designed as a piece of Roman propaganda. The original temple had been founded by Ptolemy VI, but it was the Roman emperors who set about carving their names on every available surface. The façade names Claudius, Nero, Vespasian and Domitian; the columns of the hypostyle hall record the activities of Trajan, Hadrian and Antoninus Pius; and the rear wall bears inscriptions of Septimius Severus and his wife Julia, Caracalla, Geta, Philip I and Decius. Elsewhere, the names of Marcus Aurelius and Commodus appear, and a further relief shows Titus in the traditional smiting pose of an Egyptian pharaoh. Altogether, Esna memorialises nearly three centuries of Roman rule in the Nile Valley, a roll call of Egypt's suppression by a foreign power. In one of the cruellest ironies, a column in the middle of the hypostyle hall shows Hadrian presenting a chaplet to Khnum. This rite, which involved the king offering a crown to the god in return for divine protection, dated back to the days of the pharaohs. But at Esna the crown is a Roman-style laurel wreath, and is offered together with a baton, signifying the emperor's military might.

Like all settlements in Upper Egypt, the town of Esna owes its existence to the Nile. In pharaonic times, the Nile perch (*Lates*) was worshipped locally, alongside Khnum, giving Esna its classical name of Latopolis ("perch city"). The quayside at Esna was a thriving commercial hub, and the stone quay, built under Marcus Aurelius, would have accommodated grain-ships bound for Rome. It was reinforced as late as the nineteenth century AD with blocks from Contralatopolis on the other side of the Nile. Contemporary Esna is still a town of merchants, and a centre of the weaving trade.

Tourism is also important, and there are ambitious plans to exploit Esna's potential yet further. The authorities' vision is to turn back time and restore Esna to its former glory by reuniting the quayside with the temple. This is no easy task. Until the mid nineteenth century, the temple was buried "in the accumulated rubbish of a score of centuries"[9] and the interior, "choken to within a few feet of the capitals of the columns,"[10] was used as a cotton store. It was only excavated in 1842 to provide a safe underground magazine for gunpowder, but the temple still lies a long way below street level, surrounded on all sides by the sprawling modern town. In order to clear the entire route from the temple to the river, the Ministry of Antiquities intends to demolish an entire street of shops. The demolition will threaten a rare medieval mosque. (Its minaret is already leaning at a precarious angle; with nothing being done to shore it up, it will surely collapse in the near future.) As a sweetener, the authorities are also planning to install a mains sewerage system—the giant concrete sections of pipe are lined up along the corniche. To ready the temple for its new starring role, workmen are painstakingly cleaning centuries of soot and dirt from the reliefs to expose the vivid colours. Once the whole project is finished, the temple will be a wondrous sight, directly accessible to cruise ships from the quayside, and no doubt swamped with tourists. Cleaner, more accessible, but busier and less romantic.

Future visitors to Esna may enjoy an uninterrupted walk from quayside to temple, but they will still have to get through the Esna Barrage before continuing their cruise to Luxor. Built in traditional sandstone from Gebel el-Silsila by Egyptian navvies overseen by English engineers, the barrage was completed in 1906. It was one of the last old-style barrages across the Nile, designed to regulate the river's flow (while letting silt pass through) and expand irrigation. It remains a spectacular and elegant feat of engineering. The same cannot, alas, be said for its modern counterpart, half a mile further north, designed for electricity generation and built from ugly concrete.

Waiting to get through the Esna Barrage is a characteristically Egyptian experience. Boats jostle for position, trying to get ahead of each other in the queue. Every boat is given a specified place, but wads of *baksheesh* also have something to do with who goes first. Our dahabiya is overtaken by several large cruise ships while we circle, like an airliner in a holding pattern, waiting for our turn. After three-and-a-half hours hanging back, we get the all-clear to pass through the narrow channel in the old barrage. The stone structure is redundant, its sluices all open, but its status as an historic monument has saved it from demolition.

Getting through the old barrage is only stage one. Once safely through the narrow passage and out into the pool between the two barrages, we are forced to wait again until called forwards into the lock. Scarf sellers come alongside in small wooden boats and throw their wares up on to our deck, hoping for a sale. Eventually, we enter the lock with our two tugs, the lock doors close, and the water level starts to fall rapidly. The tug to our stern is moored by rope to the side of the lock, and one of the tug-boys lets the rope out as the water level falls. But halfway down, the rope snags around the eye on the tug's foredeck, and the tug is left dangling by a single rope as the water falls away beneath it. The strain is too much and the thick nylon rope snaps under the tug's weight with a loud crack. The tug falls back down to the water surface and there is much loud shouting and cursing from the captain. The deck-hand looks dejected—he is not having a good day. Once the water level in the lock has fallen twenty-five to thirty feet, the downstream doors open and we are soon on our way northwards again. The whole business has taken nearly four hours: frustrating for Western tourists, but of no consequence to the local Egyptians. Time here in the deep south passes at the pace of the river's flow, gentle and unhurried; if Allah wills it, it will happen, if He doesn't, it won't; what cannot be accomplished today can always wait until tomorrow; and what's the hurry, anyway?

IN THE FINAL STRETCH of valley before the Theban plain, the Nile broadens out to flow between dramatic cliffs. On the east bank, beyond lush banana plantations, a towering escarpment soon gives way to distant, hazy, age-eroded bluffs, while on the west bank the limestone cliffs come right up to the river's edge. Here, the most prominent features in the landscape are two hills running parallel to the Nile. Heralding the approach to Thebes and its riches, in ancient times they marked the border between the deep south and the Thebaïd. They gave their name to the local settlement: ancient Inerty and modern Gebelein, both meaning "two hills."

The southern hill, closest to the Nile, has a forbidding, jagged outline. Its eastern flank is steep, inaccessible and scarred with ravines. Access to the summit is therefore via a narrow, stony track which winds up the hill's gentler, western side. The panorama from the top is spectacular: a commanding prospect of the river to the south and north as it rounds a gentle bend, and a clear view of the east bank. Little wonder that Gebelein in ancient times was a site of strategic importance, guarding the southern approaches to Thebes. To sanctify its significance, Egypt's early kings built a temple to the protector-goddess Hathor on the summit of the southern hill. This small stone shrine, far removed in scale and setting from the grander temples of Upper Egypt, was none the less visited by rulers throughout the dynasties.

Walking back down the hill, through the modern village of Gebelein, is like stepping back in time. Ragged barefoot children play in the dusty streets, which they share with chickens and stray dogs. Goats graze on scraps of thorny scrub and bundles of fodder dumped casually by the roadside. Donkeys are the main means of transport, supplemented by the odd pickup truck. The people are shy but curious, cheerful despite their poverty, and welcoming to visitors, despite an initial reticence. At the arrival of our tour group, the children soon organise themselves into a gaggle, begging to have their photograph taken, while other villagers simply come out to gaze at the strangers in their midst. Foreigners are a rarity here. Yet at one particular moment in Egyptian history—the civil war at the start of the third millennium BC—Gebelein was home to a remarkable community of immigrants. Their actions not only contributed to the fortunes of their adopted village but shaped the destiny of the whole of Egypt.

Their stories came to light during excavations at the northern of the two hills that give Gebelein its name. This lies further back from the river, about a mile from its southern counterpart. No temple adorned its summit. Instead, its sides and the adjacent low desert were used as the community's burial ground, for thousands of years. Hundreds of tomb shafts and graves still pock-mark its surface. Among the objects recovered from them, by Italian archaeologists in the 1930s, were the oldest known scrap of painted linen, decorated with scenes of a rowing boat and a hippopotamus hunt; and a unique stone dish carved with the image of an anteater. Both artefacts give us a sense of life as it has been lived at Gebelein since the earliest times, framed by the river and the desert. Alongside these burials from Egypt's prehistoric period, another group of graves shed light on an equally fascinating episode: the civil war that ravaged Upper Egypt after the end of the Pyramid Age. The first salvoes in this conflict were fired near Gebelein, when a local leader tried to extend his writ. What started as a minor dispute between rival governors soon escalated into an all-out fight for territory and then into a battle for the throne of Egypt. On all sides of the conflict, society was swiftly militarised: an intact burial from Gebelein includes weapons (bows and arrows) alongside the usual grave goods. And all sides looked to the outside for military support.

In ancient Egypt, anyone wishing to raise an army quickly naturally turned to Nubia. The Nile Valley beyond the First Cataract was relatively impoverished compared to Egypt, and its men were only too willing to fight in anyone's army for a price. As it happens, the Nubians were also expert archers: a bow was the very sign used to denote Lower Nubia in ancient Egyptian writing. The combination of poverty and proficiency with the bow made the Nubians the perfect mercenaries. In Egypt's civil war, Nubians were signed up by all factions.

One particular cohort was stationed at Gebelein. Gravestones from the cemetery record the names and accomplishments of members of this expatriate community. A soldier called Qedes is typical. He describes himself as "an excellent warrior who acted with his strong arm at the forefront of his troop"[11] and claims that, "As a runner I surpassed this whole town, Nubians and Upper Egyptians (alike)."[12] Such boasts came naturally to the ancient Egyptians and are commonplace among their funerary inscriptions. To this extent, Qedes had become fully acculturated. But what is remarkable about him and his fellow mercenaries is the way in which they chose to depict themselves on their gravestones: not as Egyptians, but as Nubians, with distinctive clothing, coiffures and facial features. In ancient Egypt, the general rule was that anyone who lived like an Egyptian was regarded as an Egyptian, and accepted as part of the community. This makes the case of the Gebelein mercenaries even more remarkable. Buried in the Egyptian manner, but retaining their Nubian identity, these soldiers from the upper reaches of the Nile Valley must have enjoyed considerable renown among the local inhabitants, so much so that they consciously chose to retain and celebrate aspects of their distinctive cultural identity.

Today, once again, southern Egypt is home to immigrants from the upper Nile—not seeking their fortune in warfare but fleeing it. Since the start of the Sudanese civil war in the 1990s, some four million illegal immigrants have poured into Egypt. Yet the Egyptian police who are ordered to round them up and deport them on planes back to Khartoum generally turn a blind eye. Egyptians feel a special affinity for the Sudanese—"They are our cousins," explained my guide—and besides, "they do the dirty jobs."[13]

Beyond Gebelein, the floodplain broadens out on the west bank, and much of the land is given over to the cultivation of sugar cane. This has brought employment to the region but also unexpected hazards. During the Islamist insurgency of the 1990s, extremists used the tall fields of sugar cane as hiding places from which to attack convoys of passing tourists. The Egyptian government therefore ordered that a swathe of land some five to ten yards deep be left uncultivated at the edge of any field bordering a road. Although the insurgency has been largely defeated, the restriction remains in force, accounting for one of the more curious features of the rural landscape in this part of Egypt. The presence of tourists is, of course, the result of proximity to Luxor and the monuments of ancient Thebes. Those world-famous temples and tombs eclipse all other antiquities in the region, and few visitors venture even a few miles south of the main tourist sights.

However, between Gebelein and Thebes, one site has a worthy place in the annals of Egyptian history. In classical times, Hermonthis (modern Armant) was known principally for its temple to Isis. Here, Cleopatra built a "birth-house" to celebrate the birth of her son by Julius Caesar, Caesarion. The Romans added baths and a town wall. The history of Armant, however, goes back much further. A temple was founded here in the New Kingdom, and gained a special significance from its association with a long line of sacred bulls.

The ancient Egyptians, especially in the final phases of pharaonic civilisation, were obsessed with animal worship. Everywhere they looked in the natural world they saw divine manifestations. Cats were revered as sacred to the goddess Bastet, ibises as representatives of the god Thoth. Jackals, baboons and even fish were kept in special enclosures to be worshipped, mummified and buried as acts of piety. At Kom Ombo, it was crocodiles for Sobek; at Edfu, falcons for Horus; and at Armant, it was bulls for Ra. Mummifying and burying bulls was a considerable undertaking, and an entire underground catacomb was excavated at Armant to receive the embalmed bodies of these great beasts. The so-called Buchis bulls were buried with full honours, including gravestones describing significant events in their lives (such as delivering oracles, curing eye infections and engaging in bullfights). The bulls' mothers were buried nearby in a separate vault. This strange practice was carried out continuously at Armant for a period of six centuries, from the reign of Egypt's last native pharaoh until the persecutions of the Roman Emperor Diocletian.

That we know so much—or anything at all—about the curious history of Armant is due to the dedication and munificence of an unlikely patron of Egyptology. Outside the world of archaeology, the name of Robert Mond (1867–1938) is primarily associated with industrial chemicals. Born in Cheshire in 1867, he followed in the family business, taking over from his German-Jewish immigrant father the factory that had grown from humble beginnings to become the largest producer of soda in the world. (Mond senior and his business partner were the first industrialists in England to reward their workers with one week's annual holiday with double pay.) Robert expanded the Mond interests, becoming chairman of a nickel company with mines in Ontario, Canada. He was elected Honorary Secretary for life of the Davy–Faraday Laboratory at the Royal Institution, and was a founder and benefactor of various learned societies. So he might have remained—a distinguished chemist and philanthropist—but for a serious illness contracted in 1902, soon after the birth of his second daughter. Like many wealthy Englishmen of his time and situation, he was advised by his doctor to spend the next few winters in Egypt.

For a man such as Robert Mond, this necessitated finding an outlet for his energies. So began a lifelong interest in Egyptian archaeology. (It is a nice coincidence that the word "chemistry" is derived from "alchemy," an Arabic formulation from the Greek *chemeia*, "the Egyptian art.") From his steam-dahabiya moored off the west bank, Mond excavated at Thebes for many years, during which he discovered several tombs and paid for the restoration and conservation of many more. During this time he amassed a fine collection of Egyptian antiquities which he displayed in his home in Cavendish Square, London, in a huge room decorated to resemble a pharaoh's palace.

By the winter of 1925 Mond was growing restless and in search of a new challenge. In the early weeks of 1926, he set out from Thebes with his archaeological assistant to prospect for a new site. They hit upon Armant, just ten miles south, whose ancient history was then almost entirely unknown. In three years of excavation under Mond's personal direction, and several more under his patronage, the burials of the Buchis bulls and the other ruins of ancient Armant were brought to light. A job

on the dig team at Armant was a plum posting: with so generous a benefactor, conditions were more comfortable than on other excavations. At
Christmas 1928, for example, Mond had two enormous food hampers
sent from Fortnum & Mason in London. At his own expense, he had
a paved road constructed along the ten miles from Thebes to Armant
so that he could visit the excavations two or three times a week by car,
inspect the work and record progress. Mond was just as energetic and
progressive when it came to publishing his results. For the five volumes
of his seasons at Armant, he enlisted the help of sixty-nine scholars and
scientists, a multi-disciplinary team of specialists that set a new standard
for Egyptology.

Thanks to the efforts and largesse of Robert Mond, Armant is better
known than many similar sites in the southern Nile Valley. What his
excavations showed is that Armant was never a major centre of culture
or politics, but despite—or because of—that relative insignificance, it
remained in continuous occupation from prehistoric times to the present day, an unbroken record stretching back some five thousand years. It
was the site, successively, of a pharaonic temple, Ptolemaic birth-house,
Roman shrine and Coptic church, while today an Islamic cemetery covers much of the ruins. Its modern name Armant is merely an Arabisation
of Hermonthis, which in turn preserves the name of the ancient Theban
war-god Montu. Such are the continuities in this part of Egypt: modest communities that encapsulate the Nile Valley's long and colourful
history.

FOUR

Luxor

City of Wonders

It is a place that strikes you into silence.[1]

—AMELIA EDWARDS

For many visitors to Egypt, the Nile is at its most entrancing and evocative as it flows majestically past the city of Luxor, its course unchanged since the days of Tutankhamun, Ramesses the Great and the Ptolemies—all of whom arrived here by river to moor at the quays of ancient Thebes. Now, as then, reflections of the rosy Theban Hills looming in the distance are captured in the Nile's broad waters. During the day, ferries ply the river, transporting goods, people and animals from shore to shore. The hills of the west bank, in ancient times the realm of the dead, retain an aura of mystery, belying their status as one of the great tourist destinations of the world. While the riverside of the west bank has sprouted an accretion of modern hotels, restaurants and shops to cater for visitors, beyond these, across the floodplain green with sugar-cane fields, the landscape presents a timeless picture of towering hills, dotted with tomb shafts.

The east bank, by contrast, offers an entirely man-made vista. Multi-decked tourist cruisers and traditional feluccas line the quays, several boats deep, jostling for the best position. Above them, a broad, paved promenade runs along the river's edge, backed by a busy road jammed with coaches, hooting taxis, belching pick-up trucks and horse-drawn caleches. On the far side of the corniche, hotels, shops and offices create an artificial landscape of concrete and brick. West and east, timelessness and modernity. And linking the two, connecting past and present, the constant Nile, the lifeblood of Thebes and of Egypt. As the sun sets each evening, the river turns a deep, inky blue with ripples of burnt orange, heralding the end of another daily cycle.

LUXOR IS BEST APPRECIATED from the Nile. As my boat arrives from the south, borne along gently on the river's current, the city, with its numerous sights, unfolds like a panorama. Arriving at Luxor over a century ago, Amelia Edwards described the scene thus:

> The top of another pylon [gate-tower]; the slender peak of an obelisk; a colonnade of giant pillars half-buried in the soil; the white houses of the English, American, and Prussian Consuls, each with its flagstaff and ensign; a steep slope of sandy shore; a background of mud walls and pigeon-towers; a foreground of native boats and gaily-painted daha-beeyahs lying at anchor—such, as we sweep by, is our first panoramic view of this famous village.[2]

Today, the accumulations of centuries have been cleared from around the temple pillars and the houses of the Western consuls have gone, but otherwise the view remains remarkably similar. Certainly, the experience of modern visitors on stepping ashore at the quay of Luxor is unchanged in 130 years: "the children screaming for backshish; the dealers exhibiting strings of imitation scarabs."[3]

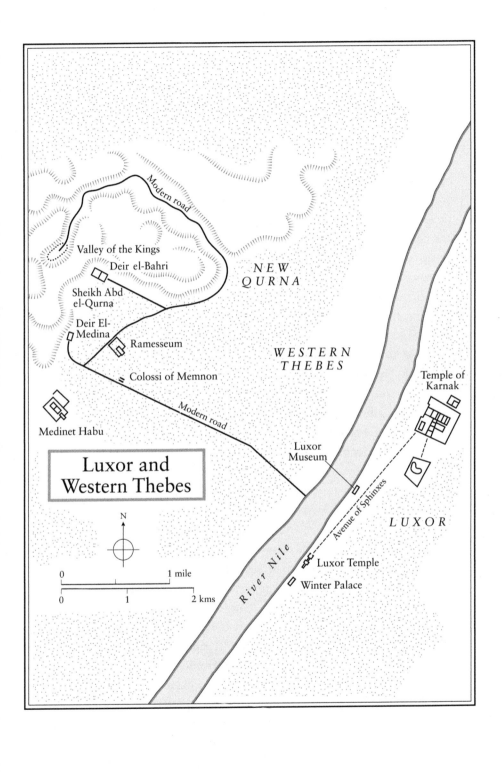

Valley of the Kings

Deir el-Bahri

Sheikh Abd
el-Qurna

Deir El-
Medina

Ramesseum

Colossi of Memnon

Medinet Habu

Modern road

NEW
QURNA

WESTERN
THEBES

Modern road

Luxor
Museum

Temple of
Karnak

Avenue of Sphinxes

LUXOR

Luxor Temple

Winter Palace

River Nile

Luxor and
Western Thebes

N

0 — 1 mile
0 — 1 — 2 kms

Above all, Luxor is a city of ancient monuments, of spectacular temples with their gate-towers and columned halls. To the ancient Greeks, it was "hundred-gated Thebes," to Egypt's Arab conquerors "the castles" (al-Uqsur, the origin of the city's modern name). An anonymous Venetian who reached Luxor in 1589 called its temples the only buildings in Egypt worthy of admiration, eclipsing in his mind even the pyramids. In exploring this city of wonders and its remarkable history, there is no better place to start than the monument which still stands at the heart of things, Luxor Temple itself. History has not been particularly kind to Luxor's defining edifice. The original "southern sanctuary" (the temple's ancient name) now stands next to the city's busiest roundabout, the last vestiges of sanctity drowned out by the din of traffic. From the roadside pavement, as I try desperately to fend off hawkers and caleche-drivers, it is difficult to recapture that sense of awe and wonder, of majesty and mystery, that cloaked the temple in its heyday; difficult to imagine the temple standing proud over the southern city, a monument to the institution of divine kingship. Luxor Temple is far better appreciated from the river. From this vantage point, the temple's undulating, elongated layout of courts and gate-towers ("pylons" to Egyptologists) is clearly discernible, running parallel to the Nile, with later additions along its northern axis. From the river, it is easier, too, to block out the modern intrusions and focus on the ancient stones.

Most pharaonic temples were laid out facing the river, both for ease of access—ancient Egyptian kings routinely travelled by boat; when they wished to disembark at a particular place, the royal barque would moor at a dock directly in front of the main temple—and for symbolic reasons, to emphasise their connection with the life-giving force of the Nile. But Luxor Temple was designed from the outset as an annexe (albeit a rather grand one) of the larger Karnak Temple, a mile and a half to the north. So it is that the main entrance of Luxor Temple faces directly towards Karnak, rather than towards the Nile. And what an entrance it is! For the façade of Luxor Temple is everyone's archetypal Egyptian monument, its massive pylon fronted by colossal royal statues and obelisks. Or, rather, obelisk. For the most jarring feature of the temple's modern appearance is its lack of symmetry. Where on the east side of the entrance there is an eighty-foot high obelisk, on the west side there is merely an empty pedestal. The story of Luxor's missing obelisk involves the very beginnings of Egyptology. Its unlikely hero (or villain) was a Frenchman at the court of Louis XV, an artist whose pornographic sketches titillated France's high society in the dying days of the *ancien régime*.

Dominique Vivant Denon (1747–1825) was born into a family of landed gentry in provincial Chalon-sur-Saône. At the age of seventeen, as all ambitious young men did, he went to Paris. There he studied design, and succeeded in being appointed a Gentilhomme Ordinaire to Louis XV. With the patronage of the king's mistress, Madame de Pompadour, he transformed himself from court artist into diplomat, serving in St. Petersburg, Switzerland and Naples. Diplomatic life may have been somewhat dull after the intrigues of Versailles, but it turned out to be a good career move for Denon, for when the French Revolution broke out in 1789 he found himself safely in Venice. Unlike many of his former circle he escaped with his life, but all his property was confiscated. Having no wish to live the remainder of his days in penury and confident of his own diplomatic skills, Denon decided to return to Paris in 1793 and put himself under the protection of a fellow artist, Jacques-Louis David, the revolutionaries' painter of choice. It was a brilliant move. Denon made the acquaintance of Napoleon Bonaparte and soon won his confidence. So much so that, when Bonaparte embarked on his great expedition to Egypt on 14 May 1798—with the purpose of wresting control of the country from the British, to undermine their dominance of trade with India—he took Denon with him as one of his closest lieutenants.

Denon's account of his travels along the Nile, *Voyages dans la Basse et la Haute Egypte*, proved an instant hit when it was published on his return to France, catapulting the land of the pharaohs to the forefront of the European imagination. His extensive drawings were no less influential, forming the nucleus of the Napoleonic *Déscription de l'Egypte*, a massive tome that marked the birth of Egyptology as a discipline. The two books, and the wave of Egyptomania that swept the cities of Europe following their publication, inspired one of Denon's young countrymen, Jean-François Champollion (1790–1832), to decipher the language of the pharaohs. After two decades of painstaking research, he made the breakthrough that correctly explained the hieroglyphic writing system for the first time.

Yet, for the great empires of nineteenth-century Europe, it was not merely enough to understand ancient Egypt: they wanted a piece of it to add lustre to their imperial capitals. On first seeing Thebes, on 26 January 1799, Denon and his men had been overwhelmed by the city's ancient monuments. As Denon recalled in his memoirs, "The army came to a stop by itself and spontaneously burst into applause, as if occupying the ruins of this capital had been the goal of our glorious mission and had completed the conquest of Egypt."[4] Among so many architectural wonders, Denon had been particularly impressed by the obelisks in front of Luxor Temple. In his diary he commented, "there is nothing on earth to compare with them."[5] Champollion, on his visit of 1828, was equally smitten. For the French, there could be no symbol more fitting of their new greatness than to have one of the Luxor obelisks erected in the heart of Paris. As one contemporary commentator put it, "The pharaohs, the Ptolemies, the Caesars, the Popes had, in turn, erected these imposing signs of Egyptian civilisation."[6] Now it was France's turn.

Negotiations with the Viceroy of Egypt, Muhammad Ali, were opened on the orders of Louis XVIII in the 1820s, with the objective of securing an obelisk for France. One of the obelisks of Alexandria, the second Cleopatra's needle, was gifted to France, but for some reason it never made the journey. It was Champollion who reawakened the idea, in 1829, but with a different monument in mind: "If one must see an Egyptian obelisk in Paris, then let it be one of those from Luxor."[7] The views of so eminent an Egyptologist could not be dismissed, so a plan was duly presented to the new French king, Charles X, with the assurance that, if Paris had one of the Luxor obelisks, "it would no longer have any reason to envy Rome."[8] The king was readily persuaded, and established a royal commission under a Monsieur Taylor to travel to Egypt. Taylor's twin goals were to negotiate the gift of the Luxor obelisk and to amass additional antiquities to enrich the collections of the Louvre. To lubricate the negotiations, he was given the enormous sum of 100,000 francs, as well as various presents for Muhammad Ali and his son. Taylor arrived at Alexandria on 23 April 1830, and was kept waiting a month before the viceroy deigned to receive him.

From the outset, the negotiations were tricky. The British had stolen a march on the French and had already put in a demand for the Luxor obelisks. But the viceroy sensed the political importance of keeping the French happy, so "He gave to France the two Luxor obelisks, confirmed the gift that he had made previously of the Alexandria obelisk, and offered in exchange to M. Barker [the British consul] the Karnak obelisk."[9] It was a deal. The Paris revolution of July 1830 threatened to scupper the agreement, but Champollion persisted in his plan and eventually the gift was reconfirmed in a letter that November from Muhammad Ali's minister: "I am commanded by His Highness to put the three aforementioned monuments at the disposal of His Majesty the King of the French with immediate effect."[10]

On 15 April 1831, an extraordinary boat named the *Luxor* set sail from Toulon, bound for the Nile. It had been built to endure two long sea voyages to and from France, to navigate the shallow waters of the Nile and the Seine, and to pass under the arches of the Paris bridges. It also had to accommodate a 250-ton obelisk in a wooden and iron cage. Exactly four months after leaving its home port on the Mediterranean coast, the *Luxor* docked at Luxor, ready to receive its colossal cargo. Unfortunately, things had not been going smoothly at the temple. On arrival at Luxor months earlier, the French engineers had been met with suspicion, their explanation—of dismantling one of the obelisks and transporting it to France—with incredulity. Once they had convinced the locals of their peaceful intentions, they had been forced to embark on lengthy negotiations with the owners of the houses that abutted the Luxor obelisk, houses that would have to be demolished before the monument could be taken down. Two weeks after the *Luxor* docked, an outbreak of cholera killed fifteen French sailors and threatened the entire project. But the engineers stuck resolutely to their great enterprise: "Nobody left his post, nothing interrupted the work, a single idea motivated us all: to remove from the ancient capital of the civilised world one of its most beautiful ornaments."[11]

Against enormous odds, by 1 September 1831 the Luxor obelisk had been encased in scaffolding. It took another month to lower it safely to the ground, and three more months to drag it to the riverbank and load it on to the waiting ship. It was now mid December, and the river level had dropped. Only when the inundation returned the following August could the *Luxor*, with its precious cargo, finally weigh anchor and embark on the long journey back to France. The ship arrived in Paris on 23 December 1833, entered dry dock and was dismantled around the obelisk. Another three years' careful work was needed before the great stone needle was ready to be installed in its new home. "On 25 October [1836], in the morning, more than 200,000 spectators filled the Place de la Concorde, all its exits, the terraces of the Tuileries and the Champs-Elysées, waiting with avid curiosity for the erection of the obelisk."[12] Fortunately the weather was dry, if a little overcast. A time capsule, consisting of a cedar box containing gold and silver coins and medallions of the king, was placed in a cavity cut in the centre of the pedestal before the obelisk was hauled into position. To crown the work, young men scaled the monument and adorned its summit with laurel wreaths and tricolours. The French state struck a commemorative medal to mark the great occasion.

Sadly, Vivant Denon had died eleven years earlier and was unable to witness the realisation of his dream. The irony would not have been lost on the wily old diplomat: an obelisk from the greatest kingdom of the ancient world now stood at the centre of the Place de la Concorde—the very spot that, three decades earlier, had witnessed the execution of the French ruling class (including many of Denon's friends and colleagues) by Madame la Guillotine. As for the British, who had coveted the Luxor obelisks for themselves, they could only look on with customary disdain. When, some fifty years later, Amelia Edwards visited Luxor Temple with its now solitary obelisk, she remarked drily that its companion was "already scaling away by imperceptible degrees under the skyey influences of an alien climate,"[13] and imagined it looking down "with melancholy indifference upon the petty revolutions and counter-revolutions of the Place de la Concorde."[14] France had acquired an appropriately imperial monument, one of the glories of pharaonic architecture. But Egypt had lost one of its architectural wonders. As the pharaohs had known only too well, the Nile could give and the Nile could take away.

In the early days of Nile tourism, Luxor Temple presented a very different picture from today's pristine attraction. Back then, the half-buried temple was "a smoky, filthy, intricate labyrinth of lanes and passages. Mud hovels, mud pigeon-towers, mud yards and a mud mosque clustered like wasps' nests in and about the ruins. Architraves sculptured with royal titles supported the roofs of squalid cabins. Stately capitals peeped out from the midst of sheds in which buffaloes, camels, donkeys, dogs, and human beings were seen herding together in unsavoury fellowship."[15] How different from the description of Luxor Temple composed for its royal builder, pharaoh Amenhotep III, in 1360 BC:

> *It is made of fine sandstone, very wide and incredibly beautiful.*
> *Its walls are of electrum, its furnishings of silver.*
> *All its gates are decorated on their thresholds.*
> *Its pylon rises up towards heaven, its flagstaffs are in the stars.*
> *When the people see it, they will give praise to His Majesty.*[16]

In an age feted for magnificent monuments, Luxor Temple ranked as one of Egypt's greatest architectural achievements. Originally conceived in 1539 BC as a monument to monarchy, the southern sanctuary was one of a series of monuments situated at the four corners of the city of Thebes, to demarcate a sacred arena in which the king would play the leading role. Over the course of the following two centuries a modest shrine was transformed into a great temple of courts and columned halls. The current façade was added by Ramesses II, its massive pylon and towering obelisk(s) expressing his uncompromising and overweening megalomania. The two seated colossi that flank the entrance do likewise. On their pedestals, decorated with images of conquered peoples, Ramesses' names are carved so deeply that they could never be erased. The walls of the massive gate-towers are decorated with scenes from the Battle of Kadesh, Ramesses' epic encounter with the Hittites. In his quest for perfection, Ramesses was also responsible for the temple's curious alignment. Having discovered that the original axis failed to line up precisely with Karnak (a mile and a half to the north), Ramesses ordered the error to be corrected in the orientation of his new forecourt. Hence the curious kink in what is otherwise a perfectly symmetrical monument.

The core of Luxor Temple is the creation of Amenhotep III's reign. Here, the elegance of form and ambition of scale reflect ancient Egyptian civilisation at the height of its aesthetic powers. There is the immense processional colonnade of fourteen gigantic stone columns, each shaped to resemble a papyrus reed in full flower. Never before in the history of ancient Egypt had such a vast edifice been conceived or constructed. To those walking beneath them, the tops of the columns must indeed have seemed to be "in the stars." Beyond the colonnade lies the most beautiful part of the whole temple, the so-called "solar court," each side formed by a double row of twelve elegant columns carved to resemble bundles of papyrus reeds. The purpose of this part of the temple was to associate the king indissolubly with the sun, the supreme creator god. Temple courts had traditionally been roofed, their dimly lit interiors creating a sense of mystery and emphasising the ineffableness of the divine. By contrast, the solar court was deliberately left open to the sky to permit the direct worship of the sun, and to allow the sun's rays to fall uninterrupted on the king and his officials.

The solar court was not just the expression of a new theology in which king and sun-god were associated in an ever-closer union. It was also the setting for the king's transformation into an immortal divine being. This was expressed most startlingly in a life-size statue which Amenhotep III commissioned in anticipation of his jubilee. Carved from a block of dazzling red quartzite (a stone with strong solar connotations) and adorned with gold, the statue showed the king emerging into the solar court at Luxor, visibly younger, radiant as the sun, and undergoing transformation into a celestial falcon. By a miracle of preservation, the statue escaped the ravages of time, buried in a deep pit in the middle of the solar court—where it was unearthed in 1989. Today, it is regarded as one of the masterpieces of ancient Egyptian sculpture, and takes pride of place in the Luxor Museum.

The solar court of Luxor Temple was both radical in its conception and extraordinary in its execution. Remarkably, it can be attributed to identifiable individuals, because a commemorative stone slab from the time of Amenhotep III names the architects responsible: the twin brothers Suti and Hor. Like their royal master, they were adherents of the sun cult, but it is the details of their lives, rather than their faith, that are most fascinating. For Suti and Hor are the only definitely attested twins in the whole of pharaonic history. Suti was the senior, presumably the elder, but to all intents and purposes the two brothers were treated as a single individual. Their very survival into adulthood—at a time when multiple births usually resulted in infant mortality—may have given them a special status and contributed to their rapid advancement. Appointed joint "Overseers of Works of Amun in the Southern Sanctuary," they shared the responsibility equally:

My brother, my likeness, his ways I trust,
He came forth from the womb with me the same day . . .
When I was in charge on the west side,
He was in charge on the east side.
We controlled the great monuments in Ipet-sut [Karnak],
At the forefront of Thebes, the city of Amun.[17]

In the midst of modern Luxor's urban sprawl, thronged by visitors and hawkers, assaulted by the din of city life, Suti and Hor's remarkable creation still stands serene, as it has for over three thousand years: a remarkable testament to the vision and energy of the ancient Egyptians, and a potent symbol of their continuing legacy.

IN EVERY AGE, Luxor Temple has been at the centre of Theban and Egyptian religion. Through pharaonic, Greek, Roman, Byzantine and Islamic rule, for over a hundred generations, the inhabitants of Thebes have come to pray among the hallowed stones of Luxor. Nowhere else on earth—not even the temple at Jerusalem—has seen such a continuity of worship, stretching back 3,500 years. As its original name, southern sanctuary, suggests, Luxor Temple began life as a holiday home for the Theban god Amun, a small pied-à-terre closely linked to, but some distance from, his main residence at Karnak. According to ancient Egyptian custom, Amun would journey south from Karnak to Luxor once a year for some rest and relaxation from the onerous duties of divinity. (That the ancient Egyptian words for "sanctuary" and "harem" are the same is no coincidence.) But in reality, Luxor Temple had another, more subtle purpose. Right from the start, Egypt's Eighteenth Dynasty royal family had embarked on a deliberate programme of architecture and spectacle designed to associate the king with Amun, and to blur the distinction between royal and divine. Luxor Temple played a vital part in the ideology which underpinned the regime.

The doctrine of divine kingship was the defining myth of the pharaonic state, the ideological glue which held ancient Egypt together. But the notion of a divine monarch was potentially undermined by a fundamental weakness: the all-too-obvious mortality of the king. The solution to this dilemma was one of the most ingenious pieces of theology ever devised by Egyptian priests. According to this myth, the king was rendered divine by means of a god-like essence (*ka*) that, at his accession, suffused his mortal body. At the king's death, the royal *ka* would pass, unaltered, into his heir, thus maintaining the divinely ordained succession. Luxor Temple became the setting of a new religious ritual, the annual Festival of the Sanctuary, which was explicitly designed to recharge the royal *ka*, so that the monarch might be rejuvenated and reaffirmed in office.

At the start of the Festival, the cult images of Amun, his consort (Mut) and their son (Khonsu) were taken from Karnak to Luxor. Originally, the images travelled overland along an avenue of sphinxes, borne aloft on the shoulders of priests, and resting at way-stations along the route. In the later Eighteenth Dynasty, they were towed along the Nile by barge, the focal point of a great river pageant. Once safely inside the precinct of Luxor Temple, the cult images were taken from their barque-shrines and installed in their new quarters. Here, in the innermost chambers of the temple, the Festival reached its culmination. Amidst the ritually charged atmosphere, the pharaoh communed in private with the god; Egypt's supreme deity and the king's divine essence co-mingled and drew strength from each other. At the end of the communion, the king would emerge into the open court of the temple, to be acclaimed by the priests and high officials of the realm as "foremost of all the living *kas*."[18]

The Festival of the Sanctuary was one of the rare occasions when ordinary citizens might share in the otherwise rarefied religious life of the court, glimpsing the sacred barque of Amun when it passed through the streets on its way to the temple. The propaganda value of a popular celebration, especially a river pageant, with the monarch at its heart was not lost on Egypt's rulers, and the Festival of the Sanctuary shaped the Egyptians' religious experience for centuries to come.

Even after the demise of the pharaohs, Luxor Temple continued to assert its role at the centre of national faith. Of all the individuals who ruled the Nile Valley after the last of the pharaohs, none was more taken with Egypt's distinctive religion than Alexander the Great. For a man convinced of his own divine origins, Egypt held a special appeal; and Luxor Temple, so closely associated with kings' god-like status, was the object of particular attention. Determined to leave his mark in this most important of sacred places, Alexander commissioned an enormous granite shrine, decorated with scenes showing him in the guise of a traditional pharaoh. At his command, the shrine was installed in the room immediately behind the communion chamber, at the very heart of the inner temple. It was as if Alexander was taking possession of the entire building, and with it, the source of the divine kingship that he so earnestly desired. A similar aspiration seems to have motivated Egypt's later, Roman rulers. The emperor Hadrian had a small mud-brick shrine built at the north-west corner of the temple enclosure, dedicated to the composite Greek–Egyptian deity Serapis; while, inside the shrine, a statue of Isis underlined the special appeal of this goddess to the peoples of the Roman Empire.

But the Romans, like Alexander, wanted not merely to beautify Luxor Temple but to appropriate it. At the beginning of the fourth century AD Luxor Temple was extensively remodelled to turn it into a Roman shrine. One of the columned halls behind the southern colonnade of the solar court was transformed into a chapel of the imperial cult. Amenhotep III's elegant columns were torn down, and a central, apsidal niche was created in the back wall, blocking the doorway. The exquisite pharaonic reliefs were covered with plaster and new paintings were commissioned showing Rome's four rulers, the tetrarchs, clad in purple robes. Inside the niche stood the cult object itself, possibly a statue of the emperor, shaded by a baldachin supported on four columns of pink granite with Corinthian capitals. The adjacent walls were plastered and decorated with scenes of Rome's imperial might, including a procession of soldiers. A neighbouring chamber seems to have been used to store the imperial standards belonging to the legion stationed at Luxor; such emblems were, like the colours of modern regiments in the British army, not mere symbols but objects of pride and veneration.

The painting of the tetrarchs seems to have commemorated an actual imperial visit to Luxor, by the emperor Diocletian, in AD 298. The visit was not just a tour of inspection but a deliberate act of foreign policy designed to pacify Rome's most lucrative province. Egypt had been particularly fractious and unsettled in the final years of the third century, witnessing a Theban revolt against Roman rule, incursions by the marauding Blemmyan tribes of the Eastern Desert, and finally a bid for independence led by a Roman official. Only a visit from the emperor himself could quell such uprisings and reassert central control. An immediate result of Diocletian's visit was the construction, in the final weeks of AD 301, of a massive military camp around Luxor Temple, to serve as the garrison for the third legion.

The pharaonic temple now occupied the central section of a great rectangular fortress, with square towers at the corners and semi-circular bastions along the four walls. This effectively placed much of the temple off-limits to the native Egyptian clergy, although priests were still allowed access to the inner sanctum—albeit by new doorways, blasted through the masonry on the temple's eastern side. Well-defended gates in the fort's enclosure wall gave access to strategic locations: the town of Luxor from the eastern gate, the river quay from the north-western. The pylon of Ramesses II, with its colossal statues and obelisks, formed a suitably imposing entrance to the camp, which was filled with barracks and storerooms on either side of the temple proper. This was not, however, a mere appropriation of a pharaonic monument for imperial ends. It was a full-scale usurpation. Distinctively Roman architectural features were added to Latinise the site. Behind the eastern gate an open square was created with columns at its four corners, each topped with a statue of the emperor. A second "tetrastyle" marked the north-west corner of the camp, while a statue of the emperor Constantine stood on a pedestal in the hypostyle hall.

To Luxor's inhabitants of the early fourth century, it must have seemed that the cult of the ruler—once a pharaoh, then a Macedonian conqueror, now a Roman emperor—would last for ever. But the winds of change were already blowing through the empire, and a new religion from the eastern Mediterranean was winning adherents at a rapid pace. Shortly after Diocletian's visit, Luxor itself felt the effects of this revolution. Two soldiers stationed in the camp, an infantryman named Sophron and a veteran called Chanatom, refused to carry out the rites of the imperial cult, protesting their Christian faith. Such a direct challenge to Roman rule could not be tolerated, and the two were put to death, together with Dalcina, the daughter of a local noble family. The three were instantly hailed as martyrs by their fellow Christians. Despite Diocletian's persecutions, Christianity gained a rapid foothold. Within little more than a decade, the empire was forced to accommodate and recognise the new religion. Although the Roman garrison remained at

Luxor for another three centuries, it did so as the military face of an increasingly Christian state.

Luxor Temple had already asborbed one change of religion. Now it did so again, while retaining its essential, sacral status. In AD 313, just a year after becoming Roman emperor, Constantine (himself a Christian convert) issued the Edict of Milan which recognised the new religion and paved the way for the conversion of the entire empire. Pharaonic religion had a strong influence on early Christianity—the iconography of the Virgin and child copied the imagery of Isis and Horus, while the key tenets of the Trinity, Resurrection and Last Judgement showed extensive borrowings from Egyptian ideas. So it is perhaps not surprising that the Egyptians were ready converts to the new faith. Churches soon sprang up throughout the Nile Valley, including no less than four within the precincts of Luxor Temple. Three were built just outside the walls of the pharaonic temple, two in the western part of the enclosure and one right in front of Ramesses II's great façade. One community of worshippers even moved into the pagan monument, building their church inside the Ramesside forecourt. They thereby commandeered a temple dedicated to Amun and his earthly incarnation, the king, for their new deity and his earthly incarnation, the Christ. The same appropriation can be seen elsewhere in Luxor Temple, where Christian symbols have been carved over hieroglyphics.

Yet, while pharaonic religion had been observed at Luxor for eighteen centuries, Christianity lasted barely three. The Arab conquest of Egypt in AD 639–41 made the country officially Islamic, although many in the countryside, including the region around Luxor, continued to hold on to their Christian faith. The man who finally won the Thebans over to Islam was al-Sayyid Youssef Ibn Abdel-Raheem, better known as Abu el-Haggag. He was born in Baghdad around 1150, a descendant of the Caliph Ali and thus of the Prophet Muhammad. With such an illustrious pedigree, his vocation as a religious teacher was never in doubt. He went first to Mecca, then to Egypt, where he studied with various Sufi groups in Cairo before travelling to Luxor. At the time of his arrival, Luxor had declined in importance and was no more than a small village set amongst impressive ruins. Legend has it that Luxor was ruled at the time by a strong woman named Sitt Towzah, and that she was far from pleased by the arrival of a charismatic foreign preacher. According to the story, Abu el-Haggag responded to her frostiness by building a wall around the village and binding it with a single thread, thus signifying his taking spiritual possession. He went on to found a centre for prayer and teaching at Luxor and lived in the town for many years. After his death in 1243, he was adopted by the locals as their patron sheikh. The church inside Luxor Temple was converted into a mosque, to receive Abu el-Haggag's bones, and it swiftly became a focus of pilgrimage. Even today, the sheikh continues to endow the place with *baraka*, divine blessing, from his resting place high above the forecourt of Ramesses II.

For all the changes that have taken place in the rites practised within Luxor Temple, one element remains constant—the importance of the River Nile. The *moulid* (festival) of Abu el-Haggag is celebrated every year, two weeks before the start of Ramadan. Over a period of two days, the people of Luxor enjoy a host of entertainments, ranging from dance and music to horse races and martial arts. The heart of the moulid is a noisy procession of boats through the temple and streets of Luxor. In 1925, the photographer Harry Burton (in Luxor for the clearance of Tutankhamun's tomb) recorded three full-sized feluccas being dragged around the temple. In more recent times, the number of boats has grown, and they now bear a closer resemblace to carnival floats, pulled by tractors and carrying local children. According to Islamic symbolism, the boats signify the quest for spiritual enlightenment, but they bear more than a passing resemblance to the barque shrines carried on the shoulders of priests during the annual Festival of the Sanctuary in pharaonic times. The moulid of Abu el-Haggag provides a tantalising glimpse of the religious life of ancient Thebes three thousand years ago and a powerful testament to the enduring sanctity of Luxor Temple. It has remained at the centre of Egypt's spiritual life and sense of identity over a period of thirty-five centuries. If a civilisation can be encapsulated in its monuments, Luxor Temple represents the history of Egypt in microcosm.

THE TEMPLE HAS ALSO PLAYED a central role in the modern engagement with ancient Egypt. Ever since the first Europeans reached the southern Nile Valley in the sixteenth century, their reports of Luxor's fabulous monuments have stirred the Western imagination. Perhaps nobody has done more to popularise the temples of ancient Thebes, nor to anchor them as archetypes of the exotic orient, than the Scottish painter David Roberts (1796–1864). His views of Egypt, and especially of Luxor, still sell in their thousands. No artist before or since has captured so effectively the timeless beauty of the Nile as it flows past the hills and monuments of ancient Thebes. Roberts' fame belies his humble origins. Born near Edinburgh, his father was a cobbler, his mother a washerwoman, three of his siblings died in childhood and he attended a local school only sporadically, enough to learn to write and gain a "small smattering of arithmetic."[19] But the young Roberts had a love of pictures and an innate talent for drawing. At the age of ten-and-a-half, he was apprenticed to an Edinburgh house-painter, and became skilled at decorative effects. The opportunity to work on the decoration of Scone Palace in 1815 gave him the break he needed, and he was engaged as a scene-painter to a touring pantomime company. Eventually, Roberts made his way to London to work at the Theatre Royal, Drury Lane, and became a founding member of the Society of British Artists.

This brought him into a circle of respected and influential fellow artists—his acquaintances included Sir Charles Barry and Ruskin, as well as Dickens and Thackeray—and he was encouraged to exhibit his paintings. His romantic style proved popular, and he was smart enough to see the potential of reproducing his work as prints, to reach a wider audience. His paintings from an extended visit to Spain in 1832–3 brought him widespread fame: he provided illustrations for the works of Sir Walter Scott, submitted designs for a new National Gallery, and was even invited to assist Barry with the decoration of the new Palace of Westminster. In 1838 Roberts was elected to the Royal Academy of Arts, signalling his full acceptance into the upper echelon of British artists. He had come a long way from the slums of outer Edinburgh.

But behind the professional success lay a private life in tatters. In 1820, Roberts had married Margaret McLachlan, and they had been blessed a year later with the birth of a daughter. But Margaret was an alcoholic, and her increasingly wayward behaviour put huge strains on the marriage. As Roberts himself recounted,

> about twelve years after our marriage I was compelled in consequence of [my wife's] abandoned and drunken habits and in order to save

myself and my child from utter destitution to break up my Establishment at 8 Abingdon Street and after placing my wife with her friends to leave England [for Spain]. But upon her solemn promise of amendment I took her back but she however relapsed into her former habits and I after trying in vain . . . to wean her from them was compelled in the year 1835 finally to separate from her and again to leave England.[20]

It was to prove a blessing in disguise. Ever since boyhood, Roberts had harboured an ambition to visit "the remote East."[21] Now he finally had the chance. In August 1838, he left London for Paris and made his way by land and sea to Alexandria, and thence to Cairo. At the port of Bulaq he hired a boat for 1,300 piastres (about £15) a month and, with the Union Jack flying at the mast, set sail up the Nile with a crew of eight, a rayyis and his faithful servant Ismail. As he travelled slowly the length of the Nile Valley, as far south as the Second Cataract, Roberts was saddened by the poverty of the people, but impressed by the scenery and overawed by the temples. His journal comes alive with his first-hand observations of Egyptian rural life: "The solitary ibis stalks lazily along the banks and there is a delicious calmness and beauty in the scene . . . We were annoyed all night with the yelping and fighting of dogs with which every town and village swarms. You need not go far to see a dead ass . . ."[22]

Despite the hardships of the trip, Roberts painted some of the most beautiful and evocative images of Egypt ever made. He was also no mere observer, but a trenchant critic of Western "consumption" of ancient Egypt (a consumption his own pictures would fuel). At Abu Simbel he was digusted by the European graffiti disfiguring the temple and remarked that tourists "have the effrontery to smear their stupid names on the very forehead of the God."[23] His passion as an artist was matched by his dedication. At Abydos, he left one of his sketchbooks on the mountain, and it took his servant Ismail four days to go back and retrieve it. In Cairo, Roberts assumed Turkish dress, cut off his whiskers and promised not to use hog-hair brushes in order to gain admission to the mosques, but as he noted, "to be the first Artist that has made drawings of these Mosques is worth the trouble of a little inconvenience."[24] But it was at Luxor that he painted his most enduring scenes—of Luxor Temple, still half-buried in sand, and of the Nile itself with its characteristic feluccas: "To the eye of a painter nothing can exceed in beauty these craft skimming along the river with their white sails spread and shivering in the wind."[25]

On his return to England (via Palestine and Syria) in July 1839, Roberts brought with him three full sketchbooks, 272 sketches, and a panorama of Cairo: in short, enough material to "serve me for the rest of my life."[26] Over the next decade, he made a series of new drawings from his sketches and published them as 247 large lithographs in the multivolume *The Holy Land, Syria, Idumea, Arabia, Egypt & Nubia*. It was the most comprehensive series of views of the Middle East ever presented, and won huge critical and popular acclaim. The paintings caught the imagination of the British public and made Egypt the most fashionable destination for the adventurous traveller.

Roberts' favourable comparison of the Nile Valley sunsets with the miserable fogs of London also struck a chord with Britain's large population of consumptives—sufferers of tuberculosis for whom the dull, dank weather of a British winter, exacerbated by choking smog, could prove deadly. Wealthier sufferers, those from the aristocracy and landed gentry, generally followed their doctors' advice and emigrated to warmer, foreign climes for the winter months. India and South Africa were ideal, but a long way away. Suddenly, Egypt offered a closer, and therefore cheaper, alternative. Luxor, with its ancient monuments, picturesque scenery and dry climate, suddenly became the quintessential health resort, "the ultimate goal of many who sought to escape the rigours of the Continental and English winters."[27] Staying at Luxor in 1881, one Englishman could not quite believe the improvement in his health:

> In about a week the sunshine and warm air of Luxor enabled me to sit in the garden, in another week I could mount a donkey, in a month I was able to ride to Karnak . . . Upon me, at all events, the effect of the climate was little short of miraculous.[28]

Among the Europeans to seek respite from poor health amidst the temples of ancient Thebes, none was more remarkable than Lucie Duff Gordon (1821–69). Eccentric, pioneer, folk heroine: her seven years living in a ramshackle house atop the roof of Luxor Temple endeared her to the local people and made her a tourist destination in her own right, adding yet further to Luxor's allure. Unlike David Roberts, she came from a wealthy, middle-class family, and a radical one. Her parents' friends included the philosopher Jeremy Bentham and Lucie herself became famous in London society for her beauty, wit and independent mind. She established herself as a professional translator and, with her husband, Sir Alexander Duff Gordon, a baronet of Scottish descent, she threw seven-course dinner parties for the capital's literary elite. The couple had three children and were comfortably off. But Lucie's life was marred by tuberculosis. In 1862, having already spent time in South Africa, she set off alone for Egypt. She was forty-one, her youngest child just three.

From the outset, the Nile Valley captivated her—not so much its ancient monuments as its people and its contemporary culture. She settled in Luxor—as its only permanent European resident—where she attended the Abu el-Haggag mosque inside Luxor Temple. The locals came to believe she had the "lucky eye," and asked her to visit new brides, pregnant cows, even houses under construction. Lucie returned the compliment, speaking up passionately and bravely for Egypt's hard-pressed peasantry against the harsh rule of its Ottoman oppressors. In the West, the Egyptian ruler Ismail was hailed as progressive because he had set about modernising the country's infrastructure. But Lucie knew at first hand the flip-side and the human cost of all this development: punitive taxes and the much-feared *corvée* (a draft of labour to work on government projects). In Luxor, out of a population of 1,000 men, 220 were taken away forcibly at six-month intervals. A third of those who went on corvée never returned. Those who stayed faced starvation or imprisonment as tax defaulters. Lucie lamented that "whole towns and villages were raided for able-bodied men who were taken away, often for years, to dig canals, build bridges, dams and railways, and work like slaves on the Suez Canal."[29] Her fierce opposition to Ismail's rule, expressed forcefully in her letters home, was unstinting and highly dangerous. The Ottoman ruler sent spies to Luxor to intercept her correspondence, but she found ways of smuggling her letters out via European visitors. Then Ismail tried to bribe her boatman into drowning her, but her local popularity saved her.

Although Lucie missed her family acutely, her new life in Luxor embraced her and she increasingly turned her back on her English home. When her husband came out to Egypt in 1864, the couple spent just three weeks together. She came to resent the hordes of European visitors that now descended upon Luxor each winter, writing scornfully, "Thebes has become an English watering-place. There are now nine boats lying here, and the great object is to *do the Nile* as fast as possible."[30] Following the publication of her remarkable *Letters from Egypt*, tourists came to seek her out as yet another attraction. In 1867 Lucie wrote to her husband, "This year I'll bolt the doors when I see a steamer coming."[31] Good health continued to elude her, but she found peace and contentment in her little house over the sanctuary at the southern end of Luxor Temple. Built originally by the English consul, Henry Salt, in 1815, the house is said to have accommodated Champollion when he visited Luxor—and, two years later, some of the French naval officers sent to transport the Luxor obelisk to Paris. By the time Lucie moved in, it was little more than a hovel, yet she called it "my Theban palace."[32] She also shared it with various uninvited guests—"The bats and the swallows are quite sociable; I hope the serpents and scorpions will be more reserved."[33] In hot weather, she lived in a room open on one side, from where she could watch the boats on the Nile and the sunset over the Theban Hills.

Lucie finally succumbed to illness and died in July 1869. When Amelia Edwards visited Luxor just five years later, Lucie's house was as she had left it, "her couch, her rug, her folding chair were there still."[34] It took a novelist's sensibility to appreciate the special allure of the place: "We were shocked by the dreariness of the place—till we went to the window. That window, which commanded the Nile and the western plain of Thebes, furnished every room and made its poverty splendid."[35] Lucie's seven years in Luxor were the longest any European had spent in Upper Egypt. Even after her house was pulled down in 1884 during the excavation of Luxor Temple, she was remembered by the local people: "every Arab in Luxor cherishes the memory of Lady Duff Gordon in his heart of hearts, and speaks of her with blessings."[36]

Another casualty of the temple's excavation was an altogether grander dwelling, the house of the British consul, Mustapha Aga. Situated between the columns of the processional colonnade, it had played host to an almost endless round of parties each winter season as wealthy, aristocratic British travellers descended upon Luxor: "In the round of gaiety that goes on at Luxor the British consulate played the leading part. Mustapha Aga entertained all the English dahabeeyahs, and all the English dahabeeyahs entertained Mustapha Aga."[37] The menu for dinner on 31 March 1874, when Amelia Edwards enjoyed the Consul's hospitality, was not atypical: "White soup (turkey); fish (fried samak); entrées (stewed pigeons, spinach and rice); roast (dall=shoulder of lamb); entrées (mutton kebobs, lambs' kidney kebobs, tomatoes with rice, kuftah); roast (turkey, with cucumber sauce); entrée (rice pilaf); second course (preserved apricots, rice and almond pudding, rice cream, sweet jelly with blanched almonds). Drinks: water, rice-water and lemonade." Followed by "pipes and coffee," and all accompanied by native musicians on "fiddles, tambourine and darabukkeh."[38] It is surprising that the invalids who came to Luxor for tuberculosis did not return home with heart disease.

Of course, well-heeled travellers could not stay at the consulate full time, nor did they want to spend weeks aboard their dahabiyas, however well appointed. What they wished for was a grand hotel in the European style, with all the comforts of home but the climate of southern Egypt.

Ever since Thomas Cook organised his first tour to Egypt in 1869, hotels have sprung up all along the Nile's eastern bank. From budget hostels in Luxor's malodorous backstreets to a five-star luxury resort on its own private island in the Nile, establishments great and small accommodate the thousands of visitors who flock to Luxor each year. Modern tourist palaces are fast muscling in, but the grandfather of them all still stands elegant and serene, occupying the prime spot on the corniche.

Since it opened its doors in January 1907, the Winter Palace has been as much a Luxor landmark as the temples of the pharaohs. Built in colonial style amid tropical gardens overlooking the Nile, the hotel's yellow stuccoed façade, replete with balconies and balustrades, presents an enduring image of early twentieth-century grandeur. But a building in so prominent a position was bound to divide opinion. In 1910 Pierre Loti, a French naval officer turned travel writer, wrote disdainfully of the Winter Palace:

a hasty modern production which has grown on the border of the Nile during the past year: a colossal hotel, obviously sham, made of plaster and mud, on a framework of iron. Twice or three times as high as the admirable Pharaonic Temple, its impudent façade rises there, painted a dirty yellow. One such thing, it will readily be understood, is sufficient to disfigure pitiably the whole of the surroundings.[39]

While the French may have bemoaned the hotel's aesthetics, the British were more interested in its mod cons. Two medical officers with the splendidly Edwardian names of W. E. Nickolls Dunn and George Vigers Worthington, who were serving at the "Luxor Hospital for Natives," wrote gushingly of the Winter Palace in their 1914 volume, *Luxor as a Health Resort*. They declared, "It is impossible to over-state the value to a visitor, be he in pursuit of pleasure or health, of such an hotel"[40] and went on to describe "a magnificent hotel fitted with all the luxuries of the age . . . a splendid modern building."[41] Understanding their readers' primary concerns, the medics singled out the hotel's bathroom and kitchen arrangements for special praise:

The hotel is well supplied with suites, with private bathrooms attached: the rooms are all lofty, large and spotlessly clean . . . The kitchens, a feature of the hotel, are all above ground, staffed by Europeans, and are beyond criticism. The water supply comes from an artesian well in the garden, sunk through the rock by the Government experts, and no other water enters the hotel with the following exception: It has been found that the Nile water is preferable for making tea and coffee, consequently a pipe conveys the water to the coffee kitchen where it passes through a Berkefeld filter and then enters directly into a boiler, from which it is drawn. It can only be obtained after it has been boiled . . . There is no occasion to advise people to use Evian water for the cleansing of their teeth—they could drink the water in the bathrooms with impunity, if so inclined.[42]

While today's guests would do well to ignore this last piece of advice, it is still true that the Winter Palace has the best views in Luxor: "The north-west front looks on to the river, the Theban plain and, beyond the plain, the Theban hills with their glorious and ever changing lights."[43] The garden may no longer include "6 acres of vegetables and fruit grown . . . under the supervision of a European head gardener,"[44] but it remains an oasis amidst the bustle and noise of downtown Luxor.

The arcades under the elegant horseshoe-shaped terrace are occupied by various boutiques. Those on the southern side sell jewellery and textiles, while the Aladdin's cave of Gaddis and Co., family-owned booksellers since 1907, still occupies the entire street frontage of the northern arcade and supplies one of the widest ranges of reading material in Luxor. Its neighbour, the venerable but ever-dingy Cheops Travel, offers guided tours of dubious quality to the west bank and tickets to the son-et-lumière at Karnak Temple. The corniche in front of the hotel remains a favoured spot for hawkers of all stripes to ply their trade. In the space of a hundred yards, I am offered "taxi," "shoes," "newspapers," "caleche," "ferry-boat" and "felucca." The list of offerings can have changed little in a century.

Inside the grand entrance of the Winter Palace, calm and decorum are restored once more: high ceilings, marble floors, silken rugs and fez-wearing attendants work their magic. On the main staircase, art nouveau ironwork spirals gracefully upwards. In the dining room, chandeliers and gilded mirrors catch the light pouring in through sumptuously pelmeted, full-length windows with their unrivalled views of the Nile. Jacket and tie are de rigueur in the 1886 restaurant, while afternoon tea is served daily at 3 p.m. in the Victorian lounge (originally the hotel ballroom). In the bedrooms, thick walls and soft bedding reduce the outside din of traffic to a distant, muffled hum (although the muezzin's call to prayer at 5 a.m. provides a rude awakening). The guests who stay in this cosseted, pampered palace of luxury are as remote from Luxor's hard-pressed citizenry as the Ottoman rulers of Lucie Duff Gordon's day.

Since marking its grand opening over a century ago with a New Year's Eve costume ball for the cream of European royalty, the Winter Palace has hosted its fair share of dilettantes and celebrities, from King Farouk to Omar Sharif, and it remains the hotel of choice for visiting heads of state and government. But perhaps nobody has graced its shady verandah more famously than George Edward Stanhope Molyneux Herbert (1866–1923), fifth Earl of Carnarvon and co-discoverer of the tomb of Tutankhamun. Born into aristocratic luxury and succeeding to the earldom at the age of twenty-four, Carnarvon added to his family's already considerable wealth through his marriage to an heiress of the Rothschild banking dynasty. As a leading member of the idle rich in those heady days before World War I, Carnarvon lived a life of unashamed hedonism.

A passion for speed—he later founded a renowned stud and became a noted patron of horse-racing—led him to take a keen interest in the newest technological innovation of the day, the motor car. But a motoring accident in Germany in 1901 left him disabled and prone to bouts of rheumatic pain in his legs, especially during the cold, damp winters at his Hampshire estate, Highclere Castle (now famous as the set for *Downton Abbey*). As a remedy, from 1903 onwards, he took to spending the worst winter months in the warmer, drier climate of Luxor; from 1907, as might have been expected, he stayed in the colonial elegance of the Winter Palace. In a typical year, he would arrive in early February and remain in residence until the end of March, a stay of six or seven weeks.

While sipping cocktails on the terrace and watching the ferries and feluccas ply the waters of the Nile, Carnarvon developed an interest in Egypt's ancient past, and found himself drawn to the burgeoning discipline of Egyptology. For their part, Egyptologists were certainly drawn to Carnarvon, for what he lacked in historical training he more than made up for in wealth. Archaeologists with high ambitions but limited resources made a beeline for the earl. And so it was in 1907 that Carnarvon was introduced to the brilliant but irascible Howard Carter, forging a partnership between patron and practitioner that would result, fifteen years later, in the greatest archaeological discovery of all time—across the Nile from the Winter Palace, in the heat and dust of the Valley of the Kings.

From the initial discovery of Tutankhamun's tomb on 26 November 1922 to the official opening of the burial chamber on 17 February 1923, Carnarvon stayed in Luxor, where he was joined by other members of his family, participants in a news story that gripped the world. Carnarvon and Carter were at the centre of this whirlwind, so on 28 February 1923, seeking a few days' peace and quiet, the earl left for Aswan. He should have stayed put at the Winter Palace. On his journey south, he was bitten on the cheek by an infected mosquito, and he inadvertently nicked the top of the bite when shaving. Blood poisoning set in and Carnarvon was hastily moved to Cairo for medical treatment; but it was too late. In the early hours of 5 April, he died at the age of fifty-seven—not from the pharaoh's curse (his co-discoverer Carter lived to a ripe old age), but from the deleterious effects of the river and its abundant insect life. Carnarvon's demise was just another case of death on the Nile.

IN THE SOUTHERN PART of Luxor, the temple and the nearby Winter Palace are the most prominent buildings. But they are not the city's only attractions. Another building, in the northern part of Luxor, holds equal fascination as a site of antique religion and modern tourism. An hour's gentle stroll along the corniche from the southern sanctuary bring you to its "mother temple." The site we know today as Karnak is the greatest religious complex in the world. It has been described as "the noblest architectural work ever designed and executed by human hands."[45] In ancient times, the Egyptians knew it simply as "the most select of places." It was no exaggeration.

The statistics alone are humbling: the site measures nearly a mile long by half a mile wide, covering an area equivalent to 168 football pitches. There are ten pylons, as many courts and at least twelve separate temples within three distinct sacred precincts. But figures scarcely do Karnak justice. Amelia Edwards summed up the effect of Karnak on the visitor with her customary literary flair: "The scale is too vast; the effect too tremendous; the sense of one's own dumbness, and littleness, and incapacity, too complete and crushing. It is a place that strikes you into silence . . ."[46] Even after Luxor Temple had been newly excavated from the accumulations of centuries, it still ranked "second . . . to Karnak for grandeur of design and beauty of proportion."[47]

The monuments of Karnak were continuously added to and rebuilt over a period of some two thousand years, the focus of royal patronage from the Middle Kingdom to the Roman Empire. The main temple, dedicated to the Theban god Amun-Ra, was founded in the Eleventh Dynasty (2050 BC), at a time of civil war in Egypt. Its royal patron, King Intef II, no doubt wished to win divine favour for his struggle for national domination. Amun-Ra was clearly pleased with the gesture, for the Thebans duly won the war, their victory ushering in a period of great cultural achievement. The subsequent Middle Kingdom saw the erection of stunning cult buildings at Karnak, foremost among them the White Chapel of Senusret I, constructed for the king's jubilee in 1888 BC.

Its beautiful relief decoration is without equal in all of Egypt. Another civil war, three-and-a-half centuries later, resulted in another Theban victory. This time, to thank their divine protector, the royal family elevated Amun-Ra to the position of state god. Karnak, his principal cult centre, became the focus of building activity on an unprecedented scale. Endowed with huge estates, it was also an economic institution of national importance, its priesthood the most powerful in the country.

The Karnak complex is laid out along two ceremonial axes, with a large sacred lake at their junction. The principal axis extends from east to west, from the sanctuary at the rear of the temple to the great gate-towers at the entrance. Along this great processional route lie a sequence of courts, embellished with obelisks, shrines and altars. The most impressive construction is undoubtedly the vast hypostyle hall of Seti I and Ramesses II—a room so vast that it makes you feel like an insect. Everyone who sees it in person comes away overawed. From David Roberts' evocative paintings to a starring role in the James Bond movie *The Spy Who Loved Me*, this great space with its 134 papyrus-shaped stone columns never fails to impress. Behind the hypostyle hall lies the holy of holies, containing a granite sanctuary installed by Alexander the Great's successor, Philip Arrhidaeus; and behind that, at the far eastern end of the main axis, is the sumptuously decorated Festival Hall of Thutmose III, complete with scenes of the king's military campaigns in Syria.

The whole sequence of courts, from east to west, was designed to track the passage of the sun across the heavens from its rising to its setting. (At dawn on a few days in early December, the sun rises directly between the gate-towers, recreating the hieroglyphic sign for the horizon, the place of daily creation, before one's very eyes.) But the orientation also had a practical, as well as a theological, purpose. For like most Egyptian temples, Karnak was a place not only of spiritual but also economic activity. Ministers and merchants, as well as priests and prophets, travelled to and from its hallowed courts. Since the principal means of communication was the Nile, it made sense for the temple to be easily accessible from the riverbank. Indeed, Karnak's great stone quay, where ships of all shapes, sizes and cargoes would have docked in ancient times, has recently been excavated in front of the temple. A short canal linked it with the river and would have allowed craft to load and unload directly in front of the temple's main entrance.

The importance of the Nile in the life of Karnak is illustrated by one of the most spectacular episodes in its long history. It began on 2 March 656 BC when a splendid flotilla set out from the royal residence at Memphis, bound for Thebes, some six hundred miles to the south. This was no ordinary convoy: its purpose was to convey Princess Nitiqret, daughter of King Psamtik I, to the great temple of Amun-Ra at Karnak. There, she would be received by the priesthood and acknowledged as the future God's Wife of Amun, the most important sacred office in Egypt after the High Priest himself. The institution of God's Wife held great religious significance and equal political importance. When held by a close female relative, it gave the king the means of controlling the Theban priesthood and, by extension, the southern half of the country. For a monarch such as Psamtik I, whose origins and power base lay in the remote north-western Delta, winning over Thebes was a key objective. So, in the ninth year of his reign, Psamtik I sent his eldest daughter to join the college of priestesses at Karnak with the aim of securing her eventual succession as God's Wife of Amun.

In overall charge of the journey was the flotilla commander Sematawytefnakht, and the next sixteen days of sailing up the Nile were to be the pinnacle of his career, the most important two weeks of his life. Planning for the journey had been going on for months in advance. Royal messengers had travelled upstream the length of the route, to persuade and cajole all the provincial governors through whose lands the flotilla would pass to supply provisions for the princess and her enormous retinue. Each governor would be responsible for providing the bread, beer, meat, poultry, fruit and vegetables to feed the convoy. In this way, the royal exchequer would be spared the entire burden of financing such a costly undertaking, and the regional potentates would be able to display their loyalty to the ruling dynasty.

By the time the day of departure dawned, all was ready. As marshals cleared the way, Nitiqret went in procession from the king's private apartments to the harbourside to embark on her voyage of destiny. Sixteen days later, the flotilla arrived safely at Thebes, to be met by throngs of people, shouting and clamouring for a glimpse of the princess. Nitiqret was taken immediately to the great temple of Karnak where she was formally welcomed by an oracle of the god Amun-Ra. She was then introduced to the incumbent God's Wife of Amun, Shepenwepet, and her heir apparent, Amenirdis, and was formally adopted by them both as their eventual successor, in the presence of "all the god's servants, priests and adherents of the temple."⁴⁸ Just to be certain, a record of the contract was made in writing. Crucially, it signed over to Nitiqret all the property of the God's Wife of Amun "both rural and urban."⁴⁹ Although Nitiqret did not expect to become God's Wife for many decades, her eventual inheritance—and with it the new dynasty's control of Thebes—had been duly secured by both religious and legal authority.

The prominence of women in the religious life at Karnak was mirrored by the ancillary buildings of the complex itself. South of the main temple of Amun-Ra, a second major shrine was dedicated to his divine consort, Mut. It is surrounded by a high enclosure wall, and in ancient times it contained hundreds of statues of the goddess Mut, represented as a lioness. Today, they are among the most familiar ancient Egyptian statues in museums the world over. They were installed by Amenhotep III, perhaps as an offering against plague, and some have suggested that there were originally 720 statues, two for each day of the year (one for each day, one for each night). But even that abundance of sculpture pales into insignificance compared with the avenue that leads on southwards from the Mut complex to Luxor Temple. This processional way, used during the annual Festival of the Sanctuary, was once lined with stone sphinxes at sixteen-foot intervals: a total of over a thousand statues.

For centuries covered in sand and debris or buried under roads and buildings, the avenue of sphinxes is once again being revealed in all its ancient glory. Starting at its southern end, in front of Luxor Temple, the avenue is being painstakingly cleared all the way to Karnak, in one of the biggest restoration projects ever undertaken by Egypt's Ministry of Antiquities. (Until the 2011 revolution, this ministry was the fourth largest recipient of Egyptian government expenditure, after the armed forces, the police and the social security ministry; it was also one of the largest generators of income.) It is an epic undertaking, and the cost has been staggering: over six hundred million Egyptian pounds to date, including compensation for those forcibly evicted from their homes and businesses, and a hefty payment to the army, the main contractor. Roads have had to be diverted, gas and water mains relaid, buildings that lay in the way compulsorily purchased and demolished. A mosque sitting alongside the avenue could not so easily be cleared away, so it has had to be underpinned. The result, if it is ever finished (work has stalled since the revolution), will be a spectacular recreation of Luxor's ancient glory, and a fabulous new addition to the tourist itinerary—even if countless lives and livelihoods have been disrupted in the process. It is, in every way, a project worthy of the pharaohs.

The religious buildings of Luxor together comprise one of the greatest treasurehouses of ancient Egyptian art and sculpture. In earlier times, artefacts were shipped off to adorn the palaces and museums of Egypt's foreign rulers—in Rome, Constantinople, Paris and London, and of course Cairo. But in the more enlightened times of the 1960s, it was decided that Luxor should have its own Museum of Art, where masterpieces from Karnak and Luxor temples could be displayed in their home city. It makes a fitting final stop on any tour of the east bank, located at the river's edge midway between the two great temples. Designed by an Egyptian, Mahmud El Hakim, the museum makes a striking addition to Luxor's distinguished architectural history. The main edifice is a simple rectangle. On the Nile side, a porch with a sun-screen as high as the whole building runs along the entire façade. Between the building and the corniche, a garden with trees and flowers provides the setting for colossal statues and blocks of relief decoration. Inside, all lighting is artificial, and objects are carefully arranged along a processional route, in the best ancient tradition. (By contrast, the time taken to build the museum and install the objects, eleven years, was characteristic of modern Egypt. The pharaohs would have done it much quicker.)

Like the temple of Karnak, Luxor Museum faces the Nile: the thread that divides yet unites the two halves of ancient Thebes. Standing in the museum's grassy grounds in the late afternoon, with the sun setting over the Theban Hills, thoughts naturally turn to the west bank of the Nile. There, in the realm of the dead, the monuments are, if anything, even more spectacular; and the stories of those who built them, plundered them, rediscovered and excavated them, every bit as extraordinary.

Hapy, god of the Nile flood, whose corpulence symbolised the river's bounty (reign of Amenhotep III, c. 1360 BC)

The Nile at Aswan: here the journey downriver begins

The *rayyis* guides our Nile
boat safely downriver

Market day, Abu Shusha, Upper Egypt

A mud-brick farmstead
on the banks of the Nile,
Upper Egypt

Fishing boat and felucca
on the Nile at sunset

The desert meets the river at Aswan

The temple of Abu Simbel which was moved to preserve it when the Aswan High Dam was built in the 1960s

"The most beautiful spot on the Nile": the temples of Philae, moved to save them from the flooding caused by the Aswan dams

Fellahin, Upper Egypt

Small boats, children and donkeys: village life unchanged for millennia at Elkab, Upper Egypt

The Winter Palace, Luxor: an elegant stopover on the journey downriver

Sunset over the Nile at Luxor

Pharonic temple, Christian basilica and mosque: religion reinvented at Luxor Temple

Karnak Temple: reflections in the sacred lake, fed by the waters of the Nile

The hills of Western Thebes, the greatest treasure-house of antiquity

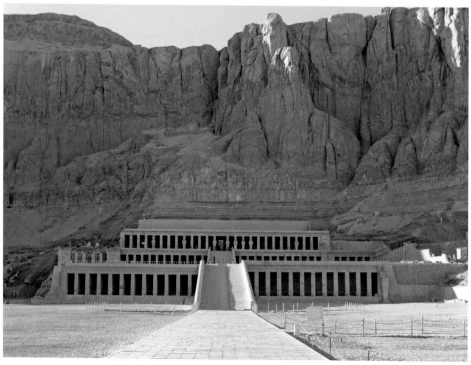

"Holy of holies": the temple of Hatshepsut at Deir el-Bahri, Western Thebes

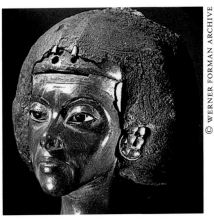

"Ozymandias": the fallen colossus of Ramesses II at the Ramesseum, Western Thebes

Queen Tiye, wife of King Amenhotep III (c. 1390–1353 BC)

The Colossi of Memnon, Western Thebes

Mons Claudianus, a Roman quarry in the desert

The painted ceiling of the temple of Hathor at Dendera

The green fields of Middle Egypt, near Abydos

Coptic papyrus from Nag Hammadi: the "Gnostic gospels" rewrite the early history of Christianity

Osiris and Isis: beautiful painted reliefs in the temple of Seti I at Abydos

Fayum portrait: a blend of Greek, Roman and Egyptian cultures

Stela of the royal family from Amarna. Akhenaten and Nefertiti promoted themselves and their daughters as Egypt's new holy family.

The solar boat of Khufu at Giza, originally buried next to the king's Great Pyramid to transport him into the afterlife

Silhouetted skyline of Islamic Cairo

The Ben Ezra synagogue, Old Cairo

Monastery of St. George, Old Cairo

Looking towards an uncertain future: (*above*) the Great Sphinx and (*below*) the Ramses Hilton, the 6 October Bridge and modern urban sprawl, Cairo

Western Thebes

Realm of the Dead

I . . . who have come to Thebes, and who have seen with
my eyes the work of these tombs of astounding horror,
have spent a delightful day.[1]

—PHILASTRIOS THE ALEXANDRIAN

W hen, in the late sixteenth century, a European traveller first sailed
up the Nile and landed on the west bank opposite Luxor, the
contrast between the past and present could not have been more stark.
Though blessed with a wide floodplain and fertile soils, the area was virtually uninhabited. The local population was as impoverished as it was
small, reflecting Upper Egypt's political insignificance and its remoteness from the great mercantile cities of the north.

Yet, in the midst of this poverty and destitution, spectacular monuments from Egypt's pharaonic past stood proudly in the landscape. Indeed, nowhere else in the entire Nile Valley—perhaps nowhere else in the world—boasts such a concentration of spectacular ancient buildings as the plain and hills of western Thebes. Dating from the New Kingdom, the golden age of pharaonic power, the temples and tombs speak of might and majesty, of a time when Egypt's treasury overflowed with gold from conquered Nubia and tribute from the Near East.

The great edifices created by kings, queens and courtiers to preserve their bodies and their memories for eternity have shaped the west bank of Thebes in countless ways. For over four thousand years, people from far and wide have come to this special place to build, visit, wonder, plunder, excavate and restore. All have left their mark.

AT THE HEIGHT of their power, the kings and queens of ancient Egypt chose Thebes, the religious capital of the country, as the location for their grandest monuments. But, while the east bank of the Nile—modern Luxor—was the main population centre, the setting for Luxor and Karnak temples, and the location for lively festivals, the west bank—where the sun sets behind the Theban Hills—was the realm of the dead, a fitting location for tombs and mortuary cults. Even today, when the money brought by mass-market tourism is driving unprecedented development throughout the Luxor region, this distinction between east and west lingers on. Directly opposite the centre of Luxor with its traffic and tourists, the ferry-dock on the west bank still presents age-old scenes of Egyptian village life: women returning from a shopping trip to Luxor with baskets balanced on their heads; children playing in the dusty streets; chickens, sheep and goats travelling to or from market; scavenging dogs. As recently as the 1990s, the whole of the west bank was like this: quieter, slower, less developed than its counterpart across the river. But the construction of a new bridge to the south of Luxor has opened up western Thebes to tourist coaches and all the associated development: budget hotels, questionable restaurants, shopping malls filled with Chinese-made souvenirs.

Away from the modern roadside excrescences, however, something of the spirit of western Thebes lingers on. The ancient monuments are still the stars of the show, their royal and noble builders the animating spirits of the place. For most visitors, the complex history of pharaonic activity can be boiled down to just four towering figures: Hatshepsut, whose dramatic terraced temple charms and awes in equal measure; Amenhotep III, whose towering colossi are the first great "sight" on every tourist itinerary; Tutankhamun, whose tiny, second-rate tomb in the Valley of the Kings yielded the greatest archaeological treasure ever discovered; and Ramesses II, whose massive mortuary temple is perhaps the most romantic Egyptian ruin, and whose matrimonial devotion produced the incomparable tomb of Nefertari in the Valley of the Queens. Every tour guide has their own entertaining if not entirely accurate stories of these pharaonic A-listers; every guide book offers potted accounts of "the female pharaoh," "Egypt's Louis XIV," "the boy-king," and "Ozymandias." But other, less well-known figures have had equally important roles in shaping the history and geography of western Thebes. Their lives and achievements also echo among the shimmering hills and dust-dry valleys.

Thebes' glory was not pre-ordained. For the first millennium of pharaonic history, including the great flowering of court culture during the Pyramid Age, Thebes was a quiet provincial backwater, scarcely registering on the national scene. Its mayors and local officials were insignificant characters in the drama of the Egyptian state. Its temples and shrines were equally nondescript, small buildings of mud brick, perhaps enlivened with the (very) occasional stone lintel or door-jamb. Its tombs were small and unspectacular, unworthy of comparison with the fabulously decorated sepulchres of Giza and Saqqara. In short, Thebes was nothing, its people nobodies. It took a national crisis—the collapse of the state at the end of the Pyramid Age and the ensuing civil war—to bring Thebes to the fore. In one of the cruellest ironies of Egyptian history, the man responsible is today one of Egypt's most forgotten rulers.

The king in question was Intef II, who reigned for half a century at the end of the third millennium BC. The reason for his relative obscurity lies in his provincial power-base: he did not, at least at the start of his reign, rule over all Egypt. Indeed, when Intef II was born, his grandfather, Intef the Great, was no more than a provincial governor, administering Thebes and its hinterland as a loyal servant of the king. But four thousand years ago, as today, the Thebans were an independent-minded people, distinctly sceptical about power exercised at a distance by a remote ruler in a northern capital. While professing loyalty to his sovereign, Intef the Great publicly challenged royal authority by styling himself Great Overlord of Upper Egypt—a dignity in the sole gift of the king. It was the start of a dream of Theban expansion that would determine the fate not only of the Intef family and their home town, but of the whole of Egypt. *or grandson?*

Intef the Great's son and namesake went one stage further, adopting kingly titles and seizing control of the desert routes behind western Thebes. These two acts effectively fired the starting pistol for a civil war that pitted north against south for the next eighty-five years. For much of that time, Intef II was the leader of the Theban rebels. He prosecuted the war against the north with a relentless intensity, his charisma and leadership inspiring fanatical loyalty among his closest lieutenants. Although he, and they, portrayed the conflict as a war of unification and a fight for the soul of Egypt, it was, in reality, little more than a power-grab by an ambitious provincial family with the resources to raise a private army. But military might, as Egyptian rulers over the centuries have well understood, conferred a distinct advantage. Intef II first secured his southern flank, by neutralising opposition in the southernmost provinces of Egypt. Then he consolidated his power-base by annexing the three neighbouring provinces. Only when he was certain of his military advantage did he take the fight to the enemy, attacking the key religious centre of Abydos. Although some of his gains were temporarily reversed, Intef II succeeded in laying the foundations for an eventual Theban victory, and for the reunification of the country under Theban control.

Having thus elevated his home town from obscure provincial backwater to aspiring national capital, Intef II proceeded to endow the landscape of Thebes with monuments befitting its new-found status. On the east bank, he inaugurated construction at the site of Karnak, founding what would become Egypt's greatest temple. On the west bank, hitherto the site for a few nondescript private tombs, Intef built himself a sepulchre of royal pretensions. Behind a pillared façade, cut into the slope of the hill, a long transverse hall gave access to a deep corridor which led to the burial shaft. Outside, in the open courtyard in front of the tomb, a magnificent stone stela with finely carved scenes and texts announced Intef II's royal titles and his kingly piety. The stela's hymn to

Ra and Hathor—sun-god and mother-goddess, twin protectors of the monarch—is as moving a piece of religious writing as ever flowed from the pen of an ancient Egyptian, hinting at a human frailty lying behind the visage of a great war leader.

But perhaps just as revealing about Intef II is a second stela, also erected in the funerary chapel of his Theban tomb. It shows the mighty soldier-king accompanied by his most trusted and trusting followers—not his human lieutenants but his hunting dogs. They carry Berber names, hinting at broader horizons of imagination beyond the Nile Valley, and the dogs' names themselves provide an insight into the character of their human master. The lead dog, with a sleek frame and elongated muzzle, was called "Gazelle," named no doubt for its swiftness. But the king's three other canine companions bore surprisingly mundane, familiar monikers: "Hound," "Kettle," and "Blackie." Perhaps in these pet names we see a certain no-nonsense attitude—a trait that would serve Intef II and his Theban successors well.

If Intef II laid the foundations for Theban prominence at the end of the third millennium BC, then two other remarkable men in the following two millennia were responsible, respectively, for creating, then defending, the city's greatness. Both lived extraordinary lives in tumultuous times. The first, Senenmut, who lived in the middle of the second millennium BC, was not Theban by birth, although he came from the nearby town of Armant, only a few miles to the south. But, named after the Theban goddess Mut, he reflected the cultural and political dominance of Thebes and it was in the great city that Senenmut's career was forged. He, in turn, helped to transform western Thebes into a setting for the greatest architectural achievements of the age.

Though Eighteenth Dynasty Egypt was an absolute monarchy, the royal court nonetheless offered prospects of advancement for men of humble origins who displayed exceptional talents. Senenmut was one such individual. His chosen career was in government administration, and like many of his time he found employment in the sprawling bureaucracy that supervised the huge estates belonging to the temple of Amun-Ra at Karnak. It was a steady job, but certainly not the passport to great wealth; when Senenmut's father died, he received only the simplest of burials, without any grave goods. By contrast, when Senenmut's mother died some years later, her funerary equipment (provided by Senenmut) included a gilded mummy mask and a heart scarab of serpentine set in gold.

The explanation for this sudden increase in Senenmut's wealth lay in the rise to power of the dominant figure of the early Eighteenth Dynasty, the female pharaoh Hatshepsut (1473–1458 BC). For a woman to rule Egypt was not unprecedented, but it was certainly highly irregular, and it ran counter to the fundamental ideology of Egyptian divine kingship. Hatshepsut was not only a woman in a man's world, she was a woman on a man's throne. She needed to surround herself with men of talent and ability, men moreover who owed their position to her and her alone. Senenmut was one such; his naming after a female goddess had proved prescient. Whether Hatshepsut admired him solely for his administrative abilities, or whether there was some deeper attraction as contemporary rumours insinuated, she promoted him to his most lucrative offices and he became her most influential courtier. He tutored her daughter and controlled access to her royal audience chamber. He managed her personal estates and held high office in her Treasury. But Senenmut's greatest achievements, and his most enduring legacy, were accomplished in his roles as chief architect and Overseer of All the King's Works. As he noted himself, "It was . . . Senenmut who conducted all the works of the king in Karnak, in Armant and Deir el-Bahri; and of Amun in the temple of Mut, in Ishry and in Luxor Temple . . ."[2]

The most significant royal building project was Hatshepsut's "holy of holies," her mortuary temple in western Thebes. Located next to an earlier temple built by Intef II's grandson, the setting was no doubt intended to associate Hatshepsut with the origins of Theban greatness. Senenmut's design echoed the earlier building, while taking it to new heights, both literally and metaphorically. His building for Hatshepsut is arranged as a series of three huge terraces, set against the cliff face. Originally, the temple was approached via a causeway, more than half a mile long, flanked for its final five hundred yards by more than a hundred sphinxes. Behind the pillared façades of each terrace, delicately carved and painted scenes record key episodes from Hatshepsut's life, real or imagined: her divine birth; her election as heir apparent; her coronation; the transport of her obelisks to Karnak; and, perhaps most famously, the expedition she sent in 1463 BC to the fabled land of Punt to bring back incense trees. The vivid details of the African landscape and the obese queen of Punt have made this tableau one of the best-known in Egyptian art.

As chief architect, Senenmut ensured that he too featured in the temple's decoration, to guarantee his own immortality. Representations of him appear in niches on the temple's upper terrace and in the Punt reliefs. He also had himself depicted, kneeling and worshipping, in the most sacred part of the temple, concealed behind the open doors of the small shrine in the upper sanctuary. This was a daring breach of protocol, verging on the sacrilegious, but Senenmut's unique position, in the construction project and at court, allowed him to get away with it. He also built himself a tomb next to the temple: although its entrance was outside the sacred enclosure, its burial chamber lay right underneath the temple's outer court. Like those closest to power throughout history, Senenmut's ambition—and self-aggrandisement—knew no bounds.

But, in another lesson of history, Senenmut's demise was as swift as his rise to power. His tomb, prepared with such care, remained empty; and his other monuments suffered posthumous persecution. Without heirs to look after his memory—he never married—his role in creating the first great monument of western Thebes was forgotten, until resurrected by Egyptologists 3,500 years after his death.

Alongside the causeway of Hatshepsut's temple, and likewise designed to share in its aura, lies the tomb of Senenmut's spiritual descendant. Though he lived eight hundred years later, Montuemhat was as deeply committed to the royal court and to Thebes. His name, too, paid homage to one of the city's deities, in this case its war-god Montu. As in Senenmut's case, it was an appropriate choice. Where Senenmut had been the architect of spectacular monuments for his royal mistress, Montuemhat was the architect of Thebes' very survival, at its darkest hour, in the chaos of a military invasion. Though largely ignored by modern commentators, Montuemhat ranks as a towering figure of his own age, and one of the most influential in the long history of Egypt. He lived during an extraordinary period bridging the eighth and seventh centuries BC, when Egypt was locked in an epic clash of civilisations with the kingdoms of Kush and Assyria.

Montuemhat was born just as the kingdom of Kush was tightening its grip over the entire Nile Valley. His career blossomed under the greatest of the black pharaohs, Taharqo, and he became Governor of Upper Egypt as well as a priest in the cult of Amun-Ra of Karnak. Montuemhat's marriage to a royal princess consolidated his position at the heart of government. But then, in the space of a mere decade, Egypt was convulsed by five successive Assyrian invasions, as warrior kings from Nineveh sought to incorporate the Nile Valley into their expanding empire.

The first test for Thebes came in 667 BC, when the Assyrians led by their king Esarhaddon conquered the whole of Egypt, from the marshlands of the Delta to the First Cataract. They imposed an imperial structure of government on Egypt, appointing governors to rule the provinces on their behalf. By dint of his remarkable political skills, Montuemhat emerged from the crisis not only unscathed but officially recognised by the Assyrians as ruler of Thebes. While paying lip service to his position as an Assyrian vassal, he deftly maintained the old order throughout his Theban realm, and seems to have negotiated successfully with the Assyrians to spare the sacred buildings of Thebes.

However, just three years later, provoked by an Egyptian counter-assault, the forces of the new Assyrian king Ashurbanipal—a man who hunted lions in his leisure time—swept down through the Nile Valley once more. After the fall of Memphis, the humiliated pharaoh turned tail and fled southwards towards Thebes, with the Assyrians in hot pursuit. Despite feverish preparations, there was only so much that could be done to resist a concerted attack by a well-prepared and well-equipped army. The Assyrians were masters of every conceivable type of military technology. In urban wafare, they were peerless: with a lethal combination of tunnels, battering rams and scaling ladders, the Assyrian army rendered even the strongest of fortifications completely ineffective. Besides sheer firepower, there was also the most lethal weapon in Ashurbanipal's armoury: psychological warfare. The Assyrians were notoriously merciless towards towns and peoples that resisted conquest. Towns that did not capitulate immediately could expect to be demolished and put to the torch, once they had fallen. Their inhabitants were likely to be slaughtered or deported to far-flung outposts of the Assyrian empire to carry out forced labour. In the face of such overwhelming force, no city in the Near East had successfully repelled an Assyrian assault. Thebes, with its largely unprotected residential quarters and vulnerable temples, stood no chance.

The expected attack was swift, fierce and unrelenting. Assyrians swarmed through the streets, butchering anyone who stood in their way, ransacking houses and looting workshops as they headed for the city's two great temples. At Karnak, they made straight for the treasury, carrying away fourteen centuries of accumulated riches to adorn Ashurbanipal's royal palace at Nineveh. The sack of Thebes reverberated through the ancient world as a cultural calamity of epic proportions. As ruler of Thebes and guardian of its ancient traditions, Montuemhat faced a daunting prospect. Yet, in the space of just eight years, workmen under his direction succeeded in rebuilding and restoring the temples of Thebes. Under his wise leadership, everything was restored to its former glory. It was his proudest achievement in a long and distinguished career.

Montuemhat survived in office to see Egypt regain its sovereignty under a new royal dynasty, and officiated at the ceremony at Karnak in 656 BC at which Princess Nitiqret was installed as the future God's Wife of Amun. Thanks to his dedication, his city—and, with it, the cultural traditions of pharaonic Egypt—survived invasion, destruction and multiple regime change.

THROUGHOUT HISTORY, the east bank of Thebes (modern Luxor) has been the land of the living, the main centre of population, while the west bank has been the realm of the dead. Yet, among the tombs where kings, queens and courtiers slumber for eternity, people have always made a living. For a few, the afterlife has proved good business. At all periods, the communities of western Thebes have been small, specialised and especially close-knit. The best-known of all such communities, and the exemplar of daily life under the pharaohs, is the workmen's village of Deir el-Medina.

It comes as a surprise to round the bend in the road and see, instead of yet more hillsides honeycombed with tomb entrances, an intact walled settlement spread out like a model village. Thanks to the thousands of documents and jottings recovered from its ruins, which record everything from laundry lists to love songs, it is the archetype of ancient Egyptian village life. And yet it was absolutely *atypical*, a community apart in every sense. The village did not grow up organically, but owed its existence to an act of royal patronage. When King Amenhotep I

(1514–1493 BC) of the Eighteenth Dynasty decided to found a new royal necropolis in a remote wadi in the Theban Hills, known today as the Valley of the Kings, he realised that he would require a dedicated work-force to construct his tomb and those of his descendants. Bringing work-ers across the Nile from the east bank was impractical, and the secrecy of the work—building the pharaoh's eternal resting-place—demanded a workforce shut off from the outside world. His solution, his foundation, was the village of Deir el-Medina. Its location is inspired: out of sight, hidden from view behind a range of hills, yet within easy walking dis-tance of both the cultivation and the Valley of the Kings. Guard-posts on the surrounding hills provided round-the-clock security (as they do today). To ensure that nobody got in or out without state sanction, a thick stone wall was built around the village by Amenhotep I's successor. Deir el-Medina is the original gated community.

Inside the walls, a main street runs the length of the village, with houses opening off either side. Each house typically had a front room for receiving visitors and a back room with a small courtyard for domestic activities. A staircase led to the roof which would have offered cooler conditions for sleeping in the heat of the summer. The basic arrange-ment remains characteristic of Egyptian village houses today.

At the beginning of each ten-day shift, the workmen walked from the village, up the hillside, along the cliff-edge path and down into the Valley of the Kings. During the working week, they camped overnight in a sheltered col, close to their place of work. At the end of the shift, they retraced their steps home to be reunited with their families. Mean-while, the women and children went about their daily business in their houses, in the village streets or at the marketplace. Over a period of some four centuries, successive generations of tomb workers and their families were born, lived and died at Deir el-Medina, until the Valley of the Kings was abandoned at the end of the New Kingdom and the village ceased to have a purpose.

In its heyday, during the Nineteenth and Twentieth Dynasties (1292–1069 BC), the community comprised about seventy families. It was a surprisingly cosmopolitan village, with workers of foreign descent from across the Egyptian empire. Life was simple, but not impoverished. The tomb builders supplemented their income (doled out as government rations) by making pieces of funerary equipment for sale to private clients, exchanging them for household goods such as sandals, clothing and furniture. Some of the village women produced textiles which, again, could be exchanged for a profit. Although they owned no land, the villagers ate better than most of their compatriots. The village employed its own fishermen who supplied fresh and dried fish, as well as its own washerwomen who did the laundry down at the riverbank. Teams of donkeys brought daily water supplies. So, although cut off from the Nile, the community retained close links with Egypt's life-giving river.

Unusually for ancient Egypt, many of Deir el-Medina's inhabitants were literate, including some of the women, and they gave free expression to their thoughts—satirical and pious, serious and frivolous—in a wide range of writings. Occasionally these were done on papyrus, but more often on fragments of broken pottery or limestone flakes (known collectively by the Greek term *ostraca*) which lay all about the village. It is thanks to the survival of these documents that we know so much about the workers and their families—more, in fact, than we know about the kings for whom they toiled.

Unlike most of the artists and sculptors who produced the great works of ancient Egyptian art and architecture, the citizens of Deir el-Medina are known to us by name. And, from this distant past, some larger-than-life characters emerge. The most infamous, by far, was the foreman Paneb. He lived in the workers' village towards the end of the Nineteenth Dynasty, and supervised the Right Side gang of tomb-builders. (Like the crew of a ship, the workers were divided into Right and Left sides.) In common with most of his fellow workers, Paneb had followed his father and grandfather into the tomb-building business. Paneb's father, Nefersenet, had worked on the tomb of Ramesses II and was a well-known local figure. While the father had enjoyed respect, the son was to gain notoriety. Paneb shared his small village house with his wife Wabet, their three sons and five daughters; but in the cramped conditions of the village, living cheek-by-jowl with other households, the opportunity for extra-marital affairs was ever-present, and Paneb seems to have found the temptation irresistible. He had sexual relations with at least three married women, leading to tensions with both his own family and his neighbours.

In his professional dealings, too, Paneb was deceitful and unscrupulous. When a vacancy for foreman presented itself, Paneb simply bribed the vizier to ensure he got the job. Then, to cover his tracks, Paneb made a complaint against the vizier which led to his dismissal. Safely installed as foreman, Paneb systematically misappropriated state resources, taking his crew away from their contracted work in the Valley of the Kings to use them on the construction and decoration of his own tomb. He stole tools from his place of work, and was even accused of having plundered the royal tomb on which he himself had worked, robbing it of a chariot cover, incense, oil, wines and a statue. He compounded his offence of theft by sitting on the dead king's sarcophagus, an act of terrible blasphemy. His detractors (of whom, by now, there were many) seized their chance to bring him to justice. The man who would have become foreman, but for Paneb's machinations, dictated a series of charges to a scribe, then laid them in writing before the vizier. The defendant's own son weighed in with accusations of adultery and fornication. Paneb was condemned on all sides, by colleagues and family members, and his criminal career had run its course. His ultimate fate is not known, but it would not be surprising if he managed to escape justice by some clever ruse. It would have been entirely in character.

The story of Paneb illustrates an important and obvious point: life in ancient Egypt had its darker side, despite the relentlessly positive image conveyed in official texts and images. The relationship between the populace and the state was not always the unquestioning, adoring obedience that the pharaohs would have had us believe. Sometimes, especially in circumstances of economic stress, the people made their voice heard. That the best-known example of civil disobedience from ancient Egypt, perhaps from the entire ancient world, involved the tomb workers of Deir el-Medina is no coincidence. This, after all, was a community more literate than most, better off than most, and, from the state's perspective, more important than most, because of the highly sensitive and secret work on the king's tomb. This special status gave the workers a combination of political clout and self-awareness that was rare, if not unparalleled, in the ancient world.

In the reign of Ramesses III (1187–1156 BC), the unwritten contract between the workers and their government paymasters broke down. Military conflict earlier in the reign had put a heavy economic burden on the state. As the king prepared for his jubilee, the government made the mistake of diverting scarce resources to the celebrations, instead of ensuring that its own employees were paid. The monthly wages of the tomb workers included their food rations, so late payment also meant going hungry. The workers did not hesitate to express their grievance, sending their foreman to remonstrate with local officials. This won a temporary victory, but merely papered over the cracks appearing in the edifice of the state.

The following year, the system of payment broke down entirely and the workers went on strike—the first recorded industrial dispute in history. Not only did they down tools, they also took part in demonstrations, marching en masse, chanting slogans, invading and occupying government buildings, setting up barricades at key installations: all the ingredients of a full-blown civil disturbance. The government seemed paralysed, unused to opposition of any kind, unable to react to such a well-articulated set of demands by so influential a group of people. In a desperate attempt to restore order, the Chief of Police was summoned to evict the protesters, but they refused to move. Eventually, with the workers' flaming torches illuminating the night sky and a local dispute threatening to escalate into a national crisis, the authorities backed down and paid the strikers their overdue rations. But it was not the end of the affair. In total, the tomb workers went on strike four times, finally demanding not just the settlement of their particular grievance but wholesale reform of the government apparatus:

> We have gone (on strike), not from hunger, but (because) we have a
> serious accusation to make: bad things have been done in this place of
> Pharaoh.[3]

This was a demand too far. But the tomb workers' dispute had laid bare the sclerosis at the heart of the Egyptian state, a systemic failure that, in the end, proved its undoing. The tomb workers of Deir el-Medina may thus be credited with the very beginnings of civic awareness, of holding the government to account. The authorities' response—denial followed by apathy, limited concessions accompanied by a security crackdown, disbelief and ultimately powerlessness—would be repeated many times in Egypt's history, culminating in Cairo's Tahrir Square in the early spring of 2011.

The showdown between the people of Deir el-Medina and the government has another modern parallel. Until the 1990s, there was still a small community on the west bank who made a living from the afterlife: not by building tombs but by plundering them. These spiritual heirs of Deir el-Medina lived in an equally close-knit, if ramshackle, village, a colourful collection of tumbledown, wood and mud-brick houses, nestled against the hillside of Sheikh Abd el-Qurna. The village of Qurna, part of the landscape for centuries, was as much a feature of the Theban scenery as the honey-coloured ruins of the pharaohs. The families, most of whom had lived at Qurna for generations, knew the Theban necropolis better than any: it was, after all, their backyard. Many an archaeologist had cause to thank these local experts for pointing the way to new discoveries. And yet, the Qurnawis were also the embodiment of everything archaeology opposes: their houses were built on top of ancient tomb shafts, preventing proper study of the surrounding area; and when a family needed an injection of funds it was the work of moments to slip through a hole in the floor, enter a tomb, and extract a choice artefact (or a section of wall-painting) to sell on the antiquities market. The tombs' guardians were thus also their plunderers. It was a situation that the Mubarak regime, at the height of its power, was determined to end.

The government's opening gambit was to try to persuade the villagers to leave, with the promise of modern houses in "New Qurna," a few miles to the north. But the Qurnawis preferred their old wooden homes with treasure in the basement to new concrete homes with hot and cold running water and a flushing toilet. Like the tomb workers before them, they simply refused to budge. After all, they boasted of having been the last Egyptians to be conquered by Napoleon's army, and a nineteenth-century traveller had described them as "superior to any other Arabs in cunning and deceit, and the most independent of any in Egypt."[4] When persuasion failed, the Egyptian government turned to force. Bulldozers arrived without notice to tear down the flimsy dwellings. The resulting scars on the landscape, as much as the plight of the villagers, brought the matter to the attention of tourists, some of whom expressed their support for the Qurnawis. This put the government in a dilemma: ostensibly, its clearance policy was designed to "restore" the Theban landscape to an imagined "pristine" condition for the edification of tourists. But, it soon transpired, many of those same tourists preferred a living landscape to an architecturally cleansed theme-park.

It was during the lull in evictions that I visited the house of the Hassans on the hillside of Sheikh Abd el-Qurna. Theirs was a typical Qurnawi family. The older brother had left home to work in the Red Sea resort of Hurghada, while a younger brother earned a modest living as a guide and selling trinkets to tourists in western Thebes. The mother and sisters spent their time, for the most part, in the back room of the house, doing the domestic chores, while the father received visitors in the front room—just as in ancient Deir el-Medina. The room was simply furnished but enjoyed the best view from a front door I have ever seen. From my perch on their upholstered settee (reserved for the most eminent visitors) I looked out over the necropolis of ancient Thebes, over the ruins of the Ramesseum, across the cultivated floodplain, to the Nile and, beyond, just visible through the haze, the columns of Luxor Temple: a World Heritage landscape framed by the wooden jambs of an old front door.

No visit to an Egyptian's house is complete without food and drink. The obligatory mint tea—strong and dark, with masses of sugar—was soon forthcoming, together with assorted snacks. (I was too preoccupied with the view to remember the food.) The conversation seemed to flow easily, even though the family had little English and I had less Arabic. All too soon it was time to leave. No house visit, before or since, has ever left quite the same impression.

Three years later, and I am once again being entertained at the Hassans' house—but everything has changed. In the face of constant harassment, they eventually gave up their battle with the authorities and accepted the offer of a concrete house in New Qurna. It is certainly more spacious, and the walls feel a great deal more solid. It must be cooler in the summer and warmer in the winter than their old hillside house. Yet, for all its modern conveniences, it is a soulless house in a soulless community. There is no panorama from the front door, and the view from the roof terrace is a line of identical roof terraces. The hospitality is as generous as before—tea and dinner (the details of which I remember well: dishes of spicy fava beans, courgettes and peppers stuffed with herbed rice, roast pigeons and plenty of home-made flatbread)—and the conversation still flows. But there is a void at the heart of this house, and at the heart of New Qurna. The people have been uprooted from their ancestral homes, and they are now exiles in their own land.

Eight years later still, and I return to Thebes after a long absence. Visiting the Ramesseum, I walk through the romantic ruins to the back of the temple, to look at my favourite view on the west bank: the hillside of Sheikh Abd el-Qurna in the bright Egyptian sunlight. But it feels as though I have taken a wrong turning, come to the wrong place. In place of the colourful houses of Old Qurna, there are just scars: vestiges of painted wood and mud brick, empty spaces where once families lived and visitors were entertained. The forced relocation of the villagers has been completed, and with it the wanton destruction of a part of Egypt's history. Instead of pristine and antique, the hillside looks violated and incomplete. I can't bring myself to track down the Hassan family. It would feel like visiting ghosts.

AS THE STORY of Old and New Qurna demonstrates, life on the west bank of Thebes has been intimately bound up with the demands of tourism—and not just in the last two centuries. Egypt in general and western Thebes in particular has been a tourist destination for two thousand years. The earliest visitors came not so much to marvel at the temples and tombs themselves, but to witness an other-worldly phenomenon famous throughout the ancient world: the singing of Memnon.

Early in his reign in the fourteenth century BC, the pharaoh Amenhotep III built himself an immense funerary temple on the plain of western Thebes. Even by ancient Egyptian standards, it was a monumental edifice, covering an area of ninety-three acres. Every court and gateway was adorned with colossal sculpture: figures of the striding king, processional avenues of sphinxes and jackals, an enormous seated statue of Amenhotep and his wife Tiye. Most impressive of all was the pair of statues framing the temple's easternmost gateway. Measuring over sixty feet tall, each statue depicted the king enthroned, flanked by diminutive figures of his female relatives: an embodiment in stone of untramelled royal power. They imparted a subtler message, too. During the annual inundation, the statues were partially submerged in water for several months each year, only to emerge again as symbols of rebirth. They also faced the rising sun, adding yet another layer to their rejuvenating symbolism. Ever since their erection, the twin statues have dominated the Theban plain, evoking awe in all observers.

Their popularity as a tourist destination in Roman times was, however, the result of an accident. In 27 BC, the northernmost of the two colossi was partly shattered by an earthquake. Thereafter, at sunrise, vibrations created inside the stone by the changing temperature and humidity caused the statue to emit a curious, twanging sound. Classical commentators linked this curious phenomenon with the legend of the warrior-king Memnon, crying to his mother Aurora, goddess of the dawn. The statues were thus identified as images of Memnon (they are known to this day as the Colossi of Memnon), and visitors came from far and wide to hear them "sing." Like countless tourists since, the Romans could not resist leaving their mark for posterity, and the colossi are carved with 107 inscriptions, 61 in Greek, 45 in Latin, and one bilingual text. Dated inscriptions span the reigns of Tiberius to Septimius Severus (20–205 AD). In a nice illustration of the cultural distinctions in Roman Egypt, most of the epigrams and poetic inscriptions are written in Greek, while the texts in Latin are more matter-of-fact. But all record the wonder experienced by their authors at hearing the singing of Memnon.

A typical inscription reads: "I, Servius . . . Clemens, in the consulate of M. Aurelius Cotta Messalinus, heard the voice of Memnon and gave thanks."[5] Another visitor wrote of the strange sound that "my very ears seized it and I recognised a song."[6] In the early days of tourism, visitors were mostly high-ranking individuals: five Roman prefects of Egypt came to hear the statue between AD 71 and 104. The other group of regular visitors was the military: the colossi were a popular excursion for soldiers en route from Alexandria to the Roman garrison south of Thebes. The down-to-earth, no-nonsense attitude of the senior military commander is summed up by the inscription of Lucius Junius Calvinus, commander of the mountain of Berenice: "I heard Memnon, with my wife Minicia Rustica, on the fifteenth of the calends of April, at the second hour, in the fourth year of our emperor Vespasian Augustus."[7]

What made the statue even more mysterious—and alluring—was its unpredictability. It did not perform every sunrise, and certainly not to order. While some pilgrims claimed to have heard the statue twice on a single morning, one prefect's wife had to wait until her third visit before Memnon uttered his baleful cry. For a few tourists, hearing the statue sing became something of an obsession. Lucius Tanicius, a centurion of the third legion of Cyrenaica (stationed in Upper Egypt), came fourteen times in a single year. The zenith of Memnon-mania—and, indeed, of the Roman interest in ancient Egyptian civilisation—was the reign of Hadrian. During his twenty-one years as emperor, all sorts of senior administrators came to Thebes and left their mark on the statues. Hadrian himself came to hear Memnon during his fateful visit up the Nile in AD 130 (see Chapter 8). When the statue duly performed, the officials in his retinue believed (or were encouraged to believe) that Memnon was recognising a fellow deity: "He noticed Hadrian, sovereign king, before the sun rose, and saluted him as he could."[8] Hadrian's long-suffering wife, Sabina Augusta, left her own inscription—in Greek. Not all Roman emperors were as lucky, though, in hearing Memnon. When Septimius Severus visited in AD 202, the colossus failed to perform, so he promptly repaired it . . . and succeeded in silencing it for ever.

The Colossi of Memnon are not the only statues in western Thebes to have inspired poetic thoughts. Equally famous in the English-speaking world is the fallen colossus of Ramesses II which lies, toppled by an earthquake, in his mortuary temple, the Ramesseum, half a mile to the north of the colossi. The Ramesseum and its gargantuan statuary first attracted the attention of the Roman historian Diodorus Siculus, who felt moved to mention them in his Histories:

> Beside the entrance are three statues, each of a single block of black stone from Syene, of which one, that is seated, is the largest of any in Egypt, the foot alone measuring over seven cubits . . . it is not merely for its size that this work merits approbation, but it is also marvellous by reason of its artistic quality and excellent because of the nature of the stone . . . The inscription upon it runs: "King of Kings am I, Osymandyas. If anyone would know how great I am and where I lie, let him surpass one of my works."[9]

Nearly two millennia later, in 1817, the young English poet Percy Bysshe Shelley attended a display in the British Museum of "Young Memnon," the head and torso of another statue of Ramesses II, recently brought to London from Thebes. That same year, inspired by Diodorus Siculus and moved by his own encounter with ancient Egypt, he published his most famous poem, "Ozymandias of Egypt." Although he had never seen the Ramesseum or the fallen colossus, his lines remain the most telling evocation in the English language of the transience of power:

"My name is Ozymandias, king of kings:
Look on my works, ye Mighty, and despair!"
Nothing beside remains. Round the decay
Of that colossal wreck, boundless and bare,
The lone and level sands stretch far away.[10]

From the Ramesseum, it is but a short taxi-ride past the ravaged hillside of Sheikh Abd el-Qurna to the most striking architectural ensemble in all of Egypt, the terraced temple of Hatshepsut at Deir el-Bahri. Excavated from mounds of debris in the 1920s and painstakingly restored over the next seven decades, it is the only west bank temple clearly visible from the other side of the river. Again, its history as a visitor attraction is a long one. Before Hatshepsut chose the dramatic embayment in the cliffs for the construction of her "holy of holies," the site was already revered as a dwelling place of Hathor, divine mother and royal protectress, worshipped in these parts as the goddess of the western mountain. Nowhere was more appropriate for a temple designed to perpetuate the eternal memory of a female pharaoh. The fact that the site also lay directly opposite Hatshepsut's additions to the great temple of Karnak lent it added symbolic potency.

The spectacular setting—a vast natural amphitheatre in the Theban Hills, backed by a towering vertical cliff face—demanded an equally spectacular design. The building that Senenmut created for Hatshepsut remains unique, and uniquely impressive, the perfect marriage of natural landscape and man-made edifice. Long after Hatshepsut's demise, her temple—especially the chapel dedicated to Hathor—remained a place of pilgrimage. In the Nineteenth and Twentieth Dynasties, women from the workers' village walked over the mountains to pray here to the goddess. They sought help and protection, for themselves and their babies. In a society where death in childbirth was common and infant mortality tragically high, divine assistance was eagerly sought in matters of family life. The small votive objects left at Deir el-Bahri—crude statues, amulets and scraps of cloth—bring us face to face with the hopes and fears of ordinary ancient Egyptians, far removed from the lofty, cosmic concerns of their rulers.

Visitors now come to Deir el-Bahri for different reasons, but—if the crowds and the trinket-sellers permit—can still be moved by the spirit of the place. Despite what the tour guides say, the best time of day to visit the temple (and just about any temple in Egypt) is between noon and two o'clock in the afternoon. The morning crowds have left, to return to their hotels for lunch, while the afternoon groups have not yet arrived. It is the hottest part of the day, so not for the faint-hearted, but also the quietest. To visit in the morning, as many do, is to run the gauntlet of legions of hawkers, plying their trade in souvenirs and fake antiquities, and of other tour groups, led by sergeant-major guides with flags or coloured umbrellas. It is not a pleasant experience. For the groups of mostly Swiss and Japanese tourists who were visiting Deir el-Bahri on the morning of Monday 17 November 1997, however, the usual ordeal was to turn into a nightmare.

Unbeknown to the guides and the tourist police on duty at the temple that morning, six armed members of the extremist group Gama'a al-Islamiyya had disguised themselves as policemen and lay in wait for the first busloads of tourists to arrive. As visitors strolled along the terraces, admiring the art and architecture, the terrorists opened fire. Terrified visitors rushed for cover, and equally terrified temple guards simply fled the scene. The Egyptian security forces were nowhere to be seen. The attack lasted an agonising forty-five minutes. Eventually, the gunmen were pursued and apprehended by the traders and other local inhabitants, aghast at the attack on their community and their livelihoods. At the end of the massacre, fifty-eight tourists and ten Egyptians lay dead. The Deir el-Bahri atrocity marked the nadir of terrorist attacks in Egypt. Over the preceding years, gunmen had attacked a bus near Nagada and had taken pot shots at a Nile cruiser in Middle Egypt. Security had been tightened—roadblocks increased, armed escorts provided for tourist buses, unauthorised travel restricted, cruises prevented from sailing north of Luxor—but the extremists had not gone away. The incident at Deir el-Bahri changed everything. The tourist industry suffered a massive decline from which it took years to recover. Scores of Theban families lost their jobs. Egyptian outrage at the attack spelled the end of support for Gama'a al-Islamiyya. After 1997, its military chief, Ayman al-Zawahiri, decided to pursue his jihad outside Egypt, as a leader of al-Qaeda.

Visitors have returned to Deir el-Bahri, but the security is tighter than ever. Now, tourists have to pass through airport-style metal detectors before they can enter the temple complex: an incongruous juxtaposition, symptomatic of the complex relationship between Egypt's ancient past and its troubled present.

Another legacy of the Deir el-Bahri massacre is that it is no longer possible to climb the cliff behind the temple and follow the ancient route over the mountain into the Valley of the Kings. Instead, visitors must now take the modern road, past the obligatory alabaster factories selling vases, model pyramids and lamp-stands cut from the distinctive, banded, translucent, honey-coloured stone. The sheer number of outlets emphasises the size of the Theban tourist industry. The names of the various factories also provide a fascinating commentary on contemporary culture. Beside the perennial stalwarts—Ramesses, Cleopatra, Nefertiti—others change their name in tune with the latest contemporary (Western) fashions. In the 1980s and '90s, one of the most prominent emporia on the west bank was the Princess Diana Alabaster Factory. It is still there, dilapidated and hanging on by a thread, but one suspects that its days, under that name at least, are numbered. It can't be long before there is a William & Kate or a David Beckham factory. Perhaps there already is.

As the road bends round to the west, towards the Valley of the Kings, it enters the heart of the Theban Hills. A narrow defile between sheer rock walls is the only route in and out of the royal necropolis, and it is easy to understand why the security-conscious pharaohs of the New Kingdom selected this place for their tombs. The remoteness and seclusion are also complemented by the particular topography of the area, which displays a host of symbolic associations so beloved of the ancient Egyptians. When viewed from across the Nile, the Theban Hills—the place of sunset—also resemble a giant hieroglyph for "horizon," and therefore rebirth. The Valley of the Kings lies directly behind the dip between the two massifs, at the very horizon point itself. And, to cap it all, towering over the valley is a majestic peak (known today as the Qurn), a natural pyramid to preside over the tombs of kings.

Tourists have been drawn to the royal necropolis since early Ptolemaic times—when the New Kingdom was already ancient history. A Greek graffito sums up the combination of emotions that many visitors feel when faced by such magnificent monuments to the dead: "I, Philastrios the Alexandrian, who have come to Thebes, and who have seen with my eyes the work of these tombs of astounding horror, have spent a delightful day."[11] Although the Colossi of Memnon were the main attraction in the Roman period, some visitors took the opportunity to explore the tombs of the "Memnonia," as western Thebes was called. Strabo recounted his visit to "tombs of kings, which are stone-hewn, are about forty in number, are marvellously constructed, and are a spectacle worth seeing";[12] while Pausanias marvelled at the steep, winding corridors of the Valley of the Kings, which he dubbed the "syrinxes." In classical times, the most prominent and easily accessible tombs attracted numerous graffiti: there are 656 Greek and Latin inscriptions in the tomb of Ramesses IV and nearly a thousand in the tomb of Ramesses VI, who was identified by the Greeks as Memnon himself. Visitors gazed in wonder at the tombs but, like many tourists today, were utterly bemused by their construction and meaning. One Roman wrote: "I have seen the peculiarly excellent workmanship of these tombs, which is unutterable to us."[13] Altogether, over two thousand Greek and Latin graffiti have been recorded in the Valley of the Kings, alongside inscriptions in Phoenician, Cypriot and Lycian, a testament to Egypt's attractiveness as an international tourist destination, even in ancient times.

By the time Orion, Governor of Upper Egypt, carved his own name in AD 537, the Roman Empire had been Christianised and a small Christian community had settled in the Valley of the Kings, converting one of the tombs into a chapel for their daily worship. The valley in summer is an unforgiving place, the steep sides of bare rock reflecting and magnifying the sun's rays, raising temperatures in the shade (if any shade can be found) to nearly 50°C. The early Coptic inhabitants chewed on the hallucinatory Balinites nut to afford them some relief from the harsh conditions and the oppressive solitude. Today, the only respite on offer is the shabby and overpriced rest-house, with its bottles of lukewarm lemonade. (To judge from their graffiti, most Greek and Roman visitors were sensible enough to visit in the cooler winter months.)

The valley's Christian inhabitants seem to have sought it out as a place of quiet contemplation and isolation; they took little interest in the tombs themselves. A millennium passed before the necropolis began, once again, to attract the attention and curiosity of foreign visitors. The first European to recognise the significance of this isolated wadi was Father Claude Sicard, head of the Jesuit mission in Cairo, who visited in 1708. He located ten open tombs, and remarked on their colourful wall paintings, which he said were "almost as fresh as the day they were done."[14] The first published account of the Valley of the Kings appeared in 1743, by the English traveller Richard Pococke. Others soon followed in his footsteps. When William Browne visited in 1792, he reported that the site had been dug over in recent decades by the son of a local sheikh, "in expectation of finding treasure."[15] It was the harbinger of things to come. For the next century and a half, the Valley of the Kings would be the focus of attention for treasure-hunters from across the Western world.

In the twenty-first century, plunder has given way once more to wonder; but, in the process, the Valley of the Kings has been transformed from a remote wadi into a major tourist attraction, losing some of its special appeal in the process. A neat arcade of shops keeps the trinket-sellers to one side of the coach park, although every visitor has to run the gauntlet in order to reach the ticket office. A little train now takes tourists from the visitor centre to the valley entrance, which is still marked by no more than a guard's hut and some iron railings. Inevitably, many of the finest tombs are closed, in an attempt to regulate the flow of visitors and preserve the tombs. The heat and humidity in some of the deeper tombs are almost unbearable. It is a wonder that the wall paintings do not simply peel off in front of one's very eyes. But the climb up and down into the tomb of Thutmose III merely strengthens one's respect for the ancient Egyptian workers who built these tombs, labouring for days on end in dusty heat in the humid bowels of the mountain by the light of flickering, sooty tallow candles. All in all, the experience of visiting the Valley of the Kings today is admirably summed up in Vivant Denon's words, written after a three-hour exploration in the spring of 1799: "A visit to Thebes was like the attack of a fever, it was a kind of crisis which left behind an impression of indescribable impatience, enthusiasm, irritation, and fatigue."[16]

WITH THE EXCEPTION of Tutankhamun's tomb, all the royal burials in the Valley of the Kings were thoroughly looted in antiquity, leaving only their wall paintings to hint at their former splendour. The tomb robberies started early, and the reason can be found in the community of Deir el-Medina. The workers who built and decorated the royal tombs had an unwritten contract with their employer, the Egyptian state: hard work and tight security in exchange for decent pay and conditions. When the government failed to honour its side of the bargain, the men of Deir el-Medina began to question why they should continue to keep the state's most carefully guarded secret, the location of the royal tombs in the Valley of the Kings. Within little more than a generation of the strikes under Ramesses III, the tomb robberies began. At first, thieves targeted the less well-guarded sepulchres on the hillside behind the Ramesseum. One night in 1114 BC, a stonemason from Deir el-Medina called Amun-panefer set out with a group of accomplices to steal treasure. Entering the tomb of King Sobekemsaf II,

> We opened their coffins and their mummy-wrappings . . . We brought back the gold we found on the noble mummy of this god, together with his pectorals and other jewellery which were around his neck . . . [17]

Their daring, blasphemous crime netted them a haul of thirty-two pounds of gold: a king's ransom indeed. The thieves got away with their misdeed for four years, until the robbery came to light and they were sentenced to death. But a line had been crossed. A royal commission set up to investigate the crime discovered that nine out of ten royal tombs had already been looted. It was open season on the royal treasures of ancient Thebes. From the workers' village, the criminal activity spread to various state and temple officials, some of whom turned a blind eye to thefts carried out under their noses, others of whom were actively involved in robbery. Even the chief guard of Karnak was implicated.

It was not long before the state itself was in on the act, pilfering the treasures of earlier rulers to fill its own coffers. During the virtual civil war that beset Egypt during the reign of Ramesses XI (1099–1069 BC), the general and head of the Theban military junta sent a letter to the scribe of the necropolis, Butehamun, ordering him to "uncover a tomb amongst the tombs of the ancestors and preserve its seal until I return."[18]

It was the beginning of a deliberate policy of state-sponsored tomb robbery. Butehamun was at the centre of it, and, fortunately for historians, he was as enthusiastic a correspondent as he was a thief. The archive of letters between Butehamun and his father Thutmose chronicles the systematic despoliation of the Theban royal tombs during the last century of the second millennium BC. The whole enterprise was organised like a military operation. The workmen who stole to Butehamun's orders had a map of the Valley of the Kings to assist them. Butehamun's office had facilities for processing the loot and re-wrapping the royal mummies after they had been stripped of all their precious accoutrements. Without a hint of apparent irony, Butehamun gloried in the titles Opener of the Gates of the Necropolis, Overseer of Works in the House of Eternity and Overseer of the Treasuries of the Kings. All over the royal necropolis, graffiti next to tomb entrances and at other key locations record the names of Butehamun and Thutmose; their fingerprints were literally all over the crime scene.

With most of the royal tombs thoroughly pillaged, the monuments of ancient Thebes were largely forgotten and left to fall into ruins, as the political and economic axis of Egypt swung northwards in the first millennium BC, towards the cities of the Delta: Tanis and Bubastis, Sais and Pelusium, Alexandria and Cairo. When the next wave of treasure-hunters turned their attention to Thebes in the early nineteenth century AD, in the wake of Napoleon's expedition to Egypt, it was the great temples that caught their imagination.

For a hundred years after Bonaparte left the Nile Valley, Egypt was turned into a battleground, not between armies but between government agents, as Europe's monarchies vied with each other to acquire the treasures of the pharaohs. From this century of plunder, one towering figure—in every sense of the word—stands out.

Giovanni Battista Belzoni (1778–1823) was born in the city of Padua, the son of a barber. Like many young Italians of the time with limited prospects, on reaching the threshold of adulthood he journeyed to Rome, to prepare for monastic orders. But fate intervened—in the form of Napoleon's invasion of Rome—and Belzoni left the city to become a vagrant, travelling through France, Germany and the Netherlands peddling religious trinkets. At the age of twenty-four he arrived in England—and caused an immediate stir. He certainly cut an arresting figure, at six foot six inches tall, with dark hair, strong aquiline features and piercing blue eyes. Sir Walter Scott called him "the handsomest man (for a giant) I ever saw."[19] Within a year Belzoni had married the love of his life, Sarah, and embarked on a theatrical career. The London stage certainly welcomed his striking looks and towering figure. On Easter Monday 1803, the playbill at Sadler's Wells theatre advertised a new act:

> Signor Giovanni Batista Belzoni, the Patagonian Sampson; Will present most extraordinary Specimens of the GYMNASTIC Art, perfectly Foreign to any former exhibitioner (His first Appearance in England).[20]

The act involved Belzoni carrying eleven people about the stage on an iron frame which itself weighed over one hundred pounds. It was so popular it ran for three months. After Sadler's Wells, the Patagonian Sampson transmogrified into "the French Hercules" for a show at Bartholomew's Fair in the City of London. Belzoni appeared as the giant in "Jack the Giantkiller" (aka "Jack and the Beanstalk") and was soon billed under his own name as "The Great Belzoni." For the next nine years, he toured the British Isles as a strongman, actor and conjuror. He also designed dramatic theatrical effects based on hydraulics. Then, in February 1813, he gave his last performance in England, at the Blue Boar Tavern in Oxford. Belzoni, ever eager for new adventures, had tired of the theatre. His old life as a wandering pedlar beckoned, and he set off on travels anew, this time with Sarah at his side.

En route to Constantinople, they travelled to Malta, where Belzoni met an agent of the Egyptian ruler. Muhammad Ali was recruiting engineers from across Europe to help him realise his ambitious plans for modernising Egypt's infrastructure. Belzoni, with his experience of theatrical hydraulics, persuaded the agent that he could build a waterwheel driven by oxen that would lift as much as four traditional waterwheels. He was encouraged to come to Egypt to prove his claims. And so, in 1815, he arrived in Cairo, for what would prove a transformational encounter with the land of the pharaohs.

At first, it must have seemed like a dreadful mistake. On his way to his interview with Muhammad Ali, Belzoni was kicked in the leg by a soldier and incapacitated for several weeks. Then a mutiny in Cairo led to looting, and Belzoni had his passport and all his money stolen.

Finally, Belzoni's waterwheel was rejected, and he found himself in a foreign city, without employment, money or contacts. But, by a stroke of great fortune, he met another government agent, Henry Salt, the British Consul-General. Salt was as ambitious for his own reputation as he was for his employer's imperial glory, and he wished more than anything to see a colossal bust of Ramesses II (known as "the Young Memnon") transported from western Thebes to London and presented to the British Museum—with Salt recognised as the donor. Belzoni seemed just the man for the job.

On 30 June 1816 Giovanni and Sarah left Cairo for Thebes, which he described on first sight as "like entering a city of giants."[21] He was equally moved by the Young Memnon, still in its original setting of the Ramesseum: "I found it near the remains of its body and chair, with its face upwards, and apparently smiling on me, at the thought of being taken to England."[22] The only tools at Belzoni's disposal were fourteen wooden poles, four palm ropes and four rollers; yet, within a few days, the statue had been successfully manoeuvred to the bank of the Nile. In the space of a week and a half, Belzoni had also discovered four new tombs in the Valley of the Kings (among them the spectacular sepulchre of Seti I, which he duly relieved of its sarcophagus). On 21 November, he set off downstream with the seven-ton Young Memnon aboard. Ten days before Christmas, he arrived in Cairo with his hoard of antiquities. (The Young Memnon duly found its way to the British Museum, but Belzoni received neither credit nor profit for his efforts.) Undaunted, he promptly set off for Nubia, to undertake another gargantuan task, the clearance of Abu Simbel. On his way there, he stopped off at Philae and noticed a rather attractive small obelisk which he fancied might suitably adorn a country estate in England. Brought back to Kingston Lacey in Dorset, it subsequently proved instrumental in the decipherment of hieroglyphics.

In his career as an acquirer of antiquities, Belzoni had found the perfect outlet for his talents. He was a skilled negotiator, able to outwit his rivals (especially the men hired by the French consul, Drovetti) and persuade suspicious locals to let him relieve them of their patrimony. He was as strong as an ox, and also resilient. A letter he wrote to his brothers from the tomb of Seti I is headed: "The Valley of Biban el-Muluk [the Valley of the Kings] near Thebes. 15 August 1818. Latitude 25°44'31"

North. Longitude 32°36'31". Shade temperature 124° Fahrenheit."[23] After leaving Egypt for the last time in early 1819, he returned to England to publish his memoirs and exhibit his discoveries. On the first day of the exhibition, held in the appropriate surroundings of the Egyptian Hall, Piccadilly, nearly two thousand people paid half-a-crown each to see the spectacle. Belzoni finally achieved the fame he deserved. As Charles Dickens put it, "The once starving mountebank became one of the most illustrious men in Europe."[24] But his fortune was to be shortlived. On an ill-fated expedition to locate the source of the Niger, Belzoni caught dysentery and died in December 1823, in Benin, at the age of forty-five. Though castigated by modern archaeologists for his methods, Belzoni nevertheless provided the British Museum with many of its finest Egyptian antiquities, and thus contributed as much, if not more, to the popularity of the subject than most professional Egyptologists.

A century after Belzoni's exploits at Thebes, when the mortuary temples had been stripped of all moveable objects, attention turned once more to the Valley of the Kings, where, archaeologists hoped, there remained some royal tombs still undiscovered. This final treasure hunt amidst the Theban Hills is, above all, the story of two protagonists, an American and an Englishman. The American was a wealthy New York lawyer, Theodore M. Davis (1838–1915). With other members of the Gilded Age, he spent his summers in a high society mansion on Ocean Avenue, Newport, Rhode Island; but his winters he spent on his dahabiya, the *Bedouin*, with his companion Mrs. Emma Andrews. He had already developed a passion for Egyptology when he succeeded, in 1902, in obtaining a permit from the Egyptian government to dig in the Valley of the Kings. Thus began his career as a private sponsor of excavations for the Antiquities Service. The Englishman was the very man who had first got Davis interested in archaeology, and who had himself been inspired by reading Belzoni: the inspector-general for Upper Egypt, Howard Carter (1874–1939). Carter was a talented excavator, but without means. (He started life as a humble Norfolk painter, getting his first experience of Egyptian archaeology as an illustrator.) In Davis, Carter had met the perfect source of funds. In their first seasons in partnership, digging in the Valley of the Kings, they found a private tomb and a box of leather loincloths: interesting, but hardly earth-shattering. When Carter was sacked as inspector-general, his successor persuaded

Davis to obtain a fresh permit, with a different archaeologist. Davis continued to bankroll excavations in the valley for another nine years. He discovered or cleared thirty tombs, including the burial of Amenhotep III's parents-in-law, Yuya and Tjuyu; the tomb of Horemheb; and a discarded embalming cache belonging to a little-known pharaoh called Tutankhamun. But eventually, disillusioned by the lack of spectacular finds, Davis threw in the towel, famously expressing his opinion that "the Valley of the Tombs is now exhausted."[25] A year later, on 23 February 1915, Davis was dead.

Carter was not so easily put off. He persuaded another wealthy backer, Lord Carnarvon, to obtain the permit; and so began another archaeological partnership which, in November 1922—and just six feet away from where Davis had stopped work, for fear of undercutting nearby tombs—uncovered the greatest treasure of all time, the burial of Tutankhamun. The story of that discovery has been told many times. After five years of fairly fruitless digging in the Valley of the Kings, Carter had persuaded Carnarvon to finance one final season. Just three days into this last campaign, under heaps of spoil from a later royal tomb, workmen uncovered a flight of steps leading downwards into the bedrock. Once the staircase had been fully cleared, an outer blocking wall was revealed, covered with plaster and stamped with seal impressions. It could mean only one thing: beyond lay an intact tomb from the golden age of the pharaohs.

Most archaeologists would have pressed on. Not Carter. Displaying the stiffest of English upper lips, he ordered the steps to be covered up again, before telegraphing Carnarvon (at home in England) to come out to Egypt immediately. If there was a major discovery to be made, it was only proper that patron and archaeologist should share it together. After what must have been an agonising wait of seventeen days, Carnarvon's train pulled into the station at Luxor, and on the morning of 26 November work to open the tomb began in earnest. Beyond the outer blocking lay a corridor filled with stone chips, which took a full day's work to clear. At the end of the corridor, another blocking wall was revealed, also covered in seal impressions. Without further hesitation, Carter took his trowel and made a small hole in the wall, just big enough to peer through. The hot air escaping from the sealed chamber caused the candle to flicker, and it took a few moments for Carter's eyes to grow accustomed to the gloom. But then, details of the chamber and its contents began to emerge. Carter stood dumbstruck. After some minutes, Carnarvon could bear the suspense no longer. "Can you see anything?" he asked. "Yes, yes," replied Carter, "wonderful things."

What came afterwards, the legacy of Tutankhamun, is more poignant. In the years following his greatest triumph, Carter maintained his home in western Thebes, "Carter House," but also spent much of his time sitting morosely in the foyer of the Winter Palace in Luxor, lost in his own thoughts. Although decorated by the King of Egypt and the King of the Belgians, and awarded an honorary doctorate from Yale, Carter never shook off the social stigma of his humble origins, and received no honours from his own country. In his last years at Thebes, to his intense irritation, tourists regarded him as a minor celebrity, as much a sight as the treasures he had discovered. Always irascible—one of his favourite expressions was "Tommy rot!"—he did not make friends easily, and was shunned by the Egyptological establishment. No letters of regret were forthcoming after his death. But, arguably, no other individual, ancient or modern—neither Intef II, Senenmut or Montuemhat, nor Belzoni or Davis—has done as much to put western Thebes on the map.

SIX

Qift and Qena
The Centre and the Provinces

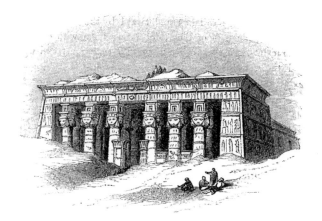

The Kuftis proved to be the most troublesome
people that I have ever worked with.[1]
—FLINDERS PETRIE

North of Luxor, as the Nile enters the great, eastward bend in its
course, the landscape of age-eroded limestone bluffs and lush
green fields is reflected in the river's gently flowing waters. Yet, by comparison with Thebes, there is a noticeable difference in the state of the
banks, canals and verges: they are strikingly free from rubbish, cleaner
here than anywhere else in the country. It is a small distinction, but an
important one, for it reflects the independent character of the people in
this part of Egypt.

The story of refuse collection is in many ways a parable of life in the contemporary Nile Valley. In the old days, people will tell you, rubbish used to be collected by private contractors, or rather by their armies of small boys who collected the refuse sacks from the roadsides at four o'clock in the morning, just before dawn. At the collecting depot, the organic waste was separated off and sold as fertiliser, earning the contractors a tidy profit. It was a successful system that suited everyone. Everyone, that is, except the authorities, who were jealous of any lucrative sector they did not control themselves. So, the contracts for rubbish collection were taken away from the private operators and given to big companies in exchange for large bribes. Service suffered, the streets and canals started to become choked with rubbish, but there was little that ordinary citizens could do: it was all part of the corruption and sclerosis of Mubarak's Egypt.

But, in the rural south of the country, the doughty locals—always independent-minded and sceptical of their distant rulers—took matters into their own hands. In the towns and villages between Luxor and Qena, the inhabitants organise rubbish collection, sorting and disposal themselves. As a result, their surroundings are cleaner and greener. It is a metaphor for the divide in Egyptian society, not just between north and south (northern Egyptians think southerners backward; southerners find their northern compatriots rude and selfish) but between the centre and the provinces. The tension between central control and provincial self-assertion is a leitmotif in Egyptian history; nowhere is it more apparent than in this part of Upper Egypt.

ON THE WEST BANK of the Nile, twelve miles north of the town of New Qurna, lies the small village of Nagada. A poor, undistinguished community of dusty streets, grubby children, hard-pressed adults, scratching chickens and semi-feral dogs, it would merit no mention at all were it not for the ancient burial ground that once lay behind it, at the foot of the western escarpment. The shallow pits that were excavated here at the end of the nineteenth century not only put Nagada on the map, they also changed our very understanding of Egypt's origins and the genesis of its great civilisation.

What the archaeologist's trowel revealed in this rural backwater were the vestiges of a long-lost and hitherto unknown culture, one as sophisticated as it was unexpected. So strange and unfamiliar were its material remains—lustrous, black-rimmed red vases; painted bowls decorated with lively scenes of hippos and hunters; and elegant cosmetic palettes of fine-grained greenish-black stone, carved in a range of curvaceous animal forms—that the excavators thought they had stumbled on a "new race." Such un-Egyptian objects, they supposed, must have been brought to the Nile Valley by invaders from the East during one of the periods of civil war that interrupted the course of ancient Egyptian civilisation. They could not have been more wrong. Subsequent discoveries at other sites soon showed that the vases, bowls and palettes uncovered in Nagada's shallow graves were not the work of foreign immigrants, but of indigenous Egyptians from the country's remote prehistoric past, people whose craftsmanship and creativity had set Egyptian culture on the path to greatness. At Nagada, the very origins of pharaonic civilisation had been dug from the gravelly soil.

Unbelievable as it seems today, for several heady centuries in the early and middle parts of the fourth millennium BC Nagada was one of the two or three most important places in the whole of Egypt. It was the location of a walled town, an innovation of communal living which betokened greater wealth and a desire to protect one's assets from jealous neighbours. The same wealth—enjoyed, as in today's Egypt, by a small, ruling class—is also seen in the nearby cemetery, where richly furnished tombs cluster together in one corner, separating the haves from the have-nots in death as in life. Even more spectacular, even more set apart, was a huge rectangular tomb of mud brick, covering thousands of square feet, its interior chambers packed with costly and exotic objects. This royal burial seems to have been made for an individual of special status, perhaps even the wife of Egypt's first king. Its location at Nagada suggests that the town had played a pivotal role in the political unification of the country, reflecting its prehistoric prominence.

But the formation of an Egyptian state spelled the beginning of the end for Nagada's fortunes. A scene of triumph scratched into the rock face in the desert behind the town suggests warfare between leading power centres of the time. Nagada's rivals in Upper Egypt, especially Nekhen, gained ground, literally and metaphorically. Nagada fell into obscurity, its leading role in the birth of Egyptian civilisation quickly forgotten. Within a few centuries of its royal tomb being built, Nagada had declined in size and splendour, a process that continued until the trowel of a late nineteenth-century archaeologist rescued it from utter obscurity.

If the discoveries at Nagada were remarkable, then so was the man responsible for them. William Matthew Flinders Petrie (1853–1942), "the father of Egyptian archaeology," excavated at more sites in the Nile Valley than any other archaeologist, before or since; and, in an age of treasure-hunters, his meticulous methods and careful recording established archaeology as a proper scientific enterprise for the first time. Nagada put him on the map as an archaeologist, and he repaid the compliment handsomely.

Like many of the great Egyptologists, Petrie was introduced to the land of the pharaohs by a curious combination of circumstances. He was born in 1853 to an electrical engineer, William Petrie, and his wife Anne, who was the daughter of the explorer of Australia, Captain Matthew Flinders. William junior—always known by his third name, Flinders—was too delicate a child to go to school, so was educated at home by his parents. This was his first lucky chance. His father had produced the first electric arc-lamp, ahead of his time, and Flinders showed an equal aptitude for science. His father was also a keen amateur surveyor—a popular pastime in Victorian Britain among the educated middle classes—and by his early twenties Flinders was travelling around southern England with his father, surveying earthworks and ancient monuments. Their measurements of Stonehenge were the most accurate yet made, and were the harbinger of things to come.

The second stroke of serendipity was William Flinders' growing fascination with the work of Charles Piazzi Smyth, Astronomer Royal of Scotland and one of the great scientific celebrities of the age. Charles Smyth's tastes were nothing if not catholic, and he mixed orthodox astronomy with distinctly unorthodox views about ancient Egypt. According to him, "the pyramid was a perfect structure, a product of divine inspiration, which embodied in its measurements a perfect system of weights and measures, among them the sacred cubit of the Israelites, the pyramid inch, and a system of prophecy."[2] Smyth's objective, through accurate measurement of the Great Pyramid, was to unlock the key to humanity's past and future. (Today's "New Age" authors like Graham Hancock and Robert Bauval stand in this long tradition.)

A fascination with science, an aptitude for surveying and a curiosity about the pyramids: all the pieces were in place, and in 1880 Flinders Petrie set out from Liverpool by ship, bound for Egypt. The resulting expedition spelled the end of Smyth's theories but the beginning of a lifelong mission for Petrie. At the end of two solitary winters at Giza, living in an abandoned tomb, Petrie's meticulous measurements thoroughly undermined Smyth's "pyramid cult"; but the looting and vandalism of ancient monuments that Petrie witnessed all around him made a profound impression. As he put it, "Egypt was like a fire, so rapid was the destruction going on. My duty was that of a salvage man: to get all I could quickly gathered in."[3] Proper excavation and recording of Egypt's manifold monuments required determination and scientific method, both of which Petrie had in abundance. But they also required funds, and he was a man of modest means. Fortunately, fate intervened once again, in the form of Amelia Edwards, romantic novelist and, ever since her trip up the Nile in 1873–4, lover of all things ancient Egyptian. When Edwards read Petrie's book on the pyramids, published by the Royal Society in 1883, it was a meeting of minds. With her encouragement and financial support, he embarked on a full-time career as an archaeologist. Over the next sixty years he worked at just about every known site along the Nile Valley, publishing his results in over a thousand books and articles.

Petrie's greatest strength—his gift to archaeology—was his insistence that even the smallest fragments, unworthy of display in a museum, were invaluable as historical evidence. His book, *Methods and Aims in Archaeology*, was seminal. But his meticulous methods went hand-in-hand with an irascible temperament. He quarrelled with his sponsors in the Egypt Exploration Fund and worked on his own for many years with private backers. His attitude to his workers was equally stern: "the people used to loiter over the dinner hour . . . so one day, when they were worse than usual, I went to meet them as they tardily came up, and dismissed them all for the half day. After that they all came as soon as they had their food."[4] His frugality, born of those first two winters at Giza, verged on asceticism, and his excavation camps, though providing an unrivalled training, were regarded with dread for their austere conditions: "Of course sheer laziness without a cause means immediate dismissal; but the break of ten minutes in the midst of the morning and afternoon seems desirable all round."[5] He was also utterly impervious to others' criticism, a trait, perhaps, borne of his home-schooling. Hence, on his digs in Egypt, his dress was individual, to say the least: "For outside work in the hot weather, vest and pants were suitable, and if pink they kept the tourist at bay, as the creature seemed to him too queer for inspection."[6]

In 1892, Petrie's mentor Amelia Edwards died and bequeathed a sum to University College London to establish the first professorship of Egyptology in Britain. She also let it be known that she wished Petrie to be its first holder. With academic status and some measure of financial security, Petrie was able to devote each winter season to excavation. His dig at Nagada in the winter of 1894 was a model of his trademark meticulousness. In three months, he and his assistant James Quibell cleared two thousand graves. Petrie carefully noted the contents of each burial, especially the pottery, on a slip of card. His scientific intuition suggested to him that by tracking gradual changes in the style of pottery, it would be possible to place the graves in their relative chronological order. So he arranged and rearranged the slips of card until each type of pottery displayed a smooth evolution in its form. The result was Petrie's famous "sequence dating system," the very first example of the now standard technique of archaeological seriation. To this day, it remains the best method for dating artefacts and tomb-groups from Egypt's prehistoric past: pots as a proxy for period.

The pottery-making prowess of Nagada's inhabitants has continued through the millennia. It was remarked upon by Arab travellers in the Middle Ages, and the nearby village of Ballas is still a renowned centre for potters. Their distinctive, pale-coloured water-jars, fired with sugarcane leaves in kilns of ancient design, are sought after throughout the region. Despite the advent of plastic canisters, pots from Ballas can still be seen perched on the heads of local women as they return from the Nile or the village water-pump.

Nagada owed its prehistoric prosperity to its special location at a point where desert trade routes meet the river and where the Nile, thanks to the bend in its course, swings further east than at any other point in its long journey to the sea. This combination of factors gave the inhabitants of Nagada relatively easy access to the gold mines of the Eastern Desert, and the ability to trade their precious ore the length and breadth of Egypt. Indeed, Nagada was synonymous with gold: its ancient Egyptian name, Nubt, meant, quite simply, "the golden." If Nagada was a gold emporium, then the centre of operations for mining expeditions was its neighbouring settlement on the opposite bank of the river. This particular town has fared rather better than Nagada over the aeons of Egyptian history. In common with only a few places in Egypt, it has kept its name down the millennia: ancient Gebt, classical Copt(os), modern Qift (pronounced "Kuft"). The longevity of its name also reflects the tenacity of its people.

Petrie chose Qift for his first excavation as Edwards Professor of Egyptology, in the winter of 1893. (It was while working here that he "eyed the hills on the opposite side of the Nile, and heard of things being found there,"[7] leading to his work at Nagada the following year.) He chose Qift, not for its standing monuments (it has none), nor for its historical importance (which was then unknown), but for its geographical proximity to the Red Sea—whence, Petrie then believed, Egypt's "dynastic people" had arrived to bring civilisation to the Nile Valley. Though his determination kept him going, the conditions at Qift were hardly conducive to archaeology. More irksome to Petrie than the usual flies, rats and dogs, were the local inhabitants: "The Kuftis proved to be the most troublesome people that I have ever worked with,"[8] he declared. The problem was partly of his own making. By the late nineteenth century, after a hundred years of Europeans looting Egypt for its ancient treasures, the Egyptians had come to realise that the sudden arrival of white-skinned foreigners with their strange clothes and equipment usually presaged the discovery of valuable antiquities. Qift had the particular misfortune (from Petrie's perspective) of a public road running right through the archaeological site—making the ancient ruins especially accessible. As a result, Petrie found the town awash with looters and antiquities dealers. Not a man to be thwarted from the important business of archaeology, he set out to teach the Qiftis a lesson. He managed to apprehend one thief, walloping him soundly. Then, Petrie "let him crawl off on hands and knees some way and then, giving shout, ran at him, when he made off like a hare."[9] But the impoverished villagers were not so easily dissuaded from the promise of making a fast buck, and they simply came back each night to steal the antiquities so painstakingly dug up by Petrie the previous day.

Despite such travails, one group of Qiftis found common cause with Petrie—each admiring the other's single-minded determination. As the archaeologist explained,

> Among this rather untoward people we found however, as in every place, a small percentage of excellent men; some half-dozen were of the very best type of native, faithful, friendly, and laborious, and from among these workmen we have drawn about forty to sixty for our work . . . They have formed the backbone of my upper Egyptian staff, and I hope that I may keep these good friends so long as I work anywhere within reach of them.[10]

He was as good as his word. "The excavation here was the founding of a tribe of workers who have been sought for by every excavator since; a 'Qufti' came to be almost the name for a good digger. There were many substantial old families here, entirely unspoiled by tourist ways, and they formed a fine stock; even their grandsons are still in my work."[11] The men from Qift whom Petrie trained as foremen passed on their skills to their descendants, some of whom are still employed as professional diggers by archaeologists working in Egypt today. "Qifti" is common parlance among Egyptologists for a skilled site foreman.

THE VILLAGE OF Qift has occupied a distinctive place in Egyptian history: never central to developments, but not insignificant either. It has been aptly described as "economically privileged but historically disadvantaged,"[12] because of its proximity to the gold mines of the Eastern Desert and the Red Sea on the one hand, and to Thebes on the other. Its southern neighbour has tended, since pharaonic times, to dominate the politics of Upper Egypt; but the country's rulers have never been able to neglect Qift, given the importance both of the Eastern Desert's mineral resources and of Red Sea trade to Egypt's economy. While provincial in many respects, Qift has been at the heart of Egypt's story for millennia. Today, the houses and streets of the typically ramshackle modern settlement encircle the ancient remains, marking a continuity of occupation that stretches back more than five thousand years. In the nineteenth and early twentieth centuries, the site—like most archaeological ruins in Egypt—was extensively mined for sebakh, the rich fertiliser that is the product of decayed mud-brick buildings. Qift's ancient structures were reduced to rubble, or grubbed out entirely. Pillaging for antiquities, as encountered by Petrie, wreaked further damage. Today the site shows only "isolated pillars of preserved antiquities surrounded by newly constructed apartment buildings, cut through by modern roads, and inhabited by herds of goats and packs of feral dogs living off the garbage deposited daily."[13] But these unpromising remains hold remarkable clues to Qift's long history.

From prehistoric times down to the coming of Christianity, the inhabitants of Qift worshipped a fertility god with a highly distinctive appearance. Known in pharaonic times as Min, his classic depiction was as a tall standing figure, swathed in tight bandages, wearing twin ostrich plumes on his head, with one arm raised behind his head, holding a flail, and the other grasping the base of his huge erect penis which protrudes through his clothing. The twin plumes (denoting divinity in general) seem to have been a later addition; but the other aspects of his appearance, especially the ithyphallic pose, predate recorded history. During Petrie's excavations at Qift in the winter of 1893–4, he uncovered a remarkable pair of colossal statues of the local fertility god. Each was crudely fashioned from a cylindrical block of stone, and bore strange signs down one side which predate hieroglyphic writing and still defy convincing explanation. The ascetic Victorian archaeologist was clearly rather embarrassed by the statues' immodesty, and could only bring himself to describe their posture as being "in the usual attitude of Min,"[14] without further comment. Usually meticulous in the publication of his finds, Petrie omitted any illustration of the complete colossi, confining himself to just the head of one statue. Nor did he provide any illustration or mention of the detachable stone penis, carefully carved to fit in a socket in one of the statues. Indeed, other than the oblique reference to Min, there is nothing to suggest the most distinctive characteristic of these remarkable survivors from the dawn of religion.

Later relief carvings of Min from Qift, dating to the reign of Senus-ret I in the nineteenth century BC, rank among the masterpieces of ancient Egyptian art, but they proved no less embarrassing to Petrie. He felt compelled to publish a photograph of one block, but covered the god's modesty, quite literally, with a wooden plaque bearing the words "temple scene of Usertsen [Senusret] I dancing before Min."[15] Line drawings of other images of Min omitted the offending member entirely.

Petrie was in a particularly delicate situation. His twelve-week dig at Qift was funded by independent financial backers in England, Jesse Haworth and Martyn Kennard, to whom Petrie sent back regular reports throughout the excavation season. He had to tread a fine line between talking up the importance of his discoveries and scandalising the very people who made the work possible. Little wonder, perhaps, that the following year Petrie founded the Egyptian Research Account to fund future excavations, thereby giving him complete independence of action (and publication).

Of the temple buildings that once housed these remarkable statues and reliefs, but little survived. Successive generations of sebakh-diggers and treasure-seekers had taken their toll. But even the small pieces of inscribed stone that remained, although dislodged from their original settings, were sufficient to rewrite chapters of Egyptian history. None is more illuminating than the series of decrees set up in the temple at Qift by successive monarchs of the late Old Kingdom. They display the tension between the centre and the provinces, between economic control and political expediency, at its most acute.

Right up until the reforms of Muhammad Ali in the early nineteenth century, the Egyptian government derived the majority of its revenue from the country's agricultural wealth. Most, if not all, land was owned, ultimately, by the state, and the state levied a share of the harvest as taxes. So the fertility of the soil, together with the regular collection of produce from Egypt's farmers, kept the government finances in a healthy surplus. In such a system, granting exemption from taxation to any landholding was a serious step, since it denied the state its revenue. On the other hand, no mark of government favour was quite as significant (or welcome, to the grantee). Throughout history, Egypt's rulers used their power to grant tax-exempt status. It was a convenient political tool to win the loyalty of influential families, towns and temples. Because of their financial and political value, exemption decrees were often prominently displayed in public buildings.

In the dying days of the Old Kingdom, several such decrees were set up in the temple at Qift, underscoring this small provincial town's wider economic and political significance. Further royal decrees followed, concerned not with tax exemption but with the promotion of royal favourites to high office. Three decrees were issued by King Neferkaura, charting the meteoric rise of a certain Shemai from obscurity to the governorship of Upper Egypt, and the commensurate appointment of his son Idy as provincial governor of Qift. A further eight decrees were announced in the space of a single day by Neferkaura's successor. Once again, all were concerned with the promotions and honours accorded to Shemai and members of his family. The reason for this extraordinary shower of royal largesse: the new king was none other than Shemai's father-in-law, and was using the full weight of his authority to reward his relatives. The Qift decrees provide a telling illustration of cronyism and of the need for the central government to buy the loyalty of the provinces—features of Egyptian politics in the twenty-first century AD as much as in the twenty-second century BC.

For a place of comparative contemporary obscurity, Qift has often found itself at the heart of Egypt's story. For example, it was on the front line of the civil war between Thebes and the northern provinces that ultimately resulted in the birth of the Middle Kingdom. Qift's rulers flip-flopped between the opposing sides, depending on which was in the ascendant, but ultimately threw in their lot with the Thebans. It was a wise choice. When the rulers of Thebes conquered all of Egypt, Qift was once again the focus of royal patronage. King Mentuhotep deployed a workforce from the town to dig new wells along the route to the Red Sea, while two generations later a successful quarrying expedition from Qift enabled the man in charge, the vizier Amenemhat, to secure his political ascendancy and ultimate accession to the throne.

Qift's undoubted heyday, though, was during the Ptolemaic and Roman periods when the establishment of a port on the Red Sea coast (Berenike), the construction of a road thence from the Nile Valley and the opening of the Red Sea trade routes from the Mediterranean to India made Qift a major trans-shipment centre. The local temple witnessed almost constant building activity from Ptolemy II down to Caracalla, as each successive ruler sought both to reward and stamp his authority on Qift. The town was noted for its cosmopolitan atmosphere, garrison troops and traders from across the Ptolemaic and Roman empires mixing with local inhabitants. (The minutiae of archaeology tell us that the Ptolemaic inhabitants ate cattle, pigs and fish, while the Romans preferred sheep, goats and birds.) In 25–4 BC, the Greek geographer Strabo—a friend of the Roman Prefect—travelled through Upper Egypt and commented on the high reputation of Qift by comparison with the degradation of Thebes (which at that point had declined to little more than a "collection of villages"[16]). Under Augustus, soldiers from the third legion were stationed at Qift, building a bridge across the Nile, and staffing, repairing and supplying the string of forts which stretched across the Eastern Desert from the Nile Valley to the Red Sea. The road from Qift to the port of Quseir was the most heavily fortified in the whole country, with watchtowers, way-stations and fortified wells, as well as small garrisons like Didyme, still well preserved today.

In addition to its military role and importance as a trading centre, Qift was also a defensive outpost against bandits (going on the run was a form of tax evasion in Roman Egypt) and, more seriously, the unpredictable nomads of the Eastern Desert who periodically threatened the state's economic interests. Augustus stationed an entire legion at Qift, while Caracalla brought in elite archers from Palmyra. But even such forces proved insufficient, and the Blemmyes temporarily overran Qift in the later third century AD, remaining thereafter a constant thorn in the government's side.

Over the centuries, Qift's combination of self-reliance and adaptability has served it well. At about the time of the Blemmyan incursions, the town also attracted early Christian converts who rebelled against Diocletian's persecutions. Although Qift was razed by the emperor as punishment, it remained unbowed and within a generation had become an episcopal seat; a large basilica and baptistery were built next to the ancient temple complex. The Qiftis likewise absorbed the coming of Islam while retaining their commercial edge. Under the Mamluks, seagoing ships were built at Qift for transport overland to Quseir, and Qift also developed a thriving manufacturing industry, specialising in sugar and soap which it supplied to the rest of Egypt. Only the rise of nearby Qus, starting in the tenth century AD, started to eat away at Qift's economic importance. By medieval times, Qus was second only to Cairo in size, a place for exiled sultans and caliphs; it had its own madrassa and mint, and a virtual monopoly on Red Sea trade.

The European mastery of the sea routes around the Cape of Good Hope in the fifteenth and sixteenth centuries greatly reduced Red Sea commerce with India (until the construction of the Suez Canal, when trade rebounded). Qus and Qift were thrown back on their own devices. With a long history to draw upon, the Qiftis settled back into their accustomed ways, as if nothing had changed. In his excavation notebooks, Petrie describes the house of a wealthy local landowner where servants ran about performing tasks and "the old scribe sat crooning over ancient airs as he cast up the accounts; it was the XIIth dynasty still alive."[17] Add a mobile telephone, and the scene would be much the same today. A second notebook entry recalls how Petrie's Qiftis quickly learned the importance of a clean water supply, saving them from the ravages of a cholera outbreak that swept Egypt one summer. Proud of its traditions but ready to embrace change, Qift exemplifies the doughty spirit of rural Upper Egypt.

When it was first founded, back in prehistory, the settlement of Qift lay right on the river. Like all villages in Upper Egypt, it depended on the life-giving waters of the Nile for its very existence. Over the centuries, however, the river has moved steadily westwards, leaving Qift some distance away from the east bank. This change in geography is, perhaps, reflected in the village's changing character. Worship of a prehistoric fertility god—appropriate for a Nile-side community—was succeeded, although not supplanted, by an orientation towards the desert and the Red Sea coast that lies beyond.

Despite its relative distance and inaccessibility from the Nile Valley, the Red Sea coast has always been important for Egypt. In prehistoric times, marine shells were brought back to settlements by the river as rare, treasured possessions. From at least the Middle Kingdom onwards, expeditions to the fabled land of Punt (probably modern coastal Sudan) set sail from the port of Mersa Gawasis or, later, Quseir. In the early Ptolemaic period, a port was founded further south, at Berenike, to trade with India. The Red Sea route to India ensured Egypt's strategic importance to its Roman, Byzantine, Islamic and colonial rulers, and provided the impetus for successive British military actions, at Abukir Bay, el-

Alamein and Suez. Since the coming of Islam to Egypt, Red Sea ports have provided the Nile Valley's pilgrims with the most direct access to the holy sites of Arabia. And, in modern times, the development of beach resorts along the Red Sea coast has given Egypt its very own "riviera," with all-year-round sun, sea and sand. In the process, once small fishing villages have been transformed into all-inclusive mega-resorts, complete with nudist beaches for Russian tourists. As a result, many ordinary Egyptians no longer feel able to take their families to the beach as they used to, even if the income from European visitors is a welcome boost to the beleaguered Egyptian economy.

The importance of the Eastern Desert is not merely as a route from the Nile Valley to the sea. The desert itself holds great riches and it is these which have led to its exploration and exploitation since earliest times. This can be seen most dramatically in the Black Mountains of the Wadi Hammamat. Due east of Qift, and roughly halfway between the river and the sea, a range of dark peaks rises up suddenly from the wadi floor. The road through the mountains, following the route of the ancient desert track, runs through a narrow defile. After a mile or so, the gulley opens out to reveal a breathtaking sight: vast, sheer quarry faces on either side, where countless blocks of fine-grained, greenish-black siltstone have been quarried away in antiquity to supply the royal workshops of pharaonic Egypt. On the north side of the road, halfway up the cliff face, lies an abandoned stone sarcophagus, its inside carefully chiselled away but its outside left unfinished when a flaw was discovered. On the south side of the road, the lower sections of the quarry face are covered with hundreds of hieroglyphic inscriptions, left by the expeditions which worked here over a period of some two thousand years. From the beginning of the Pyramid Age to the Ptolemaic and Roman periods, groups of quarrymen were sent to the Black Mountains in search of the prized stone known to the ancient Egyptians as *bekhen*. In the hot and dangerous conditions, they put their trust in Min (or, in classical times, Pan) as guardian of the Eastern Desert; many of the inscriptions depict the god receiving offerings from grateful expedition leaders or, more frequently, the kings who sent them but stayed safely at home.

The Black Mountains no longer echo to the chisels of quarrymen or the shouts of their foremen, but, a short distance beyond, riches continue to be excavated from the Eastern Desert. Bir Umm Fawakhir has been a site of gold production since late prehistoric times. Gold extracted from these mines gave Nagada its ancient moniker and its wealth. The oldest surviving map in the world, dating from the reign of Ramesses IV (1156–1150 BC), shows the Bir Umm Fawakhir gold mines. Miners' huts and a stone-built chapel from the days of the British occupation of Egypt can still be seen alongside the road. And today, once again, an Egypto-Australian company is prospecting for gold at the site.

Alongside siltstone from the Black Mountains and gold from Bir Umm Fawakhir, the Romans—the most voracious miners of the Eastern Desert's mineral resources—extracted quartz diorite from Wadi Barud and emeralds from Sikait-Zubara. But the two most remarkable quarry sites of all provided two different types of stone for the buildings of imperial Rome. Mons Claudianus, "the mountain of Claudius," lies seventy-five miles east of the Nile. Worked intermittently from the first to the fourth centuries AD, the quarries provided a particularly prized form of stone, tonalite gneiss, that was hewn into columns and basins, pedestals and pavements to adorn the imperial capital. Use of the stone seems to have been the personal prerogative of the emperor: the Pantheon has columns extracted from the living rock at Mons Claudianus. Similar columns still litter the quarry site, finished to near perfection but abandoned when faults in the stone were discovered. You can still walk through the rooms in the fortress, peer down into the well, imagine life at the quarry face. Mons Claudianus in its heyday was a hive of activity. The entire complex comprised over 130 separate quarrying sites, together with a stone-built granary, garrison, stable block, cistern, bath-house, temple and cemetery. At its peak during the reigns of Trajan (AD 98–117) and Antoninus Pius (AD 138–161), Mons Claudianus housed a population of 920 people—soldiers, officials, skilled and unskilled workers and their families. And all in a desert region whose average annual rainfall is just a quarter of an inch. The solution to maintaining a sizeable population in such an inhospitable place was to arrange regular supplies from the Nile Valley. The donkeys that carried their loads across the desert were slaughtered on arrival to provide a source of meat, thus killing two birds (or beasts) with one stone.

Even the ingenuity of the operation at Mons Claudianus pales by comparison with Mons Porphyrites, "the mountain of porphyry." It lies in the Gebel Dokhan, "the smoky mountain," twenty-five miles from the sea, among jagged mountain peaks. On 23 July AD 18, in the fourth year of the reign of Tiberius, a Roman by the name of Caius Cominius Leugas discovered a source of the most prized of all stones in the ancient world, imperial porphyry. Porphyry was the royal colour, a rich, deep purple, and was so rare that it was reused, like silver and gold. A porphyry source, even in the remotest location, could not be ignored. Mons Porphyrites began life as a series of six small quarries, served by seven villages for the workers. Later, a fortified garrison, commanded by a legionary centurion, was established at the centre of the complex to provide security. Quarrying took place more or less continuously throughout the Roman period, providing floor tiles for Nero's palace, the Domus Aurea, and a sarcophagus for his ashes. (Porphyry was also much prized by the Byzantine rulers, being used in Hagia Sophia; and its royal, sacral connotations continued into the Middle Ages—the tomb of Henry III of England in Westminster Abbey contains porphyry from Egypt's Eastern Desert.) What made the quarrying such a logistical challenge—and achievement—was the fact that the porphyry was found at the tops of the mountains. Blocks of stone had to be levered loose and allowed to roll down the mountainside along prepared slipways. At the bottom, they would be worked into shape before being hauled away along access roads driven around the contours of the mountains. Conditions at Mons Porphyrites were extreme—in summer, the temperature can reach 45°C in the shade. The vegetation is extremely sparse, yet flash floods can wreak havoc as they course through the narrow wadis. Little wonder that the quarrymen built temples to Isis and Serapis, where they could pray for protection from the ever-present dangers of injury and death.

What kept the whole operation going, for century after century, was a lifeline from the Nile Valley. Chaff and charcoal had to be imported for fuel, to supplement the meagre supplies of local timber. Workers' families living in the Nile Valley sent food parcels of freshly baked bread—though, by the time they had survived the journey across the Eastern Desert, they must have been as tough as shoe-leather. For the senior officials, luxury goods such as wine, olive oil, pine kernels and almonds were imported from the Nile Valley, together with that essential Roman condiment, fish sauce, packed carefully in ceramic containers.

More essential were the regular grain deliveries from the well-watered fields of Egypt, which provided the basic dietary staple to go with the donkey meat. Despite the Romans' remarkable ingenuity, communities in the midst of the desert like Mons Claudianus and Mons Porphyrites nonetheless relied utterly on the Nile for their sustenance.

THE EASTERN DESERT IS one of the most inhospitable and inaccessible regions of Egypt. Unlike the Sahara with its shifting sand dunes stretching to the horizon, the land to the east of the Nile is a rocky wilderness, a place of sheer cliffs and stony plains, criss-crossed by steep-sided wadis. It is a place of solitude and stark beauty. The barren desert is about as far removed as it is possible to imagine from the quintessentially riverine Egyptian landscape. Yet even in this environment the Nile exerts a powerful influence. At hundreds of places in the Eastern Desert—prominent cliff faces, rock ledges and overhangs, caves and secluded gulleys—the rocks are covered with designs, carefully pecked into the surface by the stone tools of ancient artists. The phenomenon of rock-art is well attested across North Africa and Arabia, but the rich treasure-trove to be found in Egypt's deserts is relatively poorly known. In recent years, there has been an upsurge of interest in these records from the past, and it is clear that the rock-art tradition is both ancient and long-lived.

The earliest images were made by semi-nomadic cattle herders in the early fourth millennium BC, when Egypt was just beginning its long journey to statehood. The latest images (if one discounts the picture of a Toyota Land Cruiser, etched into a rock by a very recent tourist expedition) were made in recent centuries by Bedouin tribes. In between, mining expeditions, government emissaries, traders, travellers, soldiers and explorers all left their mark. Hunters and their hunting dogs, gazelle and giraffe, tethered cattle and grazing goats, royal cartouches, prayers to Min, lewd graffiti, warriors on horseback and tribal symbols: all are to be found etched into the red-black surface of the sandstone rocks. But alongside these desert images, and equally numerous, are scenes of a distinctly Nilotic nature: crocodiles, hippos and, above all, boats. Boats of all shapes and sizes. Square-hulled boats and boats with elaborately curved prows. Boats powered by crews of rowers or hauled along by ropes. Boats carrying chiefs, deities, dancers and wild animals. Single boats and entire flotillas. All in the middle of a desert with not a drop of water in sight.

In the absence of any accompanying texts, the boats of the Eastern Desert defy easy interpretation. Their very existence indicates a strong connection with the world of the Nile Valley; their peculiar shapes and cargoes suggest a religious dimension (festival? pilgrimage? funerary ceremony? afterlife journey?). But, beyond that, it is impossible to be certain of their meaning. What is clear is that the people who have roamed the deserts to the east of Qift down the centuries have retained a close connection with Egypt's great river. Images of Nilotic life, both animal and human, burned brightly in their imaginations and found permanent expression in their art.

Perhaps the most magical, evocative and impressive of all the rock-art galleries in the Eastern Desert is the outcrop known prosaically as Site 18. Located along an ancient track, midway between two natural wells, the site is composed of piled boulders forming a natural cave. A short climb to the top of the rocky eminence affords spectacular views along the wadi in both directions, while the cave provides welcome protection, both from the fierce heat of the midday sun and from unwelcome desert animals by night. Seldom visited in modern times, Site 18 retains a palpable air of antiquity and sanctity. Those same qualities have attracted occasional visitors throughout Egypt's long history, as a roll-call of the images carved into the rocks hereabouts makes clear:

Elephants, giraffes, hippopotami, antelopes, ibexes, barbary sheep, cattle, crocodiles, birds; dog. Boats, some towed by men. Men with bows, staves, lassoes, people with upraised arms. Bukrania. Early Horus names [royal ciphers], a few probably very early hieroglyphs. Man (Pharaoh?) clubbing captive. Min. Greek inscription, Christian symbols (fish &c.). Blemyan signs, and connected with them camels, cattle, lion, sailing-boats, camel-riders. Arab inscriptions, wusûm, camels, naked woman, boat.[18]

Sheltered from the scouring effect of the sand-laden wind, the images of Site 18 remain as fresh as when they were first created, up to six thousand years ago. The figure of the god Min, and the depiction of his standard in one of the boats, emphasises the connection between desert and valley, between this remote spot and the riverside community of Qift. Adding to the air of timelessness is the fact that the most prominent designs are still picked out in the chalk used to highlight them for photography and publication in 1937.

It is a humbling experience to walk in the footsteps of the man who chalked the images at Site 18, who rediscovered them, brought them to scholarly attention and wrote the description quoted above. Persecuted during his lifetime and neglected after his death, his name merits barely a mention in the annals of Egyptology, yet he was one of its greatest pioneers. Hans Winkler (1900–45) was born in the German city of Bremerhaven. Both the date and nation of his birth were to prove unlucky. At the age of seventeen, he joined the Kaiser's army and served in World War I. He survived the horrors of the trenches and, in 1919, was finally able to fulfil his true potential, as a scholar, studying at the University of Göttingen. But Germany's post-war economic collapse and spiralling inflation proved disastrous for the Winklers, as for many families, and forced Hans to leave university. He became a miner and a political radical, briefly joining the German Communist Party. It was a decision that would come back to haunt him. Returning to his studies in 1923, he specialised in religious history and Semitic philology and went on to lecture at Tübingen University. But when Hitler came to power in 1933, the purge of "undesirables" began, and Winkler was among its first victims, being sacked from his university position on account of his brief, youthful dalliance with Marxism—a political crime compounded, no doubt, by his marriage to an Armenian. Winkler had visited Egypt once, in 1932, and now decided to go there for a longer stay, to escape persecution by the Nazis. In Egypt, as well as teaching philology at Cairo University, he pursued his interest in "folk culture" (these were the early years of scientific anthropology). Visits to Upper Egyptian villages brought him into contact with desert rock-art, and for the next few years, as a member of Robert Mond's expedition, Winkler made frequent forays into the desert to copy and record these fascinating images.

His most epic journey started at Qift in November 1936. Leaving the Nile Valley behind him, Winkler headed eastwards along the desert road to the Red Sea coast, numbering and recording the rock-art sites as he went. The first—which he duly labelled as Site 1—was the prominent outcrop of rocks on the northern side of the wadi only a few miles east of Qift, known to the locals as Qusur el-Banat. From there, he pushed further east, still following the main road, recording Sites 2 to 7 during the next week. After a week's break, perhaps to restock his supplies, he set out again along the narrower valleys to the north of the Wadi Hammamat. Winkler's progress seems to have been quite slow, even considering that he travelled by camel. He must have been making a meticulous search of the rock face at every point, noting down carved images which seemed particularly significant. It is telling that his unpublished notebooks are full of sketches—not of the fantastic boats and hunting scenes he discovered, but of later Bedouin, Coptic and Arab signs. These fascinated Winkler, and not only because he had a detailed knowledge of Egyptian folk culture. The signs which he took greatest pains to copy were those which resembled the swastika—the ancient Indian device, adopted by the Nazis as a symbol of their "Aryan" ancestry and supposed racial supremacy. The prevailing ideology of his homeland had imprinted itself on Winkler's subconscious.

After another week's break, he set out to explore the dry valleys to the south of the Hammamat road. It was on 20 December that he came to his eighteenth new site (Site 18), a place so rich in drawings that it was worth a second visit on Boxing Day 1936. The new year's season, which began after a week's break on 8 January 1937, was to be even more productive. In the space of just two days, Winkler discovered no fewer than seventeen new sites, most of them in a wadi leading to a reliable fresh water well. Further discoveries lay ahead before Winkler left the Eastern Desert on 17 January 1937. After a two-week break in the Nile Valley, he set off again, this time into the Western Desert, where he stayed for the next two months. By the time he dismounted his camel in early April, he had travelled more extensively in Egypt's deserts than any other European before him. A brilliant career as an Egyptologist and anthropologist beckoned. But Germany's invasion of Poland just two years later and the outbreak of war put paid to Winkler's hopes and dreams. He was drafted into the German army and, on 20 January 1945, just a few months before the end of the war, shot dead on active service in Poland. His work was to remain largely forgotten for the next fifty years, as Egyptologists focussed their attention on the rich sites of the

Nile Valley. Only today is the scale of Winkler's achievement once again recognised, together with the importance of his discoveries for the rich and complex history of Egypt.

Like desert travellers before him, Winkler must have relied on local Bedouin guides to find his way around. (Today, even with modern GPS, it is easy to lose one's bearings in the vast desert wilderness.) Most of the sites he visited had seen repeated use by desert people over many thousands of years, and many were still being added to by the camel-herders of Winkler's own time. A few of the best rock-art sites escaped his attention entirely, and the likeliest explanation is that they were simply unknown to his guides.

Amazingly, given the enormous changes that have buffeted Egypt since Winkler's day, and especially in recent decades, the descendants of the ancient artists live on in the Eastern Desert. The Blemmyes who confronted the Romans and the Gebadei mentioned by Pliny survive today as the Ababda tribespeople. Their territory—the stretch of Eastern Desert from Aswan in the south to Qena in the north—is exactly that described by classical writers. Suppressed by the Romans, they simply melted back into the desert landscape, there to pursue their traditional way of life—herding, guiding and trading. In the medieval period, they conveyed Islamic pilgrims from the Nile Valley to the port of Aidhab for the short journey across the Red Sea to Jeddah and thence to Mecca. Since time immemorial, they have escorted caravans travelling north and south between Egypt and the Sudan.

I will never forget my encounter with this ancient people, deep in the wastes of the Eastern Desert. Our convoy of four-wheel-drive vehicles had been travelling since dawn, through empty wadis and across rocky plains, following in Winkler's footsteps in search of rock-art. As we rounded a bend near Bir Shallul, a surprising sight lay before us: alone, in the vast emptiness of sand and stone, a small, dark tent, roughly constructed from pieces of wood, draped with thick, woollen blankets. Around the tent lay a handful of belongings: a few iron cooking pots, two old tin cans, a small earthenware jar. A few feet away, in the dust, the top half of a broken plastic toy car suggested a present brought back from some past trip to the Nile Valley. And in the entrance to the tent, sitting on the ground, only partly shaded from the sun, a middle-aged woman. I say "middle-aged" but she may have been younger: soft skin is the first victim of the unforgiving desert conditions. Her exposed face and hands were a deep, nut-brown colour; the rest of her was swathed against the sun with thick layers of deep red clothing. In her lap, she cradled a small baby—new life, even in such lifeless surroundings. But the child was not hers.

News of our arrival, unexpected and equally unwelcome, must have been borne on the desert breeze, for soon the mother appeared—a teen-aged girl with her flock of goats. She had been tending them in an adjacent wadi where an aquifer deep underground supported a small patch of thorny grazing. The girl was wearing a light, patterned dress, with a white jacket and a black headscarf. Plastic sandals gave her feet some protection against the stony ground. Suspicious of our presence, the girl quickly reclaimed her baby from its grandmother, exchanging it for a baby kid she had been nursing. Family and flocks were bound together in their battle for survival. No doubt the father was away trading in the Nile Valley or escorting a caravan. For weeks, perhaps months at a time, the girl, her baby and her mother were left alone with their goats, scratching out a living in the desert wilderness, their lifestyle unchanged for millennia. Their entire household took up just a few square feet, surrounded on every side by a vast emptiness. As carbon footprints go, it must be the smallest on earth. Yet ongoing desertification as a result of climate change may bring this ancient way of life to an end.

THE UNASSUMING LIFESTYLE and peaceful, reticent demeanour of today's desert nomads belies their historic reputation as raiders and marauders. Since time immemorial, the Egyptian authorities have regarded their desert neighbours with suspicion or outright hostility. One of the earliest surviving inscriptions from the Nile Valley, a 4,800-year-old ivory label that was attached to a pair of sandals, records "the first time of smiting the Easterner"[19] alongside an image of the king beating a desert nomad over the head. Some five centuries later, relief panels from the pyramid causeway of a Fifth Dynasty king depict starving tribespeople as a warning of what befell those who lived beyond the state's reach. A generation later still, a trusted royal official named Weni was sent on repeated occasions at the head of a conscript army to subdue the "sand-dwellers." The kings of the early Twelfth Dynasty regarded the nomads as a sufficient threat to warrant naming their Nubian command centre "Repelling the tribesmen," and inscriptions from later periods record the predations of desert tribespeople, especially against the villages of Upper Egypt. Police checkpoints and guard posts set up on vantage points above the Valley of the Kings and on the outskirts of ancient Egyptian towns were designed to prevent infiltration by "those of the desert hills."[20] As late as 1884, an English visitor to Egypt described how the southern part of the country "was in a state of anarchy"[21] in which "The Beduin on the outskirts of the desert . . . were plundering and murdering the fellahin."[22] Nineteenth-century tourists travelling by boat rarely moored for the night on the east bank of the Nile because "the shore was infested by the Beduin."[23]

Even today, settlements along the Nile Valley remain on their guard against unwanted intruders. Travellers within Egypt are used to the roadblocks and police checkpoints that monitor traffic at regular intervals along every major highway, at every intersection, and at every city and provincial boundary. But, as you drive into a town like Qena, sharp eyes will notice an additional, less obtrusive layer of state security. Standing by the roadside alongside the main bridge, dressed in everyday galabeyas but holding rifles, are the "village policemen." These are trustworthy local elders with a detailed knowledge of their villages, the routes in and out. Recruited and armed by the feared Ministry of the Interior, they are the government's eyes and ears in their local community, manning the main entrance and exit points, noting anything unusual, intercepting infiltrators and those who evade the authorities. Villagers the world over are suspicious of outsiders. In Egyptian society, and especially in the conservative communities of Upper Egypt, such distrust runs deep; it has been masterfully stoked and harnessed by successive governments, up to the present day.

Such an atmosphere, indeed the town of Qena itself, proved the perfect breeding ground for Egypt's arch spymaster, Omar Suleiman (1935–2012). One of the most notorious officials of the Mubarak era, Suleiman was born in Qena. After leaving school, he joined the army, soon after the coup that ended the monarchy and brought the Free Officers to power. In the military, his wiliness and ruthlessness found the perfect outlet. Following a master's degree in political science at Cairo University and advanced training at the Frunze Military Academy in the Soviet Union—the perfect combination for a spy—Suleiman rose swiftly through the ranks of military intelligence. Service in the Yemeni conflict of 1962 and the Arab–Israeli wars of 1967 and 1973 built his power base in the armed forces, and he became a trusted associate of Mubarak. Suleiman was appointed director of military intelligence in 1991 and director of the General Intelligence Directorate (Egypt's secret service) two years later. His quick thinking is credited with saving Mubarak's life during an assassination attempt in Ethiopia in 1995, and his diplomatic skills as a mediator between Israel and the Palestinians were highly regarded, not least by the Americans.

For a man in such a powerful position, Suleiman publicly eschewed any political ambitions, yet there was always more than met the eye. Posters supporting his candidacy mysteriously appeared in central Cairo during the 2010 presidential election, only to be swiftly taken down. Ever the consummate behind-the-scenes operator, Suleiman remained unscathed. Four days into the 2011 anti-government protests, Mubarak appointed Suleiman his first (and only) vice-president, signalling ultimate trust in his designated successor. Two weeks later, it was Suleiman who appeared on national television to announce Mubarak's departure from office, after thirty-one years. With his bushy moustache and hard, piercing eyes—often hidden behind dark glasses—Suleiman was every inch the spy chief. Believing that he was uniquely qualified to restore stability to Egypt, he tried to run for president in 2012; but his candidacy, backed by his friends in the military, was deeply unpopular with young activists and Islamists alike and was eventually disqualified by the Election Commission. In July 2012, a few days after Mohamed Morsi's inauguration as Egypt's first democratically elected president, Suleiman died unexpectedly in an American hospital while undergoing tests. Nobody had even known he was unwell. A proud and wily Qenawi, he remained secretive to the very end.

Qena's attitude to outsiders developed in spite of—or perhaps because of—its traditional role as a rendezvous for caravans of pilgrims travelling to and from Mecca. Like Qift, Qena is located at the Nile Valley terminus of a major route across the Eastern Desert, a route that was especially busy in medieval times and remains so today. Among the pilgrims who came to Qena was the man to whom the city's main mosque is dedicated. Sheikh Abd al-Rahim al-Qenawi, a Sufi holy man, died at Qena in 1196 and his tomb is a favourite place of pilgrimage. His annual *moulid* (festival) is an important event, attended by officials from throughout the Qena province. Local people have pictures of al-Qenawi in their homes, and pray to him as an intercessor. But like Heqaib of Elephantine, the original reason for his fame has been forgotten: it is enough that he is a holy man, *their* holy man.

While Egyptians come to Qena to pray at the shrine of al-Qenawi, foreign visitors to Egypt pass this way on a different pilgrimage. For them, coming principally from Luxor, Qena is best known for the road junction that leads to Dendera. There are better preserved temples in Egypt; there are more dramatically situated temples; and there are larger temples. But no other has the same allure as Dendera, a Roman temple dedicated to an Egyptian goddess. In 1828, six years after publishing his *Lettre à Monsieur Dacier*, which correctly proposed the key to the decipherment of hieroglyphics, Jean-François Champollion visited Egypt for the first time. Of all the monuments he toured, the temple of Dendera made the biggest impression. Mooring by the banks of the Nile on a moonlit night, Champollion and his party could not wait until the morning, such was their excitement at the prospect of seeing Dendera for themselves. They rushed ashore and took off across the fields, without any proper sense of direction. With their white hooded garments, guns and sabres, they must have presented an alarming sight. As Champollion himself recalled, "An Egyptian would have taken us for Bedouins."[24] On reaching the temple, they wandered among the ruins for two hours, in a state of rapture. The breathtaking architecture of Dendera made them "drunk wth admiration . . . the propylon, flooded with a heavenly light—what a sensation! Perfect peace and mysterious magic reigned under the portico with its gigantic columns—and outside the moonlight was blinding! Strange and wonderful contrast!"[25] Tragically, just seven years later, a quarter of the temple of Dendera was quarried away to provide materials for a saltpetre factory.

The reason for Champollion's high excitement at seeing Dendera for himself had little to do with its design or particular place in Egyptian history, and everything to do with a singular block of relief carving. The block in question had found its way from Dendera to Paris and was, in early nineteenth-century France, the most famous Egyptian artefact of all—more studied and commented upon than the Rosetta Stone. When

Napoleon's savants had visited Dendera in 1798, the ceiling of a small chapel high on the roof of the temple had caught their eye. Here, in a room used perhaps for night-time rituals, the ceiling decoration included a magnificent zodiac, the star signs painted in bright white against a circle of midnight blue, supported on all sides by gods and goddesses. So impressive was this relief that it merited full colour illustration in the great tomes of the *Description de l'Egypte*. In 1821, captivated by this extraordinary work of art, an enterprising French engineer made his way to Egypt, sawed the zodiac off the ceiling and shipped it back to Paris where it went on public display.

It caused a sensation. The zodiac was the talk of the city: so much so that it spawned a satirical show called "Le Zodiaque de Paris" in which actors played the different star signs, accompanied by a chorus of wailing mummies. The reason for all this interest and hype was not the design of the ceiling itself, beautiful though it undoubtedly is, but the controversy surrounding its date. Studying the illustration of the zodiac in the *Description de l'Egypte*, a noted French astronomer and mathematician had calculated that the positions of the constellations indicated a date of 15,000 BC—much older than the known antiquity of Egyptian civilisation, and considerably earlier than the canonical creation of the world (then dated to 4004 BC). Others, egged on by the Church, fervently disagreed and proposed a much younger date of 747 BC. Interpretation of the Dendera zodiac thus pitted atheists against devout Catholics, science against religion. It was Champollion who solved the riddle in the summer of 1822—by philology rather than astronomy. He correctly surmised that the accompanying hieroglyphic inscriptions held the best clue to the zodiac's date, and when he read the Roman title "autocrator" in one of the cartouches, its true age was confirmed. The revolutionary, anti-establishment Champollion found himself instantly lauded by the Catholic Church as a defender of the Christian faith. A grateful Pope Leo XII even offered to make Champollion a cardinal—an offer he politely declined.

Today, the original zodiac remains in the Louvre, one of the highlights of the museum's Egyptian collection. In its place, set in the ceiling of the shrine on the roof of Dendera, is a rather sad copy, uncoloured, unlovely, and largely unremarked. Higher up still is the temple's roof terrace with its spectacular views out across the desert plain to the Nile.

Here, the cult statue of Hathor, goddess of Dendera, would have been brought at dawn on special days, to catch the first rays of the rising sun. On my last visit, however, the terrace was closed. A German tourist had recently fallen to her death—moved by the beauty of the place, overcome by the heat, or pushed, no one could say—and even the Egyptians had felt compelled to respond to health and safety concerns.

Dendera's dedication to the mother-goddess Hathor underlines the remarkable longevity and continuity of Egyptian civilisation. At the very foundation of the Egyptian state, in 3000 BC, Hathor had been worshipped as the king's divine mother, a protector deity in bovine form who suckled and nurtured the land of Egypt and its ruler. Three thousand years later, she was still being worshipped, still appealed to as Egypt's protector. But not even a grand temple to Hathor at Dendera could save Egypt from the clutches of Rome. Everywhere in the temple are the image and name of Cleopatra, the last of the Ptolemies. As a woman on the throne of Egypt, she may have felt a particular affinity with Hathor, the mother-goddess. Indeed, the parallels between Hathor nursing her infant son Horus and Cleopatra preparing her young son Caesarion for future kingship were overt and deliberate. On the rear wall of Dendera, Cleopatra and Caesarion are shown at a gigantic scale, offering to the gods in the age-old manner of the pharaohs, triumphantly asserting the dynastic principle that had served Egypt for three millennia.

But it was not to be. Not even a planned escape across the Eastern Desert to the Red Sea coast and India could save Caesarion from his fate when Octavian's forces conquered Egypt in 30 BC. Cleopatra took her own life; Caesarion's was taken for him. The temple of Dendera was completed by Octavian, newly elevated to an imperial throne as Augustus, the first Roman emperor.

While the Romans safeguarded Egypt's pagan temples, keen to bask in the reflected glory of so ancient and venerable a civilisation, the Christians who followed them were less respectful of the past. Dendera was particularly badly affected, the faces of the Hathor-headed columns chiselled away by iconoclasts. Yet the air of sanctity, and the presence of the divine mother, somehow survives. As Amelia Edwards remarked, "Without, all was sunshine and splendour; within, all was silence and mystery."[26] Before the cutting of the Suez Canal, when Egypt was under the control of another empire, troops in the Indian Army travelling from

Calcutta to Portsmouth would pass by Dendera on their march from the Red Sea to Alexandria. British officers were amazed when their Indian sepoys bowed down and worshipped in the temple, recognising Hathor as one of their own Hindu deities.

In our twenty-first century, despite the huge investment in cleaning the interior reliefs of the soot and dirt of ages, despite the shiny new visitor facilities and interpretative signs, Dendera is more often than not deserted. It is too far away from the hotels of Luxor for most package tours, beyond the reach of most Nile cruisers, awkward to reach. But therein lies its special appeal. In the vast, empty and darkened interior, the past and present readily intertwine, and one can almost hear the chanting of Ptolemaic priestesses, Champollion's cries of delight and the prayers of Hindu soldiers in this timeless shrine to mother Egypt.

SEVEN

Abydos

Place of Mysteries

For those who love her, Abydos still has a mysterious life.[1]
—DOROTHY EADY, AKA UMM SETY

Beyond the Qena Bend, the valley of the Nile broadens out and quietens down. While the eastern escarpment runs quite close to the river, the western hills are only just visible in the far distance. The resulting wide floodplain affords excellent agriculture, making this one of the most productive regions of Upper Egypt. Here, too, is to be found the Nile Valley terminus of a vital route leading to the oases of the Western Desert, giving the region an importance as a communications hub.

But the true significance of this stretch of valley is not to be found in its natural bounty nor in its strategic location, but rather in its age-old role as a centre for the mysteries of faith. Since time immemorial, the town of Abydos has been a place of pilgrimage and worship, a focus for the religious yearnings of the Egyptians. There is something about the natural setting—perhaps it is the unaccustomed distance from the river—that gives Abydos and its neighbouring villages an enigmatic, numinous atmosphere.

The preservation of an air of sanctity is undoubtedly helped by the absence of tourists: the whole region between Luxor and Cairo is tainted by the fear of terrorist attacks; Nile cruises scarcely travel north of Luxor and tourist coaches rarely venture this far from the resort hotels with their ring-fenced security. The arrival of any tour group these days is met not so much by hawkers and guides as by gawping, incredulous locals. But for those visitors who do brave the doom-mongers, unhelpful bureaucrats and reluctant bus drivers, any inconvenience is handsomely repaid. For Abydos is still one of the most magical places in the whole of Egypt.

ON THE LOW DESERT at Abydos, about a mile to the north of the tourist café and trinket stalls, within sight of the walled Coptic village of Deir Sitt Damiana, stands an immense, looming presence: a great rectangular enclosure built of mud brick, measuring 406 feet long by 213 feet wide, its walls reaching 36 feet high in some places. Inside this vast space there is nothing but sand, banked up in drifts against the walls. Outside, especially on the eastern face, traces of whitewashed plaster still adhere to the bottom of the walls which display an alternating pattern of recesses and buttresses, creating a stark interplay of light and shade in the strong Egyptian sun. But there are no inscriptions, no reliefs, nothing to indicate the date or purpose of this mysterious building. Known to the local people as Shunet ez-Zebib, "storehouse of raisins," it is, in fact, one of the two oldest standing mud-brick structures in the world (the other is its twin enclosure, the "Fort" at Nekhen). Both were built in the reign of a shadowy king of Egypt, Khasekhemwy, who ruled over the Nile Valley around 2700 BC. As far as we can judge, the monuments were designed to celebrate and perpetuate his memory after death. The

Shunet ez-Zebib is what archaeologists term a funerary enclosure. And it is an appropriate curtain-raiser to the ancient mysteries of Abydos.

From prehistoric times, the rulers of this fertile stretch of the Nile Valley chose to be buried at Abydos. The location was not accidental. Here, on the west bank of the river, the low desert plain is backed by towering, majestic cliffs. A cleft in the rocks seems to suggest more beyond, and was believed anciently to be an entrance to the underworld—it points due west, towards the sunset. The desert at Abydos has a stillness, a magic and a mystery that are hard to describe but still palpable. Recent excavations have uncovered a sequence of brick-lined graves spanning the second and third quarters of the fourth millennium BC: the burials of prehistoric rulers, individuals who helped to shape Egyptian civilisation and set the country on its course towards statehood. Among these anonymous kings of remotest antiquity, one stands out. His tomb, larger than any other of its date in Egypt, was designed to resemble a suite of rooms in the royal palace, complete with doorways, a treasury (containing his ivory sceptre) and a wine cellar stocked with the finest imported vintages. His name is not known, although he may have used the symbol of a scorpion to denote his power of life and death over his subjects. Most remarkably, he (or, rather, his officials) was so concerned with recording the income of the royal treasury that he had small ivory and bone labels attached to all the commodities buried in his tomb—not just blank labels, but dockets with hieroglyphic signs denoting provenance, quantity and other details. The inscriptions from this early royal tomb (known prosaically to archaeologists as Abydos tomb U-j) constitute the earliest writing ever found in Egypt. They mark a key staging post in the development of pharaonic civilisation.

Within a few generations of the scorpion king's burial at Abydos, the entire Nile Valley, from the First Cataract to the marshlands of the Delta, had been unified into a single country. Following the unification, the First Dynasty of kings chose to maintain the royal necropolis at Abydos—either because they, too, hailed from the region, or because of the site's ancient and royal associations. But these First Dynasty kings were not content with a single tomb, however lavish. Each of them also commissioned a funerary enclosure—a building facing the town and temple of Abydos, where the majesty of their kingship could be made visible for all to see and where their funerary rites could be celebrated in full view and in suitable splendour. Today, only one of these funerary enclosures remains, the Shunet ez-Zebib. Its predecessors were torn down, perhaps as the final act of each royal funeral. As the last and largest of its kind, the Shunet survived when Abydos was finally abandoned in favour of a more northerly necropolis at the dawn of the Pyramid Age. The Shunet reminds us that Abydos is, above all, a place of dead kings.

Our beliefs are shaped by our surroundings, and nowhere is this more evident than in Egypt. From the rock-art of the Eastern Desert to the tombs in the Valley of the Kings, from the prehistoric painted linen of Gebelein to the moulid of Abu el-Haggag at Luxor, the Egyptians' religious rituals have always been dominated by boats. In a land defined by the River Nile, it is only natural that funeral processions, royal progresses, pilgrimages and even the travels of gods should have taken place by boat. Images of deities were housed in barque-shrines—sacred boats—even when carried on land, so dominant was the imagery of river traffic. From earliest times, when considering what lay beyond the grave, the Egyptians conceived of an afterlife journey; and, not unnaturally, they believed that journey would take place by boat. Concrete evidence for this has come to light alongside the Shunet ez-Zebib, in the form of a flotilla of longboats—fourteen have been unearthed so far—buried alongside the enclosure to serve a dead king in his afterlife. Each wooden hull was lovingly buried in a corresponding, boat-shaped pit, and covered with a skin of mud bricks which was then whitewashed to shine in the sun. Finally, each boat burial was provided with a stone anchor. From a distance, they must have looked like a fleet moored on the low desert. Carefully constructed from planks of imported coniferous wood, these boats are remarkable examples of the shipwright's craft; they are also the oldest boats in existence—dating back the best part of five thousand years.

While the boat burials and funerary enclosures were intended as public statements, designed to display and emphasise the majesty of monarchy, the kings' tombs at Abydos belonged to a more hidden realm. Their purpose was to provide the deceased monarch with everything he might need in the hereafter, from wine to women (many of the subsidiary burials which surround the early royal tombs belonged to concubines). The royal necropolis itself occupies one of the most striking locations anywhere in Egypt, on a par with the much later Valley of the Kings at Thebes. It remains exactly as described more than a century ago:

> The situation is wild and silent; close round it the hills rise high on two sites, a ravine running up into the plateau from the corner where the lines meet. Far away, and below us, stretches the long green valley of the Nile, beyond which for dozens of miles the eastern cliffs recede far into the distance.[2]

Dramatic cliffs and sand dunes form the backdrop to a stage set on which the rulers of a newly unified Nile Valley intended to play out their power and prestige for all eternity.

The rediscovery of the early royal tombs was itself a story of pride and passion, dominated by a clash of personalities, nationalities and archaeological cultures. In the late nineteenth century, Abydos attracted interest from antiquarians, not only because of its reputation as an ancient religious centre, but also because a steady stream of good antiquities was starting to emanate from the site. In the scramble to bag the best excavation permits, the concession for the royal necropolis at Abydos was secured by a French orientalist and papyrologist, Emile Amélineau (1850–1915). He may have been the leading expert of the time in Coptic manuscripts and the history of Christianity, but he was wholly unsuited to field archaeology—especially in a place as ravaged by time and tombrobbers as Abydos. At the height of his scholarly reputation, and in a move which seems inexplicable, Amélineau suspended his teaching and research at the prestigious Ecole des Hautes Etudes in Paris to direct excavations at Abydos for four years.

The result was an archaeological disaster:

> no plans were kept (a few incorrect ones were made later), there was no record of where things were found, no useful publication. He [Amélineau] boasted that he had reduced to chips the pieces of stone vases which he did not care to remove, and burnt up the remains of the woodwork of the 1st dynasty in his kitchen. The things taken to Paris were scattered as pretty presents by his partners, and finally the greater part were sold by auction . . . It was the usual French work, but with total indifference to what became of things.[3]

The author of this excoriating report was the man who stepped in and saved the early history of Abydos—none other than Flinders Petrie. Learning about what he called "the great scandal"[4] of the "affaire Amélineau," Petrie rushed to Abydos to take over the excavations of the early royal tombs, despite the fact that the concession still technically belonged to the Frenchman. But Petrie had no regard for the personal feelings of a man whom even the head of the Antiquities Service had called "a stinking beast."[5] His only concern was "to ascertain everything possible about the early royal tombs after they were done with by others, and to search for even fragments of the pottery."[6] Petrie lamented that, "Had I been allowed to work at Abydos when I asked for it in previous years, the whole of the remains would have appeared together, and we should have known much more of the early dynasties."[7] He was undoubtedly correct. Even so, what he achieved in two short seasons more than vindicated his approach. Through the systematic collection and study of the tiniest fragments, including those left on Amélineau's spoil heaps, Petrie rescued the earliest history of Egypt from utter oblivion.

It was just as well that Petrie was as determined and ascetic as he was, for not only did he have to deal with the depradations of earlier excavators, he also suffered the same trials and tribulations that had afflicted him at Qift a few years earlier:

> One stormy night a man carried off a statue of over a hundredweight from our courtyard. I tracked him and made drawings of his feet from various impressions, as the toes were peculiar. I got a local man to tell tales which led to identifying the thief. He was arrested; at the police court his feet exactly tallied to my outline . . .

> Another time a man came in the dark and shot at close range the first person who came out of our mess-hut, which was my wife. Happily she escaped.[8]

Hilda Petrie was every bit as doughty as her husband. Together, they toiled long hours in the sand and sun of Abydos, all for the sake of a more scientific approach to uncovering the past. And, after long days at the excavation site, there were few home comforts back at the dig-house. The Petries' trademark austerity shocked even a visiting clergyman, Canon Rawnsley, who recorded the following pen-portrait of the Petries' camp:

> It consists of a row of little huts, facing east and constructed of grey mud bricks and the roughest thatch. At the top, on a levelled terrace, is the common room with narrow open slits for windows, and the extreme distinction of having two wooden doors and a short flight of plank steps before it . . . We sit on empty boxes to discuss our meals. The dining room is floored with sand. It is an oblong room and down its centre is a rough trestle table. The boards are somewhat warped and stained, and on them range the bowls of food or opened tins, covered with dishes or saucers to exclude the dust.[9]

The contrast with today's excavations in the royal burial ground of Abydos could not be greater. Since the 1970s, the concession has been held by the German Archaeological Institute, which, at least before German reunification and the euro crisis, was funded on a generous scale by the German Foreign Office. When I visited the excavations, I was immediately impressed by the four-wheel-drive Mercedes-Benz Geländewagen in which the archaeologists zoomed about the low desert, from one dig site to another. Petrie, one instinctively feels, would have walked or ridden on a donkey. At the excavations themselves, the scene was much as it would have been in Petrie's day, or at any other dig in Egypt during the last century and a half: long lines of workers carrying baskets of spoil on their heads, an Egyptian site foreman watching over the digging, supervised in turn by one of the Western archaeologists. But, back at the dig-house for lunch, it was another world, one that Petrie (or, for that matter, many English teams working in Egypt today) would scarcely have recognised. Within the compound, a series of rooms and work areas surrounded a shady courtyard with flowering shrubs. The rooms themselves had doors and glass in the windows, not to mention the latest computer equipment. But the dining room was the real *pièce de résistance*: a grand, domed room, whitewashed inside and out, with a large dining table in the centre. Lunch (three courses, including, I remember, sautéed courgettes as the vegetable accompaniment) was served by waiters—not quite from silver salvers, but not far off. After lunch, visitors were taken up to the roof terrace to examine the latest finds (in this case, the wine jars from tomb U-j) and admire the view over the low desert to the Shunet ez-Zebib and, beyond it, the cultivation. Archaeology in the Nile Valley is not all threadbare blankets and corned beef.

Impressive as they are, the tombs, funerary enclosures and boat burials of Abydos, beside the bare fact of their existence, tell us little if anything about the sort of afterlife envisaged by Egypt's earliest rulers. Was it a continuation of earthly life, with all the pageantry of the royal court? Or a cosmic journey across the heavens in the company of the gods? Or something else entirely, involving a descent into the underworld? We cannot say. Even the later pyramids, some of which are inscribed with religious texts, do not give a clear picture of the afterlife. Only at the end of the Pyramid Age, as the rigid distinctions between royal and private were falling away, did a definitive concept of the hereafter emerge throughout the Nile Valley. At the heart of this new model afterlife was a dead king, Osiris, who, in his underworld realm, was transformed into the king of the dead. He was known as the Great God. Having achieved resurrection himself, his rejuvenating power brought his followers to a glorious rebirth. He was associated with the fertile Nile silt that the inundation deposited each year, bringing new life to the fields; with the sprouting grain that grew tall and fed Egypt; with water and vegetation, both vital to survival. And, above all, with Abydos. For most of its history, Abydos has been shaped by the cult of Osiris.

One of Amélineau's most important discoveries—indeed, perhaps his only real achievement at Abydos—was the very tomb that ancient Egyptian priests had identified as the burial-place of Osiris. Of course, it was nothing of the sort. It was, in fact, the tomb of King Djer, the third monarch of the First Dynasty, who reigned over the Nile Valley around 2900 BC. But, by the Middle Kingdom, when the cult of Osiris was at its most popular, the tomb was already one thousand years old, and was known to have belonged to a king from remotest antiquity. It might just as well have been built for a mythical god-king from the dawn of time. So Djer's burial was reconstructed, provided with a stone funeral bier, and promoted as a place of pilgrimage. Throngs of worshippers from all over Egypt came to present offerings at the tomb of Osiris, for century after century. The votive pottery they left behind, now smashed into fragments, gives the early royal necropolis its descriptive Arabic moniker, Umm el-Qaab, "mother of pots."

The prominence of Abydos in the religious life of Egypt from the Middle Kingdom onwards was no historical accident. It was due as much to political calculation as to ancient sanctity. Abydos had been a key battleground in the civil war between the Thebans and their adversaries in the years following the collapse of the Old Kingdom. Intef II had made the capture of Abydos and its surrounding region a strategic priority. But, in the bitter fighting, the temple and other holy places had been damaged, and this desecration was laid at the feet of the Thebans' rivals as a great act of shame. In the retrospective account written by the Theban victors, the defeat of the northern kings was presented as an act of divine retribution for their failure to protect the sanctity of Abydos. To press the point home, the Theban kings who ruled Egypt after its reunification lavished patronage on the temple of Osiris at Abydos, beautifying it and transforming it into a focus for national pilgrimage. In this way, they could present themselves as pious monarchs, their power-grab as divinely sanctioned.

In this new context, the Umm el-Qaab and adjacent areas, in addition to the year-round visits of pilgrims, also played host to an annual festival of Osiris, at which the myth of his life, death and rebirth was celebrated in grand fashion. The so-called "Mysteries of Osiris" comprised a highly charged set of processions and tableaux, led by priests and accompanied by myriad followers in a state of religious excitement. (A modern comparison would be some of the Shi'ite festivals as celebrated in Iran.) The Mysteries of Osiris took place annually at Abydos from the beginning of the second millennium BC into the Roman period— a span of two thousand years—yet there are few accounts of the proceedings, because of their secret, taboo nature. The best report we have is a veiled account written by an eyewitness, the man moreover who was put in charge of organising the festival during the reign of Senusret III, around 1820 BC. Ikhernofret was so proud of his achievement—"I did all that His Majesty commanded in executing my lord's command for his father Osiris"[10]—that he could not resist noting certain highlights of the festivities in his autobiographical inscription.

The drama seems to have unfolded in three acts, reflecting the three phases of Osiris' life (kingship, death and resurrection). First, the cult image of the god appeared, to signify his status as a living ruler. One of the temple priests—or, on occasions, a visiting dignitary such as Ikhernofret, acting as the king's personal representative—took the role of the jackal god Wepwawet, "the opener of the ways," walking at the front of the procession as the herald of Osiris. He may even have worn a jackal mask. The second and central element in the drama recalled the god's death and funeral. A "great following" escorted the cult image, enclosed in a special barque-shrine, as it was born on the shoulders of priests from the temple to the Umm el-Qaab. En route, ritualised attacks on the god's shrine were staged to represent the struggle between good and evil. The attackers were repulsed by other participants, taking the role of the god's defenders. For all its sacred imagery, this mock-battle could at times turn nasty, resulting in serious injuries. In the heat, agitation and ecstasy, zeal could easily turn to violence. The third and final act of the Mysteries was Osiris' rebirth and triumphant return to his temple. His cult image was taken back to the sanctuary, purified and adorned. The ceremonies over, the crowds dispersed and normality returned to Abydos for another year.

The central valley which divides the early royal cemetery in two was especially sacred since it formed the main processional route for the Mysteries. This was both a blessing and a curse. So powerful was the symbolism of the Osiris mysteries that participation, whether in person or vicariously, became a lifetime goal for ancient Egyptians. The easiest option for most people was attendance by proxy, in the form of a cenotaph or stela with their name on it set up along the route of the procession. As a result, the edges of the sacred way, known as the "Terrace of the Great God," became crammed with memorials, large and small, up to five or six deep. Eventually, a royal decree had to be issued to forbid monuments encroaching on the processional route, and laying down heavy penalties for transgression. Copies of the decree were set up on granite slabs at key points around the cemetery. Sometimes, even in Egypt, mystical fervour could go too far.

EVEN AFTER the official closure of Egypt's pagan temples in AD 392, Abydos retained a cult place for one of the traditional household deities, the god Bes, into the fifth century. But, with the spread of Christianity, the sacred places were gradually abandoned. Most were left to the encroaching sand. A few, including the "tomb of Osiris," were singled out for targeted iconoclasm. The vandals do not seem to have appreciated the irony: destroying the images and cult centre of one resurrected lord in the name of another. Despite the change of religion, the spirit of the place that had given Abydos its ancient sanctity seems to have survived, and the region once famed for Osiris-worship became a major centre for Christ-worship in the first and second centuries AD.

Today, the visitor travelling to Abydos by road from Luxor or Qena, along the west bank of the Nile, passes through Nag Hammadi—an undistinguished Upper Egyptian town, save for the enormous Coptic monastery on its outskirts. Once surrounded by desert, the better for solitary contemplation, the complex of buildings is now surrounded by fields, thanks to the greening of the desert made possible by the Nag Hammadi barrage. This was built by British contractors at the end of the 1920s, the last of the main Nile barrages. It incorporates a lock big enough for ships to turn around in, and 100 sluices, sufficient to irrigate some 650,000 acres of land. Perennial irrigation has brought greater prosperity to Nag Hammadi, even as the rising water table and increased salinity associated with it threaten the area's ancient remains—Coptic as well as pharaonic.

It is therefore fortunate that the most remarkable discovery of antiquities in the region occurred before the greening of the desert had really started to accelerate. In December 1945, much of the world was preoccupied with rebuilding homes and lives shattered by six years of war. This accident of timing prevented the discovery from reaching a wider audience. Subsequent political interference, litigation and scholarly rivalry meant that full publication was only achieved in 1977. Now that the story can be fully told, the objects found over six decades ago near Nag Hammadi are nothing short of explosive.

A local man called Muhammad Ali al-Samman and his brothers had saddled their camels and gone out to the cliffside behind the town, Gebel el-Tarif, to dig for sebakh—the decayed remains of ancient mudbrick buildings that make for excellent fertiliser. Digging around a large boulder, Muhammad hit a pottery jar almost three feet high. His initial reaction was one of caution and fear: belief in *jinns* (troublesome spirits) was and is alive in the Egyptian countryside, and a large jar was considered just the sort of dwelling place such beings might favour. (Think of the story of Aladdin's lamp.) But, as with the tomb robbers of old, greed soon trumped superstition, and Muhammad smashed open the jar hoping to see the glint of gold. Imagine his disappointment when, instead of coins or jewellery, he found only a collection of thirteen old papyrus books, bound in leather. He returned home with his sebakh and his strange find, before unceremoniously dumping the books and the sheets of loose papyrus next to the bread oven—where much of it was subsequently used as a handy store of kindling by his mother.

All would have been lost for ever were it not for a blood feud that engulfed the al-Samman family. (Feuds are still a common occurrence in the villages around Abydos.) Muhammad's father was murdered, and his sons took their revenge on the assailant. Fearing that the police would come calling and that the discovery of a heap of old books would get him into further trouble, Muhammad asked the local priest to take them for safe keeping. A local history teacher then saw one of the books and suspected it might be worth something, so sent it to Cairo for expert evaluation. The answer came back: the old manuscripts were indeed rare and valuable. They were quickly sold on the illicit antiquities market in Cairo. Again, they might have disappeared for ever, but for the eagle-eyed authorities who noticed the sale and moved to buy back or confiscate the books. A large part of one had already been spirited away to America, but the rest were seized and deposited in the Coptic Museum in Cairo.

What had been saved for the nation—and for scholarship—was nothing less than a collection of fifty-two texts from the early days of Christianity. Written in Coptic in the fourth century AD, they were translations of older Greek works dating back to the second century. And they were no ordinary biblical manuscripts. They included poems, myths and instructions for mystical practice. More controversial still are the non-canonical gospels, books with names like the *Gospel of Truth*, the *Gospel to the Egyptians* and the *Secret Book of James*. The *Gospel of Thomas* was written only thirty to eighty years later than the canonical gospels but preserves sayings perhaps even older than the New Testament tradition. It opens with the words, "These are the secret words which the living Jesus spoke, and which the twin, Judas Thomas, wrote down."[11] The *Secret Book of John* promises to reveal "mysteries" and "things hidden in silence."[12]

The secret words offer a radically different view of Christianity, and of Christ's teachings. For example, the *Gospel of Philip* states that "the companion of the [Saviour is] Mary Magdalene. [But Christ loved] her more than [all] the disciples, and used to kiss her [often] on her [mouth]";[13] other verses discount the Virgin Birth and bodily resurrection as naive misunderstandings. The *Testimony of Truth* tells the story of the Garden of Eden from the viewpoint of the serpent—who is regarded not as the embodiment of evil, but the bringer of divine wisdom, teaching Adam and Eve to stand up to an oppressive, jealous God and discover the truth for themselves.

Most shocking of all to the scholars and religious authorities versed in the canonical Christian tradition was a particularly mysterious text with the opaque title *Thunder, Perfect Mind*, which includes the following poem spoken by God:

> *For I am the first and the last.*
> *I am the honoured one and the scorned one.*
> *I am the whore and the holy one.*
> *I am the wife and the virgin . . .*
> *I am the barren one, and many are her sons . . .*
> *I am the silence that is incomprehensible . . .*
> *I am the utterance of my name.*[14]

The belief in God as Father and Mother—echoing the male and female principles central to ancient Egyptian theology—was commonplace among certain branches of the early church, notably the community in Upper Egypt. Emile Amélineau, in his doctoral thesis on the origins of Egyptian Christianity, had argued for a major influence of ancient Egyptian religion (which he called "paganism"). Throughout his career, his primary goal had been to find new evidence for the earliest religious concepts, and he devoted himself to studying Coptic manuscripts, not just in the libraries of Europe, but also in monasteries throughout Egypt. It is not certain if he visited the monastery of Nag Hammadi, but, given its proximity to his excavations at Abydos, it seems very likely. If only he had known that the greatest insights into early Egyptian Christianity lay buried just a few hundred yards away!

The writers of the Nag Hammadi manuscripts are today known as Gnostics—those claiming privileged insight. They asserted the identity of the divine and the human, advocated self-knowledge as the path to enlightenment, and regarded Jesus as a spiritual guide rather than the risen Lord. All in all, there are enough similarities with Buddhism to suggest that Gnostic Christianity may have been influenced by Indian beliefs as well as by Egyptian paganism. The Gnostic Gospels, as the Nag Hammadi books have come to be known, demonstrate the diversity of early Christian theology, and offer an intriguing, alternative vision for how the religion might have developed.

But this very diversity of belief and practice represented the gravest threat to the survival of Christianity in its early years. To avoid it disappearing along with the myriad of rival cults, the church fathers (and they were, indeed, mostly men) took drastic steps. They set out to create an institutional framework for Christianity—a church—that would provide for communal worship and uniform instruction to the faithful. Upper Egypt, where the traditions of asceticism, eremitism and self-discovery were especially strong, posed a particular challenge. Only by suppressing Gnosticism and its associated practices (focussed on the individual) could the orthodox leaders establish a communal church with the strength of a mass movement. One Christian tradition had to be sacrificed so that the religion as a whole might survive.

Starting in the mid second century AD, the Gnostic Gospels were denounced as heretical, and copies were systematically seized and burned in communities throughout Egypt. In Nag Hammadi, a believer in these mystical texts—possibly a monk from the nearby monastery—took a collection of the banned manuscripts and hid them from certain destruction. He put them in a jar, took them out into the desert, and buried them at the foot of the escarpment—where they remained, through the Arab conquest and the coming of Islam, until they were discovered by Muhammad Ali al-Samman nearly sixteen hundred years later.

Egyptian monasticism survived the purge, but in a cenobitic (communal) form, and within the organisational structures of the church.

In AD 451, little more than a century after the Theban St. Pachomius founded his first cenobitic monasteries in Upper Egypt, the whole Egyptian church split from Eastern Orthodoxy and Roman Catholicism over an obscure doctrinal dispute concerning the nature of Christ. Whereas Orthodoxy asserted that Christ had two natures (divine and human), the Egyptian (Coptic) church held to its monophysite belief that Christ had but one composite nature, incorporating both divine and human aspects. Despite the iconoclasm directed by Copts against the religious imagery and monuments of their pharaonic forebears, the defining belief of Coptic theology has been passed straight down from the ancient Egyptian theology of divine kingship, in which the king was both god and man in one person. In one tantalising respect, therefore, a Coptic service is not a million miles away from the ancient Festival of the Sanctuary. And a Coptic service is the only place where you can still hear the word for God, *pnoute*, uttered in the language of the pharaohs.

The religious tensions exemplified by the secret burial of the Gnostic Gospels in the fourth century AD are still rife in Nag Hammadi and the surrounding region today. The town has a majority Christian population— rare, even in Upper Egypt—and has been a flashpoint for tensions between the Christian and Muslim communities for over a decade. In recent times, Nag Hammadi has gained an unenviable reputation for inter-communal violence. In 1998, a blood feud between families led to the murder of two Copts in the Christian village of el-Kosheh, a settlement of some thirty-five thousand people close to the ancient ruins of Abydos. In response, the Egyptian authorities arrested over a thousand Copts, some of whom, it was reported, were subjected by police to mock crucifixions. When the diocesan bishop complained about the arrests, he too was arrested and charged with damaging unity between Muslims and Christians. An international outcry led to his release, but the inter-religious tensions remained high. Little more than a year later, on New Year's Eve 1999, a quarrel between a Coptic shopkeeper and a Muslim customer escalated and led to widespread looting and destruction of Christian homes and businesses. On 2 January 2000, when the rest of the world was celebrating the dawn of the third Christian millennium, twenty-one Copts were killed and forty injured in el-Kosheh. The dead were proclaimed martyrs by the Coptic Pope, Shenouda III.

Almost exactly ten years later, Nag Hammadi witnessed yet another religious atrocity. As Coptic worshippers were leaving Midnight Mass at the cathedral, on the eve of Coptic Christmas (6 January), a car pulled up and assassins fired at the crowd. Six young Christians and a Muslim policeman guarding the cathedral were killed, and another eleven people were injured. As outrage and violence spread, Coptic businesses were once again targeted. This time, under the eyes of the world, the Egyptian authorities responded more robustly, arresting three local Muslim men and charging them with premeditated murder. One was sentenced to death at a court house in Qena on 16 January 2011. His fellow defendants were due to be sentenced the following month—but nine days later the Egyptian revolution broke out that led to the fall of President Mubarak.

Those watching the events of the Arab Spring unfold in Cairo's Tahrir Square witnessed a rare display of unity as Egyptians of both faiths, Muslim and Christian, came together in defiance of the regime. Whatever the future holds for the difficult relationship between Egypt's two religious communities, and for the fate of the Copts in particular, it is likely that Nag Hammadi will be at the centre of events, for better or worse.

THE OCCASIONAL TOUR GROUP which navigates its way through Nag Hammadi and turns off the west bank road towards Abydos soon finds itself, after a six-mile straight drive through the cultivation, at journey's end. A coach-park (generally empty); a large, open-air café (ditto); and a line of stalls selling faded postcards and warm Coke: these are the inevitable precursor to the main tourist attraction at Abydos, the temple of Seti I. Although the heart of ancient Abydos lies further north, comprising the shrine of Osiris, the Shunet ez-Zebib and the Umm el-Qaab, such esoteric and faded monuments are hardly the stuff of tourism. By contrast, the limestone temple of Seti I is a real show-stopper. It is, without exaggeration, the most beautiful temple in a country of spectacular temples, the most sublime monument in a land of ancient treasures. Its very remoteness—off the beaten track, too far from the hotels of Luxor for most casual trippers—adds to its special atmosphere. The fact that, in its rear chambers, the roof remains intact means that low light levels still cast their magic, lending a heightened sense of mystery to the sacred images and texts on the walls.

And what images! In the reign of Seti I (1290–1279 BC), Egyptian artists attained the peak of perfection in the carving and painting of wall reliefs. The decoration still takes one's breath away, with its incredible subtlety and sophistication, its beautifully preserved colours. In the innermost chambers, the decoration is in raised relief—with the background stone laboriously cut away to leave the delicately modelled figures and hieroglyphs standing proud. In the front parts of the temple, completed by Seti's son Ramesses II, the style changes abruptly to sunk relief, with each figure or hieroglyph "sunk" into the background—less subtle, but much quicker to achieve. Ramesses, a great royal builder on his own account, was clearly in a hurry to finish his father's temple so he could redeploy the artists and craftsmen on his own projects elsewhere.

Unlike many Upper Egyptian temples, Seti I's sanctuary is built from fine-grained white limestone rather than the harder-wearing sandstone from Gebel el-Silsila. While this finer material permitted the most delicate carving, it also proved a curse for the front parts of Seti I's temple. Unprotected by the sand dunes which had drifted over the rear chambers in antiquity, the entrance pylon, first court, portico and much of the second court were dismantled under the Romans and burned in nearby kilns to produce quicklime. Some of the finest stone-carving ever executed by human hands ended up as Roman cement. But enough has survived to marvel at the achievement of Seti's craftsmen, and to enter into the sacred mysteries celebrated at Abydos.

Although Osiris ostensibly takes centre stage, there is no doubt that the focus of the building is Seti himself. Its texts and images, like those in every Egyptian temple, celebrate divine kingship and its central role in Egyptian theology. This was also reflected in the temple's name, "Menmaatra [Seti I] Happy in Abydos," and in its radical architecture. The temple's plan is unlike any other in Egypt, with not one sanctuary but seven. Each of Egypt's chief deities has a place: the holy family of Horus, Isis, and Osiris; the solar gods Amun-Ra and Ra-Horakhty; Ptah, the god of Memphis and of craftsmen; and, finally, predictably, Seti I himself. A further suite of side-rooms provided space for the cults of the Memphite funerary gods Nefertem and Ptah-Sokar. This bringing together of the greatest deities in the land under one roof, to honour Seti with their presence, was part of a conscious effort to establish the theological credentials of Seti's dynasty—a dynasty which had come to power not by hereditary descent, but by an agreement between military generals. The theme of dynastic legitimacy is reinforced in a long corridor to the south of the sevenfold sanctuary. Here, the decoration shows Seti's eldest son, Prince Ramesses, reading a papyrus inscribed with the names of sixty-seven royal predecessors, stretching all the way back to the legendary founder of the Egyptian state. The not-so-subtle message is one of unbroken royal succession from the beginning of the First Dynasty down to Seti I and his son—an ancestor cult with an ulterior motive.

The most curious element of Seti's architectural-cum-theological programme, however, lies behind and separated from the main temple, across what is now a stretch of desert. Aligned to the central axis of the temple, it consists of a pit containing a hall constructed from gargantuan, almost primevally large, blocks of limestone and sandstone. Originally, this hall was roofed with granite slabs supported on massive granite pillars. At the centre of the hall lay a platform surrounded by a very deep channel which was kept filled with water from an underground conduit. Behind the hall is a chamber decorated with religious scenes and texts; and the whole complex, in antiquity, was reached via a corridor from the main temple, with similar decoration. Finally, trees were planted around the perimeter of the pit. When the geographer Strabo visited Abydos in the first century AD, he had to enter via a gap in the roof, but the building was still in working order:

> And there is a well there, situated at a depth, and thus one descends to it through a vault of monoliths, of exceeding size and workmanship. There is a channel leading to this place from the Great River. Round the channel there is a grove of Egyptian acanthus, sacred to Apollo.[15]

Since its rediscovery by Flinders Petrie in the winter of 1901–2, this strange building has been dubbed the Osireion. Its ancient name was "Menmaatra Beneficial to Osiris," but actually the benefit was the other way round: it was a place where the resurrective power of Osiris could be harnessed for the eternal rejuvenation of the king's spirit. In its layout, it consciously combines the form of a Nineteenth Dynasty royal tomb with the antique symbol of the primeval mound of creation, emerging from the waters of chaos. The sacred grove of trees surrounding a watery underworld was replete with Osirian symbolism and, in Roman times, it may have been regarded as the tomb of Osiris; at that time, the Mysteries of Osiris were perhaps celebrated here, rather than on the Umm el-Qaab. Today, the god of the watery abyss and vegetation has reclaimed the Osireion: groundwater stands permanently above the floor level and reeds grow in the channel.

Anyone visiting the Osireion or the temple of Seti I in the 1960s or '70s—especially any archaeologist wishing to work there—would have heard about, more likely come across, the town's most famous mystic since the days of the pharaohs. Every bit as inscrutable as the Osireion or the secret sayings of the Gnostic Gospels, and every bit as melodramatic as the ancient Mysteries of Osiris, was the woman known to everyone as Umm Sety (1904–81). Locals regarded her with a mixture of fear and fascination, believing she practised magic. More sceptical Egyptologists were nonetheless enchanted by her, admiring her knowledge of modern Egyptian folk customs and discerning the occasional pearl of wisdom in her curious utterances about the ancient world. To tourists, she was an attraction in her own right, eccentric but harmless. In her own mind, however, she was a woman with a serious mission: to guard and preserve the temple of Seti I. Her motive was not scientific curiosity, but personal attachment. For Umm Sety believed that she was the reincarnation of an ancient Egyptian priestess, and, moreover, the lover of Seti I himself.

The strange life of Umm Sety began (if you believed her, for the second time around) on 16 January 1904, when a baby girl was born to a tailor and his wife living in a flat in Blackheath, south London. At the tender age of three, little Dorothy Eady—for that was her English name—fell down a flight of stairs and was pronounced dead. The doctor was wrong, but the accident had a profound and life-changing effect on Dorothy. Soon afterwards she began to have recurring dreams of a large building with columns, and an adjacent garden full of flowers and fruit. More disturbing, Dorothy would often sob to her parents that she wanted to go home—but, when questioned, could not say where "home" was. The Eadys' impression that their daughter had a curious inner obsession was confirmed when, on a visit to the British Museum,

Dorothy made straight for one of the cases containing an Egyptian mummy. She refused to move, insisted that she felt a kinship with the ancient Egyptians, and had to be dragged, kicking and screaming, from the gallery. Subsequently, on seeing a picture in a magazine of the temple of Seti I at Abydos, Dorothy boldly announced that she had once lived there, and insisted that there had been an adjacent garden, despite its absence from the picture or the accompanying account.

Her obsession with ancient Egypt aside, Dorothy Eady was a bright but wilful little girl. She was expelled from school for refusing to sing a hymn that included the line "curse the swart Egyptians"; to add insult to injury, she threw the hymn-book at the teacher and stormed out of the room. Not surprisingly, she had few friends; most other girls simply found her too odd. At the outbreak of World War I, Dorothy was sent by her parents to stay with her grandmother in Sussex. No doubt they hoped that the country air and some physical pursuits would do her good. They probably also needed a break from their curious, wayward daughter. True to form, however, Dorothy struck up a relationship with one of her grandmother's horses, naming it Muthotep after the chariot-horse of pharaoh Ramesses II, and talking to it like an old friend. Worse was to come.

At the age of fourteen, as she entered puberty, Dorothy's Egyptian visions took on a more sexual nature. In one, she saw the mummy of Seti I bending over her in bed and tearing open her nightdress. But, far from being scared, Dorothy became obsessed with getting in touch with her long-dead royal lover. One can perhaps understand why a lonely adolescent girl with a fixation on ancient Egypt might have been attracted to Seti I. His beautifully preserved mummy, discovered and partially unwrapped to great public excitement in the 1880s, is that of a tall, distinguished and dignified man. His aquiline nose and high cheekbones give him the look of a 1920s matinée idol, albeit one preserved in unguents for over two thousand years. But Dorothy's parents were simply bewildered by her affection for a long-dead Egyptian. They sent her to a mental asylum for a time, but to no effect. Nothing could dissuade her from the veracity of her visions.

Moving to Plymouth in 1919, when her father abandoned tailoring and decided to open up a cinema to cater to the new craze for movies, she sought out spiritualists to discuss her other life. In public, Dorothy was the singer who performed popular tunes on the stage of Mr. Eady's New Palladium. In private, she was the reincarnation of an ancient Egyptian girl called Bentreshyt, who had been abandoned by her parents (a soldier and a vegetable-seller) at the age of three and brought up in the temple of Seti I at Abydos. At the age of fourteen, Bentreshyt had become a priestess of Isis, and had met Seti I in the temple garden. Oblivious to, or dismissive of, the historical errors in her story, Dorothy Eady had subconsciously embarked on her life's quest: to return to Abydos, the place where she had once been happy.

At the age of twenty-seven, Dorothy left her parents and returned to London to work as an author and illustrator for a magazine advocating Egyptian independence. This brought her into contact with an Egyptian student in London, Imam Abdel Meguid, with whom she struck up a close correspondence. Perhaps inevitably, the couple married two years later. And so, in 1933, Dorothy Eady sailed from Southampton to Port Said to start her new life in Egypt. In Cairo, the locals called her "Bulbul" (nightingale) because of her singing voice, but her political views about Egypt's future exasperated and alienated the expatriate British community. Soon, even her husband had tired of her stubbornness (and inability to cook). Dorothy's own long-suffering mother sympathised with her son-in-law. When Dorothy had a baby boy, she insisted on calling him Sety, after her pharaonic paramour. Thereafter, according to Egyptian custom, she was always known as Umm Sety, "the mother of Sety."

Motherhood did not, however, bring solace, nor an end to her visions. Seti I started appearing to her again—this time as a living, breathing man, rather than a bandaged mummy. Dorothy's husband grew tired and not a little frightened by his wife's fixation, and they divorced after just three years of marriage. Dorothy left their matrimonial home and lived for a while (with her baby son) in a tent near the pyramids. Eventually she found a job with the Department of Antiquities as a draughtswoman, and an apartment in the village of Nazlet es-Samman, within a stone's throw of the Great Sphinx. Much to the consternation of her neighbours, the strange Englishwoman would go out at nights to pray in front of the Sphinx or sleep inside the Great Pyramid. This bizarre behaviour cost Dorothy custody of her son, to be replaced in her affections by an ever-expanding menagerie of pet animals: cats and dogs, but also geese and even snakes.

Despite her new life among Egypt's antiquities, her overriding ambition remained the same: "to go to Abydos, to live in Abydos, and to be buried in Abydos."[16] Eventually, in 1952, as the Free Officers were overthrowing the latter-day Egyptian monarchy, she visited the site of her encounters with ancient royalty. This brief, two-day visit to Abydos was followed by a two-week pilgrimage two years later. A further two years elapsed before Dorothy took the plunge and bought a one-way train ticket from Cairo to Balyana, the closest railway station to Abydos. (She climbed the Great Pyramid the night before her departure, to pray to the gods.) The Antiquities Department continued to employ her as a draughtswoman, on a meagre wage of two dollars a day, but the money was immaterial. Her new position allowed her to visit the temple of Seti I every day, and to observe the ancient Egyptian festivals as assiduously as any pharaonic priest.

Dorothy scraped together enough money to buy a one-room house in the village of el-Araba el-Madfuna, hard up against the temple. Her donkey lived downstairs, while she slept on the roof. Her appearance and customs were equally irregular. A twin-set with imitation pearls and a headscarf was her usual attire, adorned with assorted Egyptian amulets. At her favourite haunt, a local outdoor café, she sometimes appeared with a caged white cat, which she proceeded to feed eggs and milk. Her Arabic was earthy, her English eccentric.

In 1969, on reaching the age of sixty-five, Dorothy was forced to retire from the Antiquities Department. Two years later, her estranged son travelled to Abydos to try to persuade her to join him in Kuwait; but she told him, in no uncertain terms, that she preferred her humble dwelling in Abydos to more comfortable lodgings elsewhere. She never saw Sety again. King Seti, however, continued to visit her in human form on a regular basis. These nocturnal encounters she recorded in her secret diaries. Modest they are not.

To supplement her minuscule pension, Dorothy guided tourists around the temple of Seti I, regaling them with stories of the ancient rites, and speaking of Seti I and Ramesses II as if they were members of her family. (She was, of course, closer to them than to her real husband

and son.) She had few belongings—a Bunsen burner, an old teapot and a battery-operated radio for her evening fix of the BBC World Service were the only reminders of her English life—but seemed content with her lot. During the quarter of a century she lived at Abydos, she visited Cairo only once, for a single day. Abydos was where she wanted—needed—to be.

As her life drew to a close, Dorothy prepared her own tomb in her back garden: with its brick underground chamber, cement lining and concrete slab roof, it was a characteristically eccentric blend of ancient and modern Egyptian. But, when the time came, in April 1981, the local health department understandably insisted on a more regular interment, and Dorothy was buried in an unmarked grave on the edge of the local Coptic cemetery—overlooking the processional way that in ancient times witnessed the annual Mysteries of Osiris.

There is a postscript to the story of Umm Sety and her reverence for the ancient rites of Abydos. Although she has been dead for over thirty years, her beliefs live on, as I discovered on a visit to the temple of Seti I on 12 December 2012 (12/12/12), a date of apparent significance to various esoteric New Age cults. As soon as our coach arrived in front of the temple, we knew we were not the first visitors to Abydos that day: there was another minibus parked up, and its occupants were not difficult to spot in and around the temple. With their long hair (men and women alike), flowing tie-dyed clothing and expression of beatific satisfaction, they stood out from the usual tourists. Inside the seven-fold sanctuary of the temple, several of the group had made a beeline for the shrine of Seti I, and were chanting quietly in front of a relief of the king, eyes closed in mystical reverence. Others had gone behind to visit the Osireion—but on finding it rather less spiritually uplifting, had retreated back into the temple's shady chambers.

As twelve noon approached (12:00 on 12/12/12) the atmosphere inside the sanctuary suddenly changed: not from any divine intervention—at least, none that I could observe—but from the tension and increasing levels of discomfiture among the temple guards. The reason was all too plain to see in the innermost chamber of the Osiris suite. There, oblivious to onlookers, the entire party of New Age worshippers stood in a circle, taking it in turns—on the orders of their American group leader—to move into a beam of sunlight filtering down from a small gap in the roof. With arms upraised and eyes closed in spiritual concentration, each person stood in the light for only a matter of seconds. It was over almost before it had begun, but it was clearly what each had come for, why each had made this pilgrimage to a temple in the remoteness of rural Upper Egypt. As Umm Sety put it, "For those who love her, Abydos still has a mysterious life."[17]

EIGHT

Middle Egypt

Cradle of Religion

But here I am entering on the anomalies and
contradictions of Egypt, which would fill volumes.[1]

—ISAMBARD KINGDOM BRUNEL

The Nile Valley north of Abydos is today something of a backwater.
Largely rural and impoverished, and scarcely visited by tourists, its
very designation, "Middle Egypt," conveys its relative political and cultural insignificance compared with Luxor to the south and Cairo to the
north.

The landscape along the river is quite different, too—softer, more
expansive, with an "open, placid beauty."[2] The Nile flows sluggishly
through a wide floodplain, its broad channel abraded with islands in

the stream. Only at Asyut do the cliffs on both banks swing towards the river, constricting the valley at a natural pinch-point. From ancient times, Asyut has been a strategic location for the control of Nile traffic, reflected in the town's name, which means "guardian." Beyond Asyut, the hills of the eastern and western escarpments recede once more into the distance and take on a more weathered, time-worn appearance. The towns of Middle Egypt are sleepier, too, less cosmopolitan and more old-fashioned than elsewhere in the country: Asyut with its camel-market, Mallawi with its back-street artisans. Even in the university city of Minya, the Egypt of pyramids and package holidays, of mass-market tourism and a rush towards modernity, can seem a world away.

Yet there is more to this quiet stretch of fertile floodplain than meets the eye. Middle Egypt has, over the millennia, been the site of profound developments in psychology and society, developments that have shaped the course of Egyptian—and, on occasions, human—history. Since before the dawn of civilisation, this unassuming part of the Nile Valley has been a crucible of religious thought.

THERE WERE no buses for where I wanted to go; not even a service taxi. (In Egypt, these resourceful forms of transport fill a handy niche between state-run buses and taxis for private hire. They are typically rickety minibuses that wait at bus stations and in town squares for a full load of passengers and luggage before heading off to their pre-advertised destination. Depending on the popularity of the destination and the time of day, the wait can be anything from a few minutes to an hour or more.) I had just spent a fitful night in the centre of Asyut at the Hotel Zimzam, an undistinguished establishment by any standards and a fleapit in every sense of the word. As I weighed up my options, it became clear that I would have to bite the bullet and fork out for a private taxi—it was simply too far to walk. I was an impoverished student on a pilgrimage through the sites of ancient Egypt, and having got this far (Asyut is never going to be on anyone's list of "must-see" destinations) I was determined to achieve my goal. So I hailed a taxi and, in my broken Arabic, explained my unlikely destination.

About an hour later, having crossed over the Nile to the east bank and navigated a series of increasingly rural tracks, the incredulous taxi driver left me at the edge of a tiny, dusty village. He clearly thought the heat had affected my senses. But I could not have been more excited. Nobody much was about—the few inhabitants were either in the fields or shut up in their houses—so off I marched, through the village to an area of wasteground, hard up against the edge of the high desert. I thought I recognised the setting from some old black-and-white photographs taken in the 1930s by the archaeologists who had worked here. Within minutes, my excitement turned to elation when, scanning my eyes across the desert surface, I caught sight of a small irregular shard of pottery, lying on the ground. I picked it up and there it was: across its blackened surface, a faint ripple pattern, its undulations catching the sunlight. This was what I had come for—a piece of "ripple burnished pottery"; and not just any pottery, but the pottery made by the Nile Valley's first farmers. The shard in my hand was nearly seven thousand years old. I had made it to the site of Mostagedda, heartland of the Badarian culture.

When those 1930s archaeologists came to this part of Middle Egypt, the prehistory of Egypt only extended as far back as the early fourth millennium BC, thanks to Petrie's discoveries in the cemeteries of Nagada. But this new generation of excavators succeeded in pushing back the origins of Egyptian culture by another five or more centuries. On the low desert, they uncovered a series of settlements and cemeteries that bore witness to a culture even earlier than that of Nagada. They called it the Badarian, after the village of el-Badari, a few miles south of Mostagedda. Mostagedda itself yielded further remains of the same period, as did a clutch of other sites in the vicinity. (Altogether, some forty settlement sites have been found in a twenty-mile stretch of the Nile Valley south of Asyut.) The Badarian culture is now dated to the second half of the fifth millennium BC, its typical clusters of round houses representing the first settled communities along the Egyptian Nile. And you can see why they chose places like Mostagedda: high enough above the floodplain to escape the inundation, but close enough to farm the land; within easy reach of the eastern plateau, now desert, but then a savannah with herds of wild game; and well-connected, via the tracks that lead eastwards over the cliffs, to the minerals of the Eastern Desert and the marine resources of the Red Sea coast.

Settled in their farmsteads (for part of the year, at least), they were able to devote some of their time to arts and crafts, perfecting their distinctive eggshell-thin handmade pottery with its ripple-burnished decoration. This was no mere utilitarian ware, but beautiful to look at as well. (In a remarkable example of continuity, the red and black pottery pioneered by the Badarians in the fifth millennium BC was still being made in the Asyut area in the late nineteenth century AD.) The Badarians' aesthetic sense also found expression in jewellery, small items of metalwork (they were the first Egyptians to use copper, brought from as far away as the Sinai), and vases, some carved from hippopotamus tusks.

Even more remarkable, however, than the Badarians' settlements and objects of daily use were their cemeteries and grave goods. To the archaeologists' surprise, they found that nearly every Badarian burial was laid out in the same fashion: with the body curled up in the foetal position, its head towards the south, facing west. Such care and uniformity seemed to speak of an underlying set of shared beliefs. A few graves contained not just everyday items but also magical, mystical artefacts: small female figurines, formed in pottery or carved from hippo ivory. These rare objects always emphasise the breasts and pubic area, so it is not unreasonable to label them "fertility figurines." They are the earliest examples of a class of object which remained a constant feature of private worship throughout ancient Egyptian history, and they reflect the over-riding concerns of ordinary peasants in a pre-modern society: fertility, childbirth, and the survival of the next generation. Carefully laid-out burials and fertility figurines: as one Egyptologist has put it, with the Badarian culture "we unexpectedly plunge straight into a symbolic universe of incredible richness."[3] Put more simply, the Badarians invented religion.

The grave goods dug from the sand in places like Mostagedda provide, for the first time, evidence of a belief in an afterlife. The grave itself seems to have been regarded as a symbolic womb, a place of rebirth. Fertility figurines provided additional magic assistance in the quest for rejuvenation. And the objects the dead took with them were intended to serve them, practically or magically, in the next life. These objects include model clay boats, to help the dead navigate the journey into the hereafter. It is in Badarian graves that we find the first explicit link between the river and the afterlife. The Badarians' beliefs, expressed for the first time in material form, were the seed from which all of ancient Egyptian religion ultimately sprang, the origins of a remarkable five-thousand-year tradition.

The resulting edifice of belief and ritual, with its myriad gods and goddesses, developed gradually over the centuries, absorbing new influences and nuances, but remaining, essentially, highly conservative. Many of the same deities worshipped at the dawn of Egyptian history, in 3000 BC, were still being venerated under Cleopatra. Ancient Egyptian religion, forged in the crucible of social change at the end of the Stone Age, was still going strong in the early years of Christianity.

What is particularly remarkable about this longevity is that it was achieved without a single, guiding text. One might expect the so-called "religions of the book" (Judaism, Christianity and Islam) to prove relatively immutable, prescribed as they are by an unchanging and unchangeable script. Egyptian religion, on the other hand, was a creation of society, reflecting the values, hopes and fears of the Egyptian people and, more especially, of their rulers. It says much about the unchanging rhythm of life in the Nile Valley, dictated by the annual regime of the river itself, that the resulting belief system remained so stable for so long. Indeed, even today, life in the villages of Middle Egypt—in places like el-Badari and Mostagedda—has remained remarkably unaltered since the days of those first farmers, nearly seven thousand years ago. The concerns of peasant families still revolve around questions of fertility and childbirth, of ensuring a good harvest and of the survival of the next generation.

There was, however, one notable hiatus in this picture of an unchanging, eternal system of faith, a hiatus so disruptive and shocking that succeeding generations of Egyptians tried to purge it from their collective memory; a hiatus that created, almost overnight, not only a new religion but a new capital city and a new aesthetic in Egyptian art. And this revolution had its epicentre just thirty miles north of the Badarian cemeteries, at a similarly remote spot on the east bank of the Middle Egyptian Nile. It is often said that there is only one real individual in the whole history of ancient Egyptian religion. The individual in question is the pharaoh Akhenaten (1353–1336 BC), also known as "the heretic king," and the place indelibly associated with his social and religious experiment is the site of Amarna.

Today, the desert road that runs along the east bank of the Nile carries traffic from Cairo more or less directly to Amarna. But the more rewarding, certainly the more romantic way to approach the most infamous location in ancient Egyptian history is from the Nile. Boats moor up at the small village of et-Till, from where it is only a short walk to the archaeological site. It is not hard to see why this particular location would have appealed to a religious revolutionary in search of a blank canvas, a new beginning. For a start, the landscape here is especially imposing. The limestone cliffs of the eastern escarpment recede from the river bank, to create a natural amphitheatre of low desert some seven miles long and three miles wide. The hills that surround the site afford protection—both physical and symbolic—and give it an atmosphere of seclusion, appropriate for a theologically driven regime. (It is no coincidence that the ancient Egyptian word for "holy" meant, at its root, "set apart.") On a more practical note, Amarna is roughly halfway between the ancient cities of Thebes and Memphis (Luxor and Cairo), so a convenient spot from which to govern Egypt. And the site is located opposite a broad swathe of fertile floodplain on the west bank, with sufficient agricultural potential to feed a large urban population. From a religious point of view, Amarna was also ideal. It was virgin territory, uninhabited, unclaimed and therefore untainted by any other deity. And the very topography of the site seemed to enhance its special status, the shape of the eastern cliffs resembling the hieroglyphic sign for "horizon"—the place where the sun rose every day to bring new life to the world.

In a text composed to commemorate Akhenaten's "discovery" of Amarna, the king claimed to have been led there by divine inspiration; it was god, not the king, who chose it. In either case, it was the perfect setting for what Akhenaten had in mind. At the start of his reign, the king (then known as Amenhotep IV) had taken the decision to elevate one of Egypt's many deities above all the others, and make the visible orb of the sun, called the Aten, the focus of his personal religious programme. Outside the eastern wall of Karnak Temple (i.e., facing the rising sun), in the sacred city of Thebes, he had commissioned no fewer than eight new monuments to the Aten. The largest—a monumental edifice of pillared courtyards, open to the sky—was named, prophetically, Gem-pa-Aten, "the Aten is found." Though merely developing an ideology that had already gained ground during his father's reign, the new king was, in effect, announcing a radical departure. The Aten swiftly became the sole object of royal veneration.

In the fifth year of his reign, the king decided to change his name to reflect his devotion. Out went Amenhotep ("Amun is content"), with its reference to the god of Karnak, to be replaced by Akhenaten ("effective for the Aten"). At the same time, the king decided that his bold vision could not adequately be realised at Thebes, among the relics of the old religion. What he needed was a new, virgin site, one that would belong to the Aten alone. Amarna fitted the bill perfectly.

In the late spring of 1349 BC, Akhenaten paid his first official visit to the site. In a piece of pure theatre, he appeared before his assembled courtiers in a chariot plated with electrum, shining in the sunlight. As the sun-god on earth, he issued a royal decree establishing the new home for his heavenly co-regent, the Aten, and hallowed it with a spectacular offering. The entire site, Akhenaten declared, would be a monument to his god, and would be named accordingly: Akhetaten, "horizon of the Aten." Exactly one year later, on the first anniversary of the dedication, the king returned to inspect progress. Once again, he rode out at sunrise on a golden chariot, made another offering to the Aten and swore an oath that Akhetaten and everything in it would belong "to the Aten and no other, for ever."[4]

The job of the royal planners and architects was to design a sacred landscape that would do justice to this religious motivation. The result was a layout that deliberately mirrored the passage of the sun's orb across the sky, an earthly reflection of the underlying rhythm of Akhenaten's universe. To this end, a series of grand ceremonial buildings was laid out along a "royal road," a wide boulevard that ran parallel to the river from the king's private residence at the northern edge of the plain to his office and state apartments further south. The king's daily chariot ride up and down the royal road at the start and end of each day not only symbolised his close association with the sun-disc; it also provided the people of Akhetaten with a regular piece of ceremonial, something to take the place of the religious festivals of yore. By elevating the Aten as the sole focus of official religion, Akhenaten's purpose, it seems, was to cut a swathe through the theological accumulations of earlier centuries and purify Egyptian religion, taking it back to the mythical pristine state it had enjoyed at the time of creation. The irony was that in order to refine Egyptian religion, Akhenaten had to destroy it.

One of the starkest breaks with tradition was the promulgation of a prescriptive text, the "Teaching," which set out the parameters of Akhenaten's new faith. The best known element of the Teaching is the so-called Great Hymn to the Aten. More than three thousand years after it was composed, probably by the king himself, it still ranks as one of the masterpieces of religious poetry:

> *You shine forth in beauty on the horizon of heaven,*
> *O living Aten, the creator of life!*
> *When you rise on the eastern horizon,*
> *You fill every land with your beauty.*
> *Beautiful, great, dazzling,*
> *High over every land,*
> *Your rays encompass the lands*
> *To the limit of all that you have made . . .*
>
> *The earth is bright when you rise on the horizon,*
> *And shine as Aten of the daytime.*
> *You dispel the darkness*
> *When you send out your rays.*
> *The Two Lands are in festival . . .*
> *All the herds are at peace in their pastures,*
> *Trees and plants grow green,*
> *Birds fly up from their nests . . .*
> *Fish in the river leap in your presence,*
> *Your rays are in the midst of the sea . . .*
>
> *How manifold are your deeds,*
> *Though hidden from sight,*
> *Sole god, apart from whom there is no other,*
> *You created the earth according to your desire, when you were alone.*
> *All people, cattle, and flocks,*
> *All upon earth that walk on legs,*
> *All on high that fly with wings . . .*

Your rays nurse every pasture;
When you rise they live and prosper for you.
You made the seasons to foster everything of your making:
Winter to cool them, heat that they might taste you.[5]

But this tone of rapturous exultation masked a darker, more repressive side to Akhenaten's theology. After a decade on the throne, he decreed that all references to traditional deities were to be removed from official documents; even the titles of the Aten itself were purged and purified. At the king's instigation, a systematic programme of state-sponsored iconoclasm was launched throughout Egypt. Armies of the king's henchmen broke open tomb-chapels and burst into temples, to deface the sacred texts and images. Armed with chisels and cue cards, they shinnied up obelisks to hack out the figures and names of the traditional deities, paying special attention to Amun-Ra, whom the Aten had supplanted as chief god. Personal names that included the element "Amun" were also targeted, even though they included Akhenaten's own father, Amenhotep III. Individuals scrambled to protect themselves, subjecting treasured personal possessions to self-censorship and even changing their own names to escape the wrath of Akhenaten's cultural revolution.

Not only were all the old certainties overturned, but the architectural backdrop to people's lives was fundamentally altered, too. For the Aten, whose power was manifest in sunlight itself, the traditional form of Egyptian temple, with its roofed courts and dark, hidden sanctuary, was utterly inappropriate. Instead, Akhenaten ordered the construction of open-air temples. In their vast courtyards, offering tables and altars were piled high with bread, meat, vegetables and other foodstuffs to nourish the Aten as he passed overhead. The largest of these temples, the massive "House of the Aten," occupied 750 feet of street frontage along the Royal Road and stretched back nearly half a mile. It even had its own slaughterhouse to keep the altars stocked with choice cuts of meat.

In one sense, the entire site of Akhetaten was a temple to the Aten, since the visible orb of the sun could be observed and worshipped overhead at any time of day. However, Akhenaten's Teaching sought to remove worship of the Aten from the popular sphere, by asserting that the only path to salvation lay through the king himself as the god's intermediary:

There is none other who knows you,
Only your son . . .
Everyone who has passed by since you founded the earth,
You have raised them for your son,
The one who has come from your body . . .
The Son of Ra who lives on Truth, the Lord of diadems,
Akhenaten, whose life is long.[6]

As dictators have discovered down the centuries, a purified form of belief serves very effectively as a vehicle for elevating the status of the ruler and his family. Under Akhenaten the royal family became a holy family, supplanting the traditional pantheon. The royal chariot drive had taken the place of the gods' processions, while statues of Akhenaten and his wife Nefertiti replaced images of deities. In the tombs of favoured officials, the age-old formula designed to ensure a perpetual supply of offerings for the deceased was no longer addressed to Osiris, god of the dead, but to the king, and occasionally to Nefertiti as well.

The wealthier residents of Akhetaten kept statues and images of the royal family in their household shrines, and the size of one's shrine was a public measure of one's loyalty to the regime. On the outskirts of Akhetaten, five large ritual complexes, each dedicated to a prominent female member of the royal family, ensured a permanent and highly visible royal presence whichever way the inhabitants turned; while in the main residential district there was a Chapel of the King's Statue for public worship by ordinary citizens.

But faith operates in private as well as in public. As in every religious revolution since, there were people in Akhenaten's own time and in his own city who refused to let go of their old beliefs. While outwardly they may have subscribed to the new doctrine, in the privacy of their own homes they continued to put their trust in the traditional deities. Amulets of the mother-goddess Hathor, of the household god Bes, even of the old state god Amun, have been found in the ruins of Akhetaten's humble dwellings. In the end, Akhenaten's religious revolution was a personal one, it failed to capture the hearts and minds of most Egyptians, and it did not survive his death.

Before the king was even cold in his grave, the traditional temples were reopened, their priesthoods reinstated and new cult statues commissioned (paid for by the royal treasury). The counter-revolution was swift and total. The House of the Aten was abandoned, its statues of the king and queen torn down and smashed. The royal court decamped from Akhetaten, never to return. Today, thanks to the city's rapid construction, brief occupation, swift abandonment and cursed memory, Akhetaten—modern Amarna—is a time capsule. Its buildings, great and small, its granaries and graves, even its rubbish heaps, are testament to one of the most extraordinary episodes in the Nile Valley's long history: a failed religious revolution that, had it succeeded, would have altered not only Egyptian culture but the entire trajectory of human civilisation.

That Akhenaten's bold experiment ultimately failed tells us as much about the Egyptians, as much about the human spirit, as its brief, brash duration. On the other hand, the rapturous tone and descriptive imagery of the Great Hymn to the Aten exerted a profound influence on later religious authors, not least the Jewish psalmists. (Compare, most notably, Psalm 104.) And the monotheism inherent in Akhenaten's religion found fertile ground elsewhere in the Middle East, and, not long afterwards, in Egypt itself.

ON THE WEST BANK of the Nile opposite Amarna lies a monument from another remarkable period in the history of Egyptian religion. The tomb of Petosiris at Tuna el-Gebel is famous today for its hybrid decoration, combining traditional Egyptian funerary motifs with a distinctly Greek style of representation. Petosiris himself lived at a time of transition, in Egyptian politics, culture and religion. He witnessed a series of cataclysmic events in the history of the Nile Valley: the second Persian invasion of 343 BC, a failed Egyptian insurrection, the conquest of Egypt by Alexander the Great, and finally the country's incorporation into the Mediterranean empire of the Ptolemies. All the while he devoted his energies not, as Akhenaten had done, to overturning the established orthodoxies, but to preserving them.

A few miles to the north of Tuna el-Gebel, the city of Hermopolis (modern Ashmunein) was in ancient times a cult centre of Thoth, the god of wisdom and writing. Two very different animals, the baboon and the sacred ibis, were regarded as manifestations of Thoth; and in the fourth century BC, which saw the height of popularity of animal cults throughout Egypt, the ibis took centre stage at Hermopolis. A vast area next to the temple was set aside for rearing flocks of sacred ibis. When a bird died, even the tiniest part of eggshell, feather or nest was carefully gathered up by the temple priests for sale as a votive offering. Pilgrims came to Hermopolis in their thousands to worship Thoth, and the priests turned a good profit from their trade in religious ephemera—as attested by the costly decoration of Petosiris' tomb. Petosiris makes no mention in his autobiographical inscription of the economic benefits of his priestly office, but he does give an account of his temple duties, emphasising his diligence in a time of uncertainty and unrest. Even though "nothing was in its former place, since fighting had started inside Egypt, the South being in turmoil, the North in revolt . . . all temples without their servants; the priests fled, not knowing what was happening,"[7] Petosiris dutifully "spent seven years as controller for this god, administering his endowment without fault being found."[8] It is, perhaps, thanks to men like Petosiris, with his Middle Egyptian parochialism and his unshakeable adherence to tradition, that pharaonic religion survived, unscathed, through successive invasions and occupations by Persians, Macedonians and Romans.

Without exception, every foreign ruler who set foot in the Nile Valley in ancient times was intrigued, beguiled and ultimately won over by the might and mystery of its native beliefs. None was more entranced than the Roman emperor Hadrian. His visit to Egypt in the summer and autumn of AD 130 not only proved a turning point in his own reign, but also—unexpectedly—led to the creation of the last pagan god of the ancient world. Once again, Middle Egypt was the setting.

Hadrian was born in AD 76, three years before the destruction of Pompeii. At the age of four, he may have witnessed the opening of the Colosseum in Rome, marked by one hundred days of spectacles. Four years later, he was in the city for the triumphant return of Domitian, fresh from his conquest of Germania. Hadrian himself, like many Roman men of his time, entered the army, serving with distinction in the Danube campaign of AD 101 and rising rapidly through the ranks. Military success brought with it political recognition, and Hadrian was appointed, successively, praetor, provincial governor and consul. Eventually, this outstanding soldier was adopted by Trajan as his heir and succeeded to the imperial throne of Rome on 9 August 117, at the age of forty-one. So began a reign marked by restless energy and insatiable curiosity, and by a heady mix of militarism, religious toleration and an extravagant private life. At the northern extremity of his empire, Hadrian built a massive wall to keep out the barbarian hordes (Hadrian's Wall). In the centre of Rome, he built an unprecedented temple to all the gods of the empire (the Pantheon). And in the hills above the city, he established a private pleasure-dome (Tivoli). These exceptional projects aside, the most striking feature of his reign was the frequency of foreign tours. Hadrian spent at least half of his time as emperor away from Rome and Italy, exploring the remoter parts of his empire.

It was during one of these royal progresses, through the lands bordering the Black Sea, that Hadrian met a beautiful Bithynian boy called Antinous. A country lad, about twelve years old, from the forested uplands of Bithynia, Antinous had tightly curled hair, high cheekbones and a sensuous mouth. Hadrian was captivated by him, and took him into his imperial retinue. Since boyhood, Hadrian had been obsessed with reviving Hellenistic culture; his friends had even nicknamed him Graeculus, "the little Greek." Now, with Antinous, he saw himself perpetuating the traditions of classical Greek male-to-male relationships: he was the older man, the *erastes*, while Antinous was the beautiful youth, the *eromenos*. Other commentators were less charitable, regarding the intimate relationship with suspicion and speaking of Hadrian's "burning passion for his notorious attendant Antinous."[9]

Whatever the true nature of their friendship, Antinous and Hadrian became constant companions, travelling the empire together. In the late summer of AD 130 they reached Egypt. It was to prove a fateful visit. The emperor's intention seems to have been to inspect the entire Nile Valley as far south as Philae and, in good Hellenistic tradition, to found a fourth Greek city (to stand alongside the ancient foundations of Naucratis, Alexandria and Ptolemaïs) at a site of his own choosing. The imperial progress began at Canopus, a city at the mouth of one of the Nile's main branches, and passed via the trading community of Naucratis and the religious centre of Heliopolis. By the second half of October, the flotilla had reached Hermopolis. It was here, in Middle Egypt, that ancient Egyptian religion began to exert its peculiar influence on the emperor and his companion.

The inundation of AD 130 had been lower than normal. In fact, it was the second year in succession that the river's flood had been inadequate. Egyptians knew only too well that a third successive low Nile would mean famine and misery for the whole land. Something needed to be done to placate the god of the Nile and ensure a return to its accustomed bounty. It was in this atmosphere of foreboding that Hadrian and Antinous arrived at Hermopolis a few days before the annual Festival of the Nile, celebrated on 22 October. This coincided with the date when the Greeks marked the drowning of Osiris—a mythical act of sacrifice which had led to a glorious and eternal resurrection.

In circumstances which remained forever shrouded in mystery, the Festival of the Nile that year would be remembered not for the usual pageantry, but for a shocking event: the death by drowning of Antinous. Hadrian maintained that it was a tragic accident. Others speculated that Antinous had gone to his death willingly to achieve a kind of immortality, for himself or for Hadrian. (Classical authors, including Herodotus and Tertullian, had written about an Egyptian belief that those who drowned in the Nile received divine honours.) Whatever the cause, the tragedy had a dramatic effect on the emperor. According to contemporary accounts, his grief "knew no bounds."[10] He set up statues to Antinous in Egypt and throughout the Roman world. He declared that he had seen a star which he took to be the resurrected youth. He had a poem composed in honour of Antinous. And, as an eternal monument, he fulfilled his ambition by founding, on 30 October AD 130, a new Greek city in Egypt, at the very spot where his companion had drowned. Its name, Antinoopolis.

When Antinous perished beneath the waters, there was little on the east bank besides a cluster of mud huts and a modest provincial temple built by Ramesses II. But within seven years of his death, a spectacular city had arisen in its place, one of the civic wonders of the Roman world. The two main streets were lined with over a thousand stone columns, in Hadrian's own words "made as they used to be made by our forefathers and also as they are made by the Greeks."[11] The main temple had a façade eighty-two feet wide. All across the city there were dozens, if not hundreds, of statues of Antinous, including a colossal one cast in bronze that stood on its pedestal for over two centuries. Giving full rein to his love of antiquity and Greek culture, Hadrian gave Antinoopolis a constitution modelled on that of Naucratis, the first Greek city in Egypt. Settlers—lured to the site by the promise of free grain and a child support scheme—were exempted from the poll tax and the tax on goods in transit. Uniquely, non-Greeks could become citizens of Antinoopolis: Hadrian's way of spreading the benefits (as he saw them) of Hellenism among the native Egyptian population. To boost the city's economy, a desert road was built to the Red Sea coast (although it never competed with the shorter route to Qift). Last, but not least, the city was given the privilege of holding a regular games, the Antinocia, celebrated according to rules laid down by Hadrian himself.

Hand in hand with the foundation of Antinoopolis went the foundation of a new cult of the deified Antinous. In death, the boy from Bithynia was explicitly merged with Osiris and worshipped as a god of resurrection. On an obelisk from Antinoopolis that now stands on the Pincio in Rome, one of the last examples of an extended, high quality text composed in Egyptian hieroglyphics includes a prayer by "Osiris-Antinous" to the ancient Egyptian sun-god Ra-Horakhty to reward Hadrian with a long life. Antinous is described as "The god Osiris-Antinous, the justified, is become a youth with perfect face . . . on whom the eyes rejoiced,"[12] while Hadrian calls himself "beloved of the inundation god."[13] The Nile had claimed one Roman citizen and ensnared another.

Accident or sacrifice, Antinous' drowning seems to have appeased the great river, for the following year the inundation was exceptionally bountiful, in Hadrian's own words "causing the production of abundant and beautiful crops."[14] The emperor himself left Egypt in the spring of 131, after a stay of nearly eight months. A Roman coin issued afterwards shows him in military uniform, standing on a crocodile (symbolising the Nile Valley). Whether Hadrian had conquered Egypt or vice versa is debatable.

Long after Hadrian's death and the end of the Roman Empire, Antinoopolis retained a reputation as a religious and magical location. It became a centre of early Christianity (as did Amarna, a few miles to the south), and medieval Arab writers associated it with sorcery. Following in its founder's footsteps, later citizens of Antinoopolis became Christian martyrs and Muslim sheikhs. The spirit of sacrifice and devotion remained with it to the end. After the Arab invasion, Antinoopolis was plundered for its stone; in Egypt's nineteenth-century push for modernisation, the columns of Hadrian's great city were a handy source of building material for the sugar factory at nearby el-Roda, for a dam at Asyut, and for quicklime quarries throughout Middle Egypt. Today, little remains of Hadrian's monument to the love of his life. Antinoopolis (known to the Arabs as Sheikh Ibada) is as desolate and empty as it was two millennia ago when a death in the Nile led to the birth of Egypt's last pagan god.

The cult of Antinous spread from its remote epicentre in the Nile Valley across the Roman world. Antinous became the focus of popular worship from Holland to Cyprus, and from Naples to the Black Sea. Not surprisingly, he was especially revered in his homeland of Bithynia. He also had his own temples and priesthoods in Middle Egypt, at Hermopolis and Oxyrhynchus, at Tebtunis in the Fayum, and even in Alexandria. The numerous statues of Antinous—sometimes soft and feminine, sometimes muscular and virile—even impressed Christian writers. Clement of Alexandria remarked on their "unsurpassed beauty,"[15] while St. Jerome called Antinous "a boy of uncommonly outstanding beauty."[16] (It is no coincidence that one of the finest surviving statues is today in the Vatican Museum.) Some post-classical commentators even went so far as to compare the self-sacrifice and resurrection of a youth from Bithynia with the self-sacrifice and resurrection of another young man from another provincial town of the Roman Empire: Nazareth.

WITH ITS FIRST democratically elected president having been drawn from the ranks of the Muslim Brotherhood and with Cairo's al-Azhar University regarded as one of the world's great centres of Islamic teaching, Egypt is undoubtedly a leading Muslim nation. In every city and town throughout the Nile Valley, the cry of the muezzin calling the faithful to prayer five times a day is a defining feature of the soundscape. As in other Islamic countries, Friday, not Sunday, is the day of rest. In recent years, the proportion of women wearing the veil has increased markedly, even in cosmopolitan downtown Cairo, as has the number of men who get out their prayer mats and prostrate themselves in the middle of the street when "Allahu akbar" reverberates from the nearest loudspeaker.

Amidst all these outward signs and sounds of Islam, it is easy to forget that, for three centuries, Egypt was a Christian nation. Indeed, between the proscription of the pagan cults and the Arab conquest, Egypt was one of the leading centres of Christianity. It still has the largest Christian population of any Middle Eastern country—well over eight million people, or 10 per cent of the population—and its Christian history, as the Nag Hammadi codices show, is richer and more illuminating than most. Besides the apostle St. Mark, whose bishopric at Alexandria is still the ecclesiastical headquarters of Egyptian Christianity, two figures, one ancient and one modern, have played a decisive role in shaping the Christian faith of the Nile Valley. Both came from Middle Egypt.

In AD 251, a boy was born to wealthy landowner parents in the village of Cooma near Ihnasya el-Medina (a city then known by its classical name, Herakleopolis Magna). Although a few pagan temples remained open, notably at Philae, Egypt was already largely Christianised, and Herakleopolis was no exception. The boy's parents died when he was about eighteen, leaving him in the care of his unmarried sister. Whether it was the trauma of losing his mother and father, or the trauma of living with his sister, the young man—whose name was Antony—decided soon afterwards to follow the words of Jesus, sell all he had, and give it to the poor. And, being a landowner, he had quite a lot to sell. Some of the family estate he gave away to neighbours, but the rest he sold, donating the proceeds to the local poor. He then placed his sister with a group of Christian virgins—so much for fraternal feelings—and took himself away to become the disciple of a local hermit.

In the third century AD, monasticism had already become an established way of life among the Christian community in Egypt. The harsh, uninhabitable wastes around Lake Mareotis near Alexandria offered an unrivalled setting for solitary contemplation and prayer, and the desert landscape was dotted with lone anchorites, fasting and praying in the wilderness. Antony decided to follow this tradition, going out into the alkaline Nitrian Desert west of Alexandria (whence the ancient Egyptians collected the natron used in mummification) and staying there for thirteen years, cut off from civilisation. There, according to his later biographer Athanasius, Antony was visited by the devil, who afflicted him with laziness and boredom (understandable, in the circumstances), and tempted him with imaginings of women. Like all good Christian hermits, Antony rebuffed the devil through the power of prayer. Even so, he felt compelled to move into a nearby tomb where local villagers brought him food. After more tempting by the devil, Antony retreated back into the desert to a more distant mountain on the edge of the Fayum, not far from his birth place. There he lived in an abandoned Roman fort for the next two decades. Nobody was allowed to enter his cell; his only means of communication with the outside world was a small crevice, through which parcels of food could be passed and blessings given. When, one day, he emerged from the fort, he was reported to be healthy and serene; and he was promptly hailed as a holy man.

In his new role as a leader of the Desert Fathers, Antony undertook missionary work in the Fayum, confirming Christians in their faith, and visited those imprisoned for their faith in Alexandria, in defiance of the authorities. When they refused to martyr him, he returned to his old fort and became a focus for pilgrims seeking forgiveness, healing or enlightenment. But Antony was a hermit at heart, and the constant visits kept him from his prayers. So he retreated further into the desert until he found an isolated well where he settled down, cultivated a garden, and made rush mats. Unfortunately, the disciples and pilgrims continued to arrive, so Antony engaged in manual labour to purify his soul.

His fame spread far and wide throughout the Byzantine Empire. The Emperor Constantine asked Antony to pray for him, and Antony's sayings were collected, written down and disseminated to the faithful. He prophesied the persecution of Christianity and its ultimate victory. When he felt that death was near, he instructed his followers to bury his body in an unmarked grave on the top of a mountain. There, his remains were reportedly dug up in AD 361 and taken to Alexandria. They were later transferred to Constantinople and, in the eleventh century, given by the Byzantine emperor to a French count, who had them re-interred at La Motte Saint Didier (duly renamed Saint-Antoine-en-Dauphiné). It, in turn, became a place of pilgrimage; miraculous healings, especially of skin infections, were attributed to St. Antony. The biography of his life, translated into Latin, became one of the best-known works of Christian literature, and his temptation in the wilderness was a popular subject in religious art. Antony's fame spread the concept of monasticism throughout western Christendom. The great monastic orders of western Europe thus owe their inspiration to a man from Middle Egypt. From a village on the Nile to a town in south-eastern France: Antony has travelled a long way and his impact on the development of Christianity, in Egypt and Europe, has been profound.

In twenty-first-century Egypt, monasteries are once again popular retreats for young Copts. The renaissance of monasticism, and the survival of Coptic Christianity in the face of persecution and official indifference, owes much to a second Christian leader from Middle Egypt—a man in whose life St. Antony's example played an influential role. Nazeer Gayed Roufail was born on 3 August 1923 in a village called Salaam ("peace") in the governorate of Asyut. He was the youngest child of eight, and his mother died shortly after his birth. Nazeer was forced to leave his home town to be raised by his older brother Raphael in the Delta city of Damanhur. After Coptic elementary school and American middle school, the young Nazeer moved to Cairo for his secondary education and became active in the Coptic Sunday-school movement. His first teaching role, appropriately, was at St. Antony's church in the Cairo suburb of Shubra. Nazeer was academically gifted and, at the age of twenty, he was accepted into the University of Fuad I (now Cairo University) to study English and history. But his summer vacations he spent at the monastery of St. Mary in the Western Desert.

While still an undergaduate, Nazeer was accepted into the Coptic Theological Seminary in Cairo. After graduation from university, he continued taking night classes at the seminary while teaching English, history and social sciences at a Cairo high school during the day and attending graduate courses in archaeology and Classics at university. The dean of the seminary recognised Nazeer's exceptional abilities (he spoke fluent Arabic, English, Coptic and French, and could read Greek, Latin and Amharic), and appointed him to a full-time lectureship in Old and New Testament studies in 1950. Nazeer remained dedicated to the Sunday-school movement, establishing a youth group at St. Antony's church.

After four years' teaching and leading the Christian community of Cairo, Nazeer decided to follow St. Antony's example and retreat to a monastery. These were the early days following the Free Officers' coup, and Egypt was in a state of turmoil and transition. Nazeer chose to go to the so-called Syrian Monastery in the Nitrian Desert, where St. Antony had first adopted an anchoritic lifestyle, and was duly given the name Father Antony the Syrian. For a period of six years from 1956 to 1962 he lived as a hermit in a cave some miles from the monastery. During this time he was ordained priest and, on emerging from his ascetic lifestyle, was appointed bishop and dean of the Coptic Orthodox Theological Seminary. He took as his episcopal name Shenouda, in honour of a renowned fifth-century Coptic scholar and monk, St. Shenouda the Archimandrite. Under Bishop Shenouda, attendance at the seminary trebled, the students being inspired by his great learning and his support for reformist measures.

When the Coptic Pope Cyril VI died in 1971, Bishop Shenouda was an obvious choice as successor. He was duly enthroned in the recently completed St. Mark's Cathedral in Cairo as the 117th Pope of Alexandria and patriarch of the See of St. Mark. To signal his commitment to ecumenism, one of his first acts was to visit the head of the Greek Orthodox Church, becoming the first Coptic leader to do so since the schism between the two churches fifteen hundred years earlier. Shenouda also signed a joint declaration of faith with the Vatican, and travelled widely to visit Coptic communities in North America, Europe and Australia.

But it was at home in Egypt that his leadership and courage were most acutely needed. During the late 1970s, the threat of Islamic extremism had been growing, and a massacre of Christians in Cairo prompted Shenouda to criticise the Egyptian regime in public for its complacency. In response, in early 1981, President Sadat rescinded the decree recognising Shenouda as pope and banished him to a desert monastery. Shenouda, however, was right: a few months later, Sadat was assassinated by Islamic extremists at a military parade. Eventually, Shenouda was reinstated by the new Egyptian leader, Hosni Mubarak. But still the persecution and attacks against Christians continued, including the massacres at Nag Hammadi in January 2000 and January 2010. Some younger Copts lamented Shenouda's powerlessness to stop these attacks, and censured him for his friendly relations with the Mubarak regime. Nonetheless, when he died on 17 March 2012, a year after the Egyptian revolution that saw Muslims and Copts standing together in Tahrir Square, Shenouda was widely mourned by his flock as one of the great popes and a defender of their faith, and by Muslims and Christians alike as a noted Egyptian leader of the twentieth century. Even the Muslim Brotherhood hailed him as a national icon. An estimated hundred thousand mourners filed past his body as it lay in state in St. Mark's Cathedral and, as he had wished, he was laid to rest in the monastery of St. Pishoy in the Wadi Natrun.

Though little known in the outside world, Coptic popes are as familiar and revered among Egyptian Christians as the Pope of Rome is among Catholics. Every Coptic home and business has a picture of the Pope of Alexandria on the wall—more often than not, a faded postcard or calendar hanging in the front room or office. Many Copts carry small cards with the pope's image. In the drawer of my desk, as I write, there is just such a card with the smiling face of Pope Shenouda, given to me many years ago by a young Copt in the Middle Egyptian city of Minya.

It was only my second visit to Egypt, and I was on my guard. I assumed (as Western visitors to Egypt quickly learn to) that any Egyptian who accosted me in the street must be wanting to sell me something, wanting to take me to someone else who wanted to sell me something, or simply wanting baksheesh. So when a young man about my age sidled up to me walking down Minya's main thoroughfare, I adopted my stoniest of faces, looked straight ahead and carried on walking. Only this time it seemed to have no effect. Still he maintained his friendly conversation (or monologue—I was refusing to engage, for fear of being drawn away to yet another perfume shop or papyrus factory). Eventually, he realised the problem, explained that he wasn't trying to sell me anything and, by way of proof, showed me the inside of his wrist. There, somewhat smudged and a little faded, but still immediately recognisable, was a small tattooed cross. For Joseph was a Copt, and therefore—it went without saying—trustworthy and sincere. Every Coptic man I have since met in Egypt has been similarly tattooed: a statement of personal faith, of solidarity with a beleaguered community, and of quiet defiance in the face of prejudice, hostility and sometimes personal danger.

Over the next few days, that chance meeting with Joseph led to introductions to all his other friends—university students, and all Copts. I drank fresh lemonade with them in their digs (as shabby and untidy as any student room anywhere in the world), and talked with them about Egypt, England, and our different problems. Eager to share and celebrate their faith with a sympathetic visitor, they took me to Minya's Coptic cathedral, with its brightly coloured murals of Christ and the saints, and facilitated my attendance (suitably chaperoned) at a Coptic service. It was a strange, fascinating and memorable experience. Coptic churches, like mosques, separate the faithful according to gender: women on one side of the aisle, men on the other. To an observer used to an Anglican service with its careful choreography, reverent silences and limited congregational participation, the Coptic way of worship was utterly alien: participatory, noisy, somewhat chaotic. At the back of the church, families chatted, caught up on gossip, played with their children, came and went, all during the service. Not that one could blame them, for the liturgy was long and rambling. Most of it was conducted in Arabic, although certain prayers and holy words were still intoned in Coptic—the direct descendant of ancient Egyptian. I was thrilled to hear priests declaim the word *pnoute* ("God"), just as they did in the days of the pharaohs. How remarkable it is that, sixteen hundred years after the last hieroglyphic inscription was carved, the sacred words of ancient Egypt are still uttered, even if the religion they once described has long vanished.

But that link with the past is under threat. Ever since the Arab conquest of the Nile Valley in the mid seventh century AD, Egypt's Muslim rulers have taken an increasingly intolerant view of their Christian subjects. An Ottoman-era decree restricting the building of new churches or the repairing of old ones has been enforced by successive Egyptian governments, so that many Coptic places of worship have fallen into dereliction. (The historic churches of Old Cairo have been saved from utter ruin only by their status as major tourist attractions.) Individual Copts suffer discrimination in the employment market, while official indifference has left Coptic communities to fend for themselves in the face of attacks by Islamic militants, felt most keenly in Middle Egypt where many towns have a large Christian population.

One such town is Abu Qurqas, on the west bank of the Nile between Hermopolis and Minya. My visit, at the invitation of one of Joseph's student friends, was a stark illustration of the travails of the Coptic community. Under Mubarak, just obtaining permission to visit an Egyptian in their own home—if they lived outside the main tourist centres of Aswan, Luxor or Cairo—was a laborious process: copious paperwork and a personal interview (for visitor and host alike) at the local police headquarters. It seemed—indeed, was—heavy-handed and intrusive, but when I finally made it to Abu Qurqas, I could understand something of the authorities' nervousness. A few weeks before my visit, an Islamic mob had attacked one of the town's Coptic churches, setting light to the ground floor which now stood charred and empty. (Fortunately, the sacred books and furniture had been rescued before the fire took hold, and carried upstairs to the room above the church for safe keeping.) In another incident, a Copt had been taken into the surrounding fields and shot.

Yet, in the midst of all this violence and persecution, the Coptic community remained as friendly and welcoming to strangers as ever. The hospitality I enjoyed on that brief visit has never been matched. In the front room of my Coptic friend's family home, what seemed like their entire week's food supply was laid before me in a banquet of epic proportions: dish after dish of classic Egyptian country cooking, until I could physically eat no more. In a further display of hospitality, my Coptic friend, having accompanied me back to my hotel in Minya (the police permit to visit Abu Qurqas did not extend to an overnight stay), promptly turned up the following morning to walk me to the service-taxi stand and put me on the right minibus for the journey to Mallawi and Amarna. He even insisted on paying the fare. In a country famed for its hospitality, it seems that a little tattooed cross on the inside wrist is the surest guarantee of all.

NINE

The Fayum

A Lake in the Desert

This district is the most noteworthy of all in respect of its
appearance, its fertility, and its material development.[1]

—STRABO

A t the northern end of the Nile Valley, just before the great river
reaches the apex of the Delta and divides into several channels on
its way to the sea, lies an anomaly in the geography of Egypt. To the
west of the Nile and surrounded on all sides by the Libyan Desert, a
low depression presents a contrasting picture of leafy abundance. With
its well-watered fields and flower gardens, its palm groves and irrigation channels, the region called the Fayum is an oasis. But, in contrast
to the other oases of the Western Desert, the Fayum receives its water

not from underground aquifers but from the Nile itself. The valley's sweet waters enter the Fayum via the Bahr Yusuf, the subsidiary river that flows parallel to the Nile through much of Middle Egypt. When the Bahr Yusuf reaches the low-lying Fayum, it debouches into a great lake, Birket Qarun. It is this remarkable geographical feature—a lake in the desert—that has shaped the history of the Fayum and that gives the region its special character.

From the earliest times, the people of the Fayum revered their lake and the fertility it brought. They identified it—not the River Nile—as the primeval waters where the universe began, and they worshipped its most fearsome denizen, the crocodile, as the very power of creation, to be honoured above all other gods. The Fayum's main town, Shedyt (modern Medinet el-Fayum), became famous for its sacred crocodiles, so much so that the Greeks later named it Krokodilopolis, "crocodile city."

For the ancient Egyptians, the lake and its surrounding region were synonymous; the Fayum was known, simply, as *ta-she*, "the lake." Classical authors, who named the lake Moeris, marvelled at its size and splendour. The Greek geographer Strabo called it "wonderful," likening it to "an open sea in size and like a sea in colour."[2]

Today, the nine-thousand-year-old body of water is ailing. Its deep waters no longer sustain the huge shoals that attracted fisherfolk from earliest prehistory. Its saline shores no longer offer fertile soils for agriculture. But the unique landscape created by Birket Qarun remains as alluring as ever. This lake in the desert has much to teach us about the fundamental bond between water, land and people that is at the heart of Egyptian history, and that holds the key to the country's future.

OVER TWENTY-FIVE MILLION Egyptians still make their living on the land. Despite growing urbanisation throughout the Nile Valley and an expanding tourist industry along the Red Sea coast, one-third of Egypt's burgeoning population continues to be employed in agriculture. In ancient times, the proportion was much higher—most estimates for ancient Egypt are around 90 to 95 per cent. Life in the countryside has followed the same pattern for thousands of years—farmers preparing the soil with hand-hoes, vegetable beds lovingly created with raised edges to trap the Nile's water, egrets probing for worms in the newly irrigated fields, men on donkeys, mud-brick houses and dirt streets. Tilling the soil has been the predominant way of life in Egypt for most of its history; the lowly fellahin have created the country's wealth and provided the foundations of its civilisation.

The prerequisites for successful agriculture are, of course, fertile soil and water. Egypt is blessed in having both, thanks to the Nile. Were it not for the river, Egypt would be nothing but desert. As it is, Egypt is in effect a linear oasis, a narrow strip of cultivation—the Nile's floodplain— hemmed in on both sides by arid wastes. Throughout the Nile Valley, from the First Cataract to the shores of the Mediterranean, the demands of agriculture have shaped the landscape. Over the millennia, successive parcels of floodplain have been turned into natural flood basins, divided by dykes and criss-crossed by irrigation channels. Diesel-powered water- pumps have all but replaced ox-powered waterwheels and human-powered shadufs as the main technology of irrigation, but moving fresh water from the river to the fields remains the underpinning activity of Egyp- tian agriculture. The Nile is the source of all life, but it has taken human ingenuity to harness its bounty.

There is one part of Egypt, however, where the effects of the Nile are felt only remotely and where agriculture has flourished thanks to the pres- ence of a different body of water. This most unusual area is the Fayum, the source of its fertility and productivity Egypt's only natural lake. For thousands of years, Birket Qarun has been fed by the Nile, rising and falling, expanding and contracting in unison with the river's regime. The very name Fayum is a corruption of the Coptic *pa-yom*, meaning simply "the lake," for the region as a whole is inextricably linked with its source of life. Ever since the first lake formed around 7000 BC, people have lived along its shore. The shallow waters afford excellent fishing, and early communities of fisherfolk made their temporary homes on high ground to the north and west of Birket Qarun. While fish were the mainstay of their diet, they supplemented these lacustrine resources with hunting and gathering in the fertile pastures around the lake edge. Bird life has always been abundant in the Fayum, and in earlier times herds of antelope and other game also frequented the lake margins. For Stone Age peoples, the Fayum must have been a veritable Eden.

The Fayum holds a special place in the story of Egyptian civilisation, not so much for its early fisherfolk (whom archaeologists call Qarunian), but for their successors (Fayumian), who flourished around two thousand years later, at the beginning of the fifth millennium BC. They seem to have come from the Western Desert, driven eastwards in search of better ecological conditions by the deteriorating climate and advancing desertification. They found what they were looking for when they reached the shore of Birket Qarun. The traces of their remarkable way of life have all but vanished, swallowed up—like so many Egyptian antiquities—by modern development. Their main settlement, on the lake's northern shore, now lies under fields: "Nothing is left but a desolate ploughed area where a litter of potsherds and flint cobble still bear witness to one of the few excavated Neolithic settlements in Egypt."[3] The settlement itself had no permanent dwellings, but rather a concentration of hearths, suggesting that the people lived in temporary structures of wood and straw, flimsy but portable homes such as their nomadic ancestors would have erected at each new hunting or fishing encampment. Yet, despite this temporary architecture, the Fayumian people lived a sedentary way of life. Indeed, they are the very first people anywhere in Egypt to have settled down to live on the land. Against all the odds, some of the remains of their revolutionary lifestyle have survived the ravages of seven millennia. A short distance from the ploughed-up settlement, some shallow depressions in the desert surface hold a remarkable secret: grain bins, lined with matting, some of them still containing kernels of barley and emmer (a primitive form of wheat). The high elevation and dry desert climate have provided the perfect conditions for the preservation of organic materials. These silos are the earliest evidence for agriculture in Egypt, and their Fayumian creators were the first people in the Nile Valley to till the land and raise crops.

Despite the fact that agriculture was a novel technique, imported from the Fertile Crescent, Egypt's earliest farmers were impressively productive. They arranged their grain bins in groups, suggesting communal effort to bring in the harvest; one group contained 109 silos. Each bin, around four feet across and two feet deep, carefully plastered with mud and lined with basketry, could hold eight hundredweight of cereals, representing the yield of two to three acres of land. So the most ambitious group of Fayumian farmers seem to have tended a sizeable holding of two to three hundred acres. When originally excavated, one of the bins still contained a sickle, its wooden shaft set with flint blades.

Agriculture did not, however, entirely displace an older way of life. In 5000 BC, Birket Qarun was around four times its present size, some fifty miles wide, and fishing remained an important activity for the Fayumian people. The animal bones found in the village hearths—from turtles, hippos, crocodiles, bittern and wild geese, as well as from domesticated cattle, goats and sheep—show that hunting and animal husbandry were also valuable sources of food. Altogether, the impression is that the Fayum's farmers enjoyed a rather comfortable living by the shores of Birket Qarun. They ate a wholesome and varied diet, grew flax to weave into linen and traded precious objects from far and wide, including seashells from the Red Sea and the Mediterranean, and stone cosmetic palettes from Nubia. In their taste for bodily decoration and pottery (red-coated and burnished), they set the trend for later phases of Egyptian culture. In their mastery of agriculture, they laid the foundations for the glories of pharaonic civilisation.

Most of the Fayumian granaries have been destroyed by a modern road and two large irrigation canals. The area containing the last remaining grain bins had also been zoned for agriculture, but was saved from destruction at the last minute. When the farmer realised the significance of the pits on his land, he agreed to work around them. It is ironic that "the earliest evidence of agriculture in Egypt was almost destroyed by ploughing."[4]

Over the succeeding centuries and millennia, the Fayumians' innovation became the mainstay of the Egyptian economy, and the lands around Birket Qarun were some of the most productive in the country. From the beginning of the second millennium BC onwards, the Egyptians began to regulate water flow into the lake, by means of dams and canals. This trend reached its peak circa 1900 BC, when the lake was artificially expanded to extend the irrigated area and bring more land under cultivation; so impressive were the results that the Fayum region became known as *mi-wer*, "great lake." The driving force behind this major civil engineering project was King Amenemhat III, and he remains a powerful, if ghostly, presence in the Fayum.

Our minibus ground to a halt next to an improbable-looking, if productive, patch of land, near a small Fayum village called Biahmu. Water gurgled along an irrigation canal down one side of the field, drawn from a nearby canal by an invisible, though clearly audible, diesel pump. A camel munched lazily on a heap of fodder under a stand of palm trees. Within the field margins, a crop of lucerne grew lush and tall. And there, in the middle of the cultivated area, incongruous against this scene of agricultural bounty, stood an enormous pedestal, its back towering thirty or forty feet into the air. This old heap of stones was, in fact, the remains of a monument that was once the most famous in the Fayum. The pedestal, now empty and unadorned, once held a colossal double-statue of Amenemhat III. From its lofty height, the king looked out over the farmlands he had brought into being. Elsewhere in the Fayum, the king built further edifices to mark his achievement: a temple on the western edge of the cultivation, sited as if to hold back the encroaching desert by magical means; and, to the south-east of the Great Lake, a pyramid, its mortuary chapel so large, complex and multi-roomed that classical authors dubbed it "the Labyrinth." Today, the Labyrinth is nothing more than a series of muddy lines in the soil, the pyramid has collapsed into a pile of bricks, and the temple is losing its battle with the sand dunes. The double-statue of Biahmu is no more, but its colossal pedestal survives, surrounded by crops, an enduring testament to the long history of intensive agriculture in this part of Egypt.

Uniquely in the annals of pharaonic civilisation, we have a first-hand account of life on the land in the lush fields of the Fayum. In the early twentieth century, during the excavation of a tomb in the hills of Thebes, archaeologists uncovered a mass of discarded, crumpled papyri that had been dumped into the tomb shaft before it was sealed. Among this refuse was a collection of letters and household accounts belonging to a man named Heqanakht. He lived in the early years of the Middle Kingdom (circa 2000 BC) and farmed land on the edge of the Fayum, in a place with the poetic name of "jujube-grove" (*Nebsyt*). At the same time, he held the post of priest in the mortuary cult of one of the king's viziers, and this official duty took Heqanakht periodically away from home to the great southern city of Thebes. It was during these sojourns in Upper Egypt that Heqanakht wrote letters back to his family—letters which subsequently ended up in the rubbish filling the shaft of the vizier's tomb. Heqanakht's casual correspondence provides a remarkable window on his world, that of a successful Egyptian farmer four thousand years ago.

At the time he wrote home, Heqanakht was probably well into his thirties, distinctly middle-aged in ancient Egyptian terms. He was already married for the second time and was master of a large household of relatives and dependants. He must have been fairly well educated by the standards of the age, certainly literate enough to write some or all of his own letters; he resorted to employing a professional scribe only when something more formal was required. For the most part, his letters reflect his chief preoccupation, which was farming. They are dominated by economic matters, ranging from the collection of debts to the distribution of grain, and they underline his worries at leaving his business interests in the hands of others. His tone is concerned, but also impatient and hectoring: "Take great care! Watch over my seed-corn! Look after all my property! Look, I count you responsible for it. Take great care with all my property!"[5] In particular, Heqanakht was anxious to ensure that the steward of his estates, a man named Merisu, made the necessary and timely preparations for the coming agricultural year. Heqanakht instructed Merisu not to siphon off any of the grain held in reserve to pay the rent on a parcel of farmland, and to investigate the possibility of renting additional land if the circumstances looked favourable.

As a successful businessman, Heqanakht had financial dealings with at least twenty-eight different people, sixteen of them neighbouring farmers. Alongside these professional relationships, Heqanakht's life was full of personal interest and intrigue. His large household included eighteen dependants and three servants. Among his employees were a foreman, a steward (Merisu), a household scribe and a fieldhand in charge of cattle. Heqanakht's extended family, all living under his roof, comprised his mother and another senior female relative; a younger brother; a son and daughter by Heqanakht's previous marriage, and two daughters by his second marriage; and the new wife herself. Like Egyptian men down the centuries, Heqanakht showed particular reverence towards his mother, sending her special greetings and reassuring her about his well-being. Like Egyptian men down the centuries, too, Heqanakht also betrayed more than a touch of favouritism towards his son, telling his other relatives, "Whatever he wants, you shall make him content with what he wants."[6]

In this large and rivalrous household, the atmosphere seems to have been claustrophobic and febrile. One of the main causes of tension was the attitude of Heqanakht's relatives to his new wife. A long way from home, Heqanakht clearly worried that the others were ganging up on the new arrival. Believing that one of his female servants had behaved particularly badly towards his wife, Heqanakht had the unfortunate girl promptly dismissed. He then accused his family of not protecting the wife against the maid's malice because they regarded the former as a slut and a parvenu.

The domestic intrigue reflected in Heqanakht's letters proved so compelling that Agatha Christie used it as the basis for her murder mystery novel, *Death Comes as the End*. Whether resentment ever boiled over into murder, we shall never know, but the Heqanakht letters certainly provide a vivid picture of life on a Fayum farm—a picture that still rings true today. Four thousand years after Heqanakht, the inhabitants of the Fayum retain a reputation for being clannish and rebellious.

AGATHA CHRISTIE WAS NOT the only woman of her generation to be entranced by Egypt and its ancient culture. Less famous by far, but much more influential in the history of Egyptology, was an almost exact contemporary of Christie's, a woman by the name of Gertrude Caton-Thompson (1888–1985). Born at a time and into a social set which expected women to do nothing more onerous than be an exemplary hostess, Gertrude defied all expectations by becoming an archaeologist. Abandoning the wealth and privilege of her background, she made her name excavating on the shores of Birket Qarun. And, to the chagrin of many of her male contemporaries, her work succeeded in rewriting the origins of Egyptian civilisation.

Despite losing her father when she was just five years old, Gertrude enjoyed a charmed childhood. With her brother and widowed mother, she lived in an eleven-bedroom house which boasted a forty-foot billiard room, stables and three-and-a-half acres of garden. The family went to dances with the Astors at Cliveden, hunted in the Christmas holidays and spent summers in France and Scotland. Like many of their social set, they were drawn to the winter climate of Egypt, and it was in 1907 that Gertrude first visited the country. She returned four years later and stayed at the Winter Palace in Luxor, describing it as "a haven of peace in its orange-scented garden, with glorious views across the Nile to the Theban Hills."[7] But Egypt cast a darker spell, too. During World War I, Gertrude's sweetheart, a captain in the British army, was killed in the Western Desert near the Baharia Oasis. Yet, despite these early influences, nothing suggested that Egypt would become Gertrude's abiding interest.

All that changed in 1915, during a visit to Paris. Gertrude seems to have been entranced by the Egyptian collections of the Louvre and the Egyptianising architecture of the Napoleonic city. Returning to London, she took Arabic lessons and embarked on a course in prehistoric archaeology at University College, where she met Flinders Petrie, then at the height of his career as Professor of Egyptology. In 1921, Gertrude persuaded her mother to allow her to join Petrie's excavations in Egypt. The contrast with her gilded youth could not have been more stark. Second-class travel was a novelty, and the Petries' spartan lifestyle she treated as a great adventure. It was the golden age of Egyptology, and Petrie introduced the young woman from the Home Counties to the wonders of excavation in the land of the pharaohs. She visited Carter and Carnarvon's dig in the Valley of the Kings—just a year before their discovery of Tutankhamun's tomb—then accompanied the Petries to their own dig at Oxyrhynchus in Middle Egypt. It was to prove a disappointment: not because of the Petries' asceticism or the dirt and filth of the place itself, but because Oxyrhynchus, with its abundant Greek and Roman remains, offered little for a woman whose chief interest was the Palaeolithic period.

In typically resourceful fashion, Gertrude upped sticks and left Oxyrhynchus—on her own—to dig at Helwan. Throughout her archaeological career, she displayed a doughtiness impressive even by the standards of the time, and especially for a woman: "It was my habit," she explained, "to carry a pistol in case of an encounter with an angry hyena. At night the weapon lived under my pillow."[8] On excavations, she slept in an abandoned tomb, which she happily shared with a family of cobras. It was that same indefatigable spirit that led her, in 1924, to discover the first stratified prehistoric settlement site ever excavated in Egypt—not in the Nile Valley, but on the remote northern fringes of the Fayum.

In archaeological circles, the Fayum had become known as a source

of flint tools, but nobody had shown much interest in their precise provenance. Nobody, that is, except Gertrude Caton-Thompson. Having
identified a promising site, she returned to London to begin preparations
for a full-scale archaeological expedition. Petrie promised her five of his
best Qiftis (though irascible, he recognised a fellow archaeologist when
he saw one), and she selected her own personal companion. Together, the
two women headed back to Egypt—via Trieste, on the Orient Express.

In the winter of 1924, Egypt was in uproar following the murder in
Cairo of the British Governor of Sudan. In the opinion of the colonial
authorities, it was no place for a member of the fairer sex. No sooner had
Gertrude arrived than she was advised to leave. But where fainter hearts
would have capitulated, she circumvented, ignoring the British authorities and going straight to the Egyptian governor of the Fayum to secure
his personal protection. He advised her to take camels, but she insisted
on sticking with the second-hand (but chauffeur-driven) Ford she had
purchased in Cairo. Once again, her intuition proved well-founded,
and the car was a great success. Having finally arrived at the dig site,
she embarked on her first solo season of excavation, an experience she
adored.

Those two months changed our understanding of Egyptian prehistory. The dig produced the first Neolithic pottery ever discovered in
Egypt, together with flint tools, grinding-stones and cereal remains: in
summary, the earliest evidence of a settled agricultural lifestyle in Egypt.
Two further seasons in the Fayum uncovered the grain silos of the Fayumian farmers, found quite by chance when Gertrude was scraping back
the desert surface to investigate the underlying geology. The mats lining
the pits were in such good condition that she was able to lift ten intact
and send several back to England. Gertrude made important discoveries from other periods, too: the gypsum quarry used by the plasterers
who worked in the decorated tombs of the Pyramid Age, and a Ptolemaic irrigation system that had succumbed to the encroaching desert.
Interested not merely in archaeology but also in the environmental setting, Gertrude and her companion undertook a geological expedition—
by camel—to the neighbouring depression of Rayana in temperatures
reaching 49°C in the shade. To avoid the excessive heat, they returned to
camp by night, relying on Gertrude's instinct for direction to see them
safely back when their guide got lost among the dunes.

The climate and the bleak surroundings were not the only tribulations. For her third excavation season, Gertrude traded in her second-hand Ford for a state-of-the-art, six-wheeled Morris truck, recommended by the British army for desert travel. Never one to take someone else's word for it, Gertrude took the precaution of trying the vehicle out on a military testing ground in the Midlands, and was suitably impressed. But the sand dunes around Birket Qarun proved altogether more taxing than the hills around Birmingham, and at the end of the season Gertrude brought a court case against the Morris Motor Company, demanding full compensation for the expenses incurred in extracting her vehicle from the Sahara and towing it back to Cairo. Morris swiftly capitulated.

After such adventures, Gertrude wrote, without a hint of irony, "it had been realised by my mother that my archaeology was not a passing hobby."[9] Indeed, after her pioneering work in the Fayum, Gertrude went on to excavate at Great Zimbabwe, in the Transvaal, in the Belgian Congo and Uganda, and in Kenya with Louis Leakey. She was appointed to the Council of the Royal Geographical Society, awarded the Rivers Medal by the Royal Anthropological Institute and elected a Fellow of the British Academy.

She never lost her sense of adventure, nor her love for the finer things in life: on the day the Battle of Britain began, she was in London to go shopping and have her hair done at Harvey Nichols. Her background had given her the utter self-assurance and confidence that anything was possible, any obstacle could be overcome, and she used those qualities to advance the cause of women intellectuals as much as to push back the frontiers of science. Gertrude Caton-Thompson finished her memoirs at the age of ninety-one, and died at the ripe old age of ninety-seven, indefatigable to the last.

Gertrude chose the Fayum because of her interest in Egyptian prehistory. But she could easily have selected it for another reason: as Petrie's excavations in the 1880s had shown, the Fayum had, in pharaonic times, played home to more than its fair share of determined and influential women. While the kings of ancient Egypt held court at Memphis or Thebes, their wives and daughters exercised power, behind the scenes, from a palace on the south-eastern edge of the Fayum. The site known today as Medinet el-Gurob, "town of the crows," was in ancient times called "the harem of the Great Canal," or more simply "the harem of the Lake." It was well named, for it lay on the edge of the desert, overlooking a major irrigation canal. Indeed, the diversion of the Bahr Yusuf from its northward course into the Fayum basin, initiated at the beginning of the New Kingdom, was controlled from Gurob.

Texts suggest that there was a harem-palace in the Fayum from at least Middle Kingdom times. The kings of the Twelfth Dynasty enjoyed fishing and fowling on Birket Qarun, and the lake shore provided the perfect location for a pleasure palace. (It is tempting to believe that Amenemhat III's frequent visits to the Fayum may have been prompted as much by the presence of a harem-palace as by his interest in hydraulic engineering.) But it was the creation of an Egyptian empire in the New Kingdom, and especially the Eighteenth Dynasty fashion for diplomatic marriages, that spurred the establishment of a major institution for royal women at Gurob. When, as a result of military campaigns in Syria–Palestine, Thutmose III returned home with a clutch of Near Eastern princesses as well as a haul of booty, he needed somewhere to house them and their extensive retinue of attendants. His solution was to build a new harem-palace at Gurob—a palace that his exotic concubines could call home; where the royal children could be brought up in a safe and secure environment; and, just as important, where the royal women and their retainers could engage in worthwhile and economically productive activity.

The resulting complex, situated within a twelve-acre walled enclosure, comprised two large buildings. One, a residential wing with spacious columned halls, housed the living quarters for the royal women, their children and servants. The other, an administrative-cum-industrial wing, provided storage facilities and workshops. (There were also offices for the harem-palace bureaucrats, all of them male—what aspiring Egyptian man would not have been attracted by a job with the title Overseer of the Young Women of the Lord of the Two Lands?) In ancient Egypt as in medieval Europe, the manufacture of fine textiles was an activity closely associated with aristocratic women, and the harem-palace of Gurob became a major centre of weaving. Flax grown on the rich farmlands of the Fayum provided the raw material, and the finished product—Gurob linen—was highly sought-after throughout the Nile Valley. A papyrus found at Gurob refers to "royal linen, head-cloths, bag-tunic and triangular cloths, all of the first quality."[10] Glass—another

elite product with long-standing royal connotations—was also manufactured at Gurob (the royal potteries of Sèvres in Bourbon France offer
an instructive parallel), as were jewellery and cosmetics. To supplement
its manufacturing activities, the harem-palace of Gurob owned its own
buildings and estates; was supported by central taxation; and received
regular supplies from the royal treasury, delivered by boat to the harbourside just outside the palace walls. In short, it was a major economic
institution in its own right.

Unfortunately for the kings of Egypt, this combination of economic
independence, geographic isolation from the capital and a clutch of rival
wives and their children all under one roof made the harem-palace a
dangerous place. It provided a fertile breeding-ground for conspiracies,
stoked by the jealousies of the king's multiple wives and their offspring.
Two full-scale harem plots are attested in the annals of ancient Egypt,
but one suspects there must have been more. The conspiracy against the
Sixth Dynasty King Pepi I (2300 BC) by one of his own wives was resolved
by a secret judicial hearing. By contrast, the plot against Ramesses III,
1,150 years later, ended in the king's assassination, his throat slit from side
to side. One of his sons was sentenced to death, together with a clutch of
senior harem officials.

In happier times, the palace at Gurob would have played host to a
succession of exotic and dazzling royal women: Princess Gilukhepa of
Mittani, a diplomatic bride for Amenhotep III, who arrived in Egypt
with a retinue of 317 women; the king's favourite wife Tiye, to whose
statue belonged the beautiful painted ebony head, found at Gurob, that
is now one of the treasures of the Egyptian Museum in Berlin; and the
Hittite princess whose marriage to Ramesses II concluded the world's
first peace treaty.

The palace at Gurob flourished for some three hundred years, until
the dying days of the New Kingdom. It remains the only site in Egypt
where both buildings on the ground and inscriptions confirm the existence of a harem. The buildings themselves, protected by the dry climate, survived relatively intact until the late nineteenth century AD. And
the tradition of pleasure palaces in the Fayum did not stop there. The
last king of Egypt, Farouk, was a fanatical sportsman and a notorious
womaniser. Both pastimes came together on the shore of Birket Qarun,
where he built a hunting-lodge and retreat. Known as Auberge Fayum,

it hosted royal parties until the final days of the Egyptian monarchy. In 1945, it was the location for high-level negotiations between the Egyptian and British authorities; no less a personage than Winston Churchill graced its halls.

After the Free Officers' coup of 1952, Auberge Fayum was renamed Auberge du Lac, but it retained its colonial ambience and hedonistic atmosphere well into the 1970s. Today, it has been given a new lease on life, refurbished as a five-star hotel and health resort with stunning views over Birket Qarun. It is particularly popular as a weekend getaway for wealthy Egyptians. The pharaohs would have approved.

AFTER THE EXPANSION in cultivation during the Middle Kingdom and the diversion of the Bahr Yusuf at the beginning of the New Kingdom, the third great wave of land reclamation in the Fayum took place under Ptolemaic rule. From initially dismissing the region as "the marsh," the Ptolemies came to value the Fayum for its potential to increase agricultural production and thus the wealth of Egypt. They started the process of shrinking Birket Qarun by controlling the inflow of water from the Bahr Yusuf, and reclaimed the resulting land by means of drainage ditches, canals and dykes. Sweet Nile water was pumped on to the new fields by means of Archimedes screws, manned around the clock. As a result, the area under cultivation grew rapidly and the Fayum became one of the richest areas of farmland in Egypt. It was particularly prized for its vineyards, orchards and market gardens. (Today, it remains a major area for flower-growing, and most of the flower waters and essential oils sold in the bazaars of Cairo originate in the Fayum.)

Much of the new farmland was apportioned to army veterans, brought in from other places in Egypt and from the wider Mediterranean. This process transformed the ethnic mix of the Fayum and led on occasions to open hostility between communities. A few of the new settlements, such as Samareia, had Jewish names, reflecting the origin of their particular settlers. Most of the landowners were Greek, while the irrigation workers and humble fellahin were Egyptian. Half the population were veterans and their families, half civilians. Added to this mix were tourists from across the Ptolemaic lands, drawn by the attraction of feeding the sacred crocodiles of Krokodilopolis with fried fish and honey cakes sold by the enterprising priests. (A Roman-period papyrus recounts how "Lucius Memmius, a Roman senator, who occupies a position of great dignity and honour, is making the voyage from Alexandria to the Arsinoite Nome to see the sights. Let him be received with special magnificence and take care that . . . the customary tit-bits for Petesouchos and the crocodiles . . . be provided."[11]) All in all, the Ptolemaic Fayum was a cultural and linguistic melting-pot, a microcosm of the wider Nile Valley under Hellenistic rule.

Among the newly founded settlements was the city of Karanis. Located on the north-eastern edge of the Fayum, on the border between cultivation and desert, it covered an area of 185 acres and flourished for over seven centuries, from 270 BC to AD 500. Excavations at the site in modern times have yielded major quantities of both archaeological and documentary evidence, making Karanis one of the best-understood settlements of the ancient Mediterranean world. In its multistorey houses lived mostly poor farm-workers who toiled in the fields to bring in an annual grain harvest to benefit absentee landlords. Children were sent to work in the fields at an early age, and families supplemented their meagre income by keeping a few farm animals themselves and rearing flocks of pigeons in large dovecots on behalf of wealthy patrons.

In such miserable conditions, it is little wonder that the inhabitants of Karanis sought divine assistance. In its heyday, the city boasted two temples, the southern dedicated to two local crocodile gods, Pnepheros and Petesouchos, and the northern to the compound Greek–Egyptian deity Zeus-Ammon-Serapis-Helios. There was also a cult centre for the Thracian horseman-god Heron, and perhaps even a Mithraeum, while a wall painting from a household shrine showing Isis suckling the infant Horus directly foreshadowed the Christian iconography of the Virgin and child. The citizens of Karanis, it seems, were covering all their spiritual bases.

But the Fayum's Ptolemaic renaissance was shortlived. By the reign of Ptolemy II, with the state increasingly distracted by foreign policy crises, the essential infrastructure of irrigation started to be neglected. Canals silted up, farmland turned back to desert and the population shrank. Only the Roman conquest of Egypt saved the Fayum from further decline. Soon after seizing power, and recognising the potential of the region to supply Rome with grain, the emperor Augustus ordered the Roman army into the Fayum to repair the irrigation system. The turnaround was swift. Cities like Karanis boomed again, boosted by economic links with neighbouring communities and with the great Mediterranean port of Alexandria. Grain production soared; with 10 per cent of Egypt's cultivable land, the Fayum became known as the breadbasket of the Roman Empire. Large numbers of army veterans were granted land, swelling the population. But it was not all rosy. The Roman emperors grew greedy and started to tax the population of the Fayum more heavily than other Egyptians—twice the average, in fact. Eventually many people moved away to avoid serfdom. In AD 165 a plague killed much of the remaining population. By the late second century, social order had started to break down. Papyri from the town of Tebtunis, one of the largest settlements in the region, record extortion, theft, disappearances, and even an attempted gang murder.

Set against this picture of societal decline is an extraordinary cultural heritage, reflecting the Fayum's multi-ethnic, polyglot population. Romans and Egyptians moved in the same social circles (even if the Romans were generally wealthier), and both communities wrote in Greek. This complex, composite identity was expressed most creatively—and in true Egyptian fashion—in the funerary customs of the Graeco-Roman Fayum. Perhaps the most celebrated objects of the period from anywhere in Egypt are the extraordinary mummy portraits from Hawara, the site of Amenemhat III's pyramid complex on the edge of the Fayum. In classical times, burial near the fabled Labyrinth was a particular privilege, and Hawara served as the cemetery for the urbanised elite of the regional capital. The gilded mummy masks, which feature Graeco-Roman portraiture in a quintessentially Egyptian context, bring us face to face with the higher echelons of Fayum society. They also tell poignant personal stories.

An example is Artemidorus, a man of about twenty years, with large brown eyes under arched bushy eyebrows, a long aquiline nose, full lips, sunburned skin and dark brown hair brushed forwards in the style fashionable during the reign of the emperor Trajan. In his mummy portrait of about AD 120, painted in encaustic on lime wood with gold-leaf decoration, Artemidorus is shown wearing a white tunic and a creamy white mantle over his left shoulder. In one person, he thus combines a Greek name, Greek identity (his father was also called Artemidorus), a Romanised portrait, and an adherence to Egyptian funerary customs.

The woman buried with him (his wife?) had the Egyptian name The-moutharin, adding a further twist.

About a century earlier, during the reign of Augustus, another young man with a Greek name was buried in the cemetery at Hawara. In his mummy portrait, Syros son of Herakles harked back to Ptolemaic imagery—an indication, perhaps, that he resented the recent Roman conquest?—with his sculpted cheekbones and large ears set high on the sides of his head. Most striking, however, was the prominent Egyptian imagery with which he chose to have his portrait adorned: a row of cobras with solar discs on their heads, a winged scarab-beetle, sphinxes, a human-headed *ba*-bird, the goddess Nut, the mummy laid on a bier, and the gods Anubis and Horus leading the deceased into the presence of Osiris. There is no hint of Romanisation, but rather a conscious rever-ence for the beliefs and customs of ancient Egypt. All the more surpris-ing, therefore, that Syros' companion in death (and most probably his close friend in life), a young man called Mareis, should have chosen to be painted sporting a fashionable Roman hairstyle of curls brushed forwards on to the brow. In the Graeco-Roman Fayum, identities and friendships bridged ethnic and cultural divisions in often complex ways.

A final mummy mask from the Fayum is of a young woman of deli-cate features. She was aged in her late teens or early twenties when she died around AD 40. The only ornamentation on her portrait is a pair of large earrings, each comprising a pearl suspended from a gold disc. An inscription in Greek next to her face names her as "Hermione, teacher of grammar." In her mixed Egypto-Graeco-Roman community, her role would have been to promote the Greek cultural traditions of the ruling elite, which included a thorough knowledge of grammar. Her mummy mask, together with her complete mummified body, was discovered by Flinders Petrie at Hawara in 1888. Hermione looked like just the sort of woman of whom Petrie approved, a "studious and meek schoolmis-tress without a trace of show or ornament."[12] He duly sent her, and her mask, to Girton College Cambridge, to inspire its female students to yet greater feats of self-effacing erudition. It is one of the great ironies of Egyptology that Hermione was discovered in the very year in which Gertrude Caton-Thompson was born—a woman who, under Petrie's own tutelage, would equal his discoveries in the Fayum and strike a blow for an altogether different kind of female scholarship.

The Fayum portraits represent the region's cultural zenith, but since the fall of the Roman Empire the Fayum has experienced mixed fortunes. Like other remoter parts of Egypt, it attracted early Christian settlers, and was particularly popular with those seeking an ascetic lifestyle. Christianity put down deep roots (the region eventually boasted thirty-five monasteries), and the inhabitants of the Fayum did not take kindly to the Arab invasion of AD 639. The region remained a hotbed of rebellion and was the last part of Egypt to be fully subdued by the Arab conquerors. Little wonder, then, that the Fayum was by turns plundered and neglected by Egypt's Muslim rulers. Invading Fatimid armies laid waste to the region in 969, and thereafter it continued a long decline into the Ottoman era. In 1245, when the local governor commissioned a survey of the hydrology for his masters in Cairo, he reported a region almost completely abandoned; the Fayum was at its lowest ebb in over six thousand years. At the beginning of the reign of Muhammad Ali in the early nineteenth century, when Egypt began its emergence into the modern age, there were only 60 villages in the Fayum—compared with 114 under Ptolemaic rule, two thousand years earlier.

Prosperity only returned to the Fayum in the late nineteenth century, when modern transport and communications finally reconnected this remote region with the rest of Egypt. The British brought the railway in 1893, to be followed by the first metalled road from Cairo in the 1930s. As a result, once-small villages have burgeoned into substantial towns. The regional capital, Medinet el-Fayum, occupies the same location as its pharaonic and classical predecessors (Shedyt and Krokodilopolis), but it presents a thoroughly modern picture, typical of any growing city in Egypt. Mud-brick buildings have been replaced by ugly concrete boxes, more often than not with steel rods projecting rustily from an unfinished top storey; the streets are clogged with traffic, more cars than carts; and pollution hangs in the air, eating away at what few ancient ruins remain. Gone, in this sprawling town, is the sense of a community rooted in an agricultural way of life; gone, too, the temples with their pools for sacred crocodiles. In fact, just about the only indication of Medinet el-Fayum's great antiquity is a lone monument, marooned on a roundabout on the main route into town. A towering round-topped obelisk, smooth-faced and entirely undecorated but for the royal name of its builder King Senusret I, it once stood sentinel outside the village of Abgig, a few miles to the south-west. There, it pointed towards the spot where the Bahr Yusuf leaves the Nile Valley and enters the Fayum depression—a marker, perhaps, to celebrate the fertility of the Fayum under pharaonic rule. Its removal to a charmless roundabout in Medinet el-Fayum signalled, unwittingly, a new crisis in the history of the Fayum.

The construction of the High Dam at Aswan and greater extraction of water for irrigation have starved Birket Qarun of its lifeblood. Without a steady influx of fresh water, evaporation from the lake surface has turned its water increasingly saline—to the point where it is no longer good for irrigating the fields, nor even for sustaining much in the way of fish stocks. As concerned locals will testify, Birket Qarun is slowly dying. And, as livelihoods are threatened, poverty and lack of opportunity all too easily breed resentment and extremism, as other parts of Egypt have learned to their cost.

On my last visit to the Fayum, an escort of armed soldiers was deemed necessary, all the way from Cairo. When we announced that we wanted to see the mud-brick pyramid of Senusret II, the minibus driver was reluctant to drive through the nearby town of Lahun, for fear of being attacked. His relief when we finally left the town behind us and saw the pyramid on the horizon was palpable. But the soldiers were not so relaxed. Before we were allowed out of the bus and anywhere near the pyramid, they jumped out of their jeep and fanned out across the landscape. Only when they had taken up positions on every elevation, guns trained outwards, were we finally allowed to walk to the pyramid enclosure. Even then, a few minutes, just enough to jog around the perimeter and take a few photos, was all that the guards' nerves could take. Before we knew it, the bus horn was blaring and we were being hurriedly beckoned back for a quick getaway. No member of the Egyptian security forces wanted to linger for long in the Fayum. Only when we were safely back on the road to Cairo did the soldiers begin to relax.

Against this backdrop of insecurity and environmental degradation, the destiny of the Fayum looks uncertain, if not bleak. But this lake in the desert has seen many ups and downs in its nine-thousand-year history, and has always proved resilient, despite periods of great adversity. Perhaps the rescue of those Neolithic grain pits from the farmer's plough will come to be seen as a turning point: by honouring its origins, the Fayum may have a brighter future.

TEN

Cairo

Egypt's Capital

[Cairo] is the glory of Islam, and
is the marketplace for all mankind.[1]

—AL-MUQADDASI

Cairo is the largest city in Africa, in the Middle East and in the Arab world. This metropolis of at least seventeen million people—a number rising by up to a million every year—is as populous as many countries. Although the kings of ancient Egypt succeeded spectacularly in building the greatest monuments the world has ever seen—still visible from large parts of Cairo as hazy triangles on the horizon—they never had to contend with running and organising a conurbation of more than a few tens of thousands of souls. In its size and scale, Cairo is an experiment in urban living unprecedented in Egyptian history—an order of magnitude bigger than any other settlement in the Nile Valley. It is an unbelievable press of humanity: an overcrowded, dilapidated, noisy, smelly, frenetic, impossible city; yet its inhabitants go about their daily lives with resigned good humour, demonstrating the resilience that has characterised the Egyptian people throughout their long history.

As you approach Cairo by river, from Upper Egypt, the southern tip of Roda Island with its ancient Nilometer marks the beginning of the city in both a geographical and an historical sense. From Roda, the historic city spreads northwards and eastwards on the east bank of the river, while in more recent times Cairo has engulfed the islands in the Nile and once-distinct villages and towns (such as Giza) on the west bank, as well as vast tracts of desert in all directions. The southern tip of Roda, or more particularly the stretch of Nile bank immediately opposite, known as Old Cairo, is also the place where Egypt's capital began, where the heirs of the pharaohs established a new centre of administration for the entire Nile Valley.

Although it has pharaonic monuments aplenty in its museums and public squares, Cairo proper is a post-pharaonic foundation, the one major settlement in Egypt that does not owe its origins to the country's ancient civilisation. Cairo is an Arab creation, founded by Arab conquerors, home to venerable mosques and madrassas, headquarters of the Arab League. But to think of Cairo as only an Arab city would be to underestimate its cultural complexity. Like all of Egypt, it embodies many different histories and traditions, many influences and contradictions; and it is this extraordinary mix that gives Egypt's capital its distinctive character and its special appeal.

OPPOSITE THE SOUTHERN TIP of Roda Island, a couple of blocks east of the Nile in Old Cairo, there is a vast area of wasteland, bounded by fences and strewn with rubbish. In a rapidly expanding city, it is distinguished only by its lack of buildings. What keeps it free from development—for the moment—is its history. For this unlikely, unprepossessing spot is all that remains of the first Arab settlement in Egypt, one that would expand and develop into the greatest city in the Arab world. This is the site of Fustat ("tent" in Arabic), where in AD 641, just nine years after the death of the Prophet Muhammad, the victorious Arab forces of Amr ibn al-As pitched their camp and established their new capital, having invaded Egypt two years earlier and, after a series of battles, seized the country from its Byzantine rulers. The nearby mosque of Amr, long since rebuilt, is all that remains of Fustat; its construction symbolised the incorporation of Egypt into the Islamic realm, and a new dispensation for the entire Nile Valley. Egypt's current position as the voice of the Arab world traces its origins to this barren expanse in southern Cairo.

The Arabs may have brought a new religion to Egypt, but they followed ancient traditions when choosing a location for their capital city. From the very dawn of Egyptian history in 3000 BC, when the Nile Valley and Delta were unified under a single king at the beginning of the First Dynasty, the country was ruled from "the junction of the Two Lands"— the apex of the Delta where the Nile splits into several channels on its way to the sea. This was the obvious place from which to govern such a geographically extensive territory, as it lay within relatively easy reach of all parts of the country and of Egypt's vulnerable north-eastern border. The first kings of Egypt called their capital Inebu-hedj ("white walls"), after the whitewashed palace compound at its physical and symbolic heart. In later generations, the city came to be called after another royal monument, the nearby pyramid of Pepi I, Men-nefer ("established and beautiful"), a designation which the Greeks corrupted into "Memphis." By whichever name it was known, the pharaonic settlement remained Egypt's principal seat of administration for nearly three thousand years until the foundation of Alexandria in 332 BC. Yet today, the site of Memphis is as bleak and empty as Fustat. As Amelia Edwards lamented, "this is all that remains of Memphis, eldest of cities—a few huge rubbish heaps, a dozen or so of broken statues, and a name! . . . Memphis is a place to read about, and think about, and remember; but it is a disappointing place to see."[2]

Under the Ptolemies, Memphis declined. Under the Romans, it virtually disappeared, superseded as a strategic base by a massive fortress built further north, at a site called Babylon-in-Egypt. The round towers of the western gate and the semicircular bastions of the Water Gate still

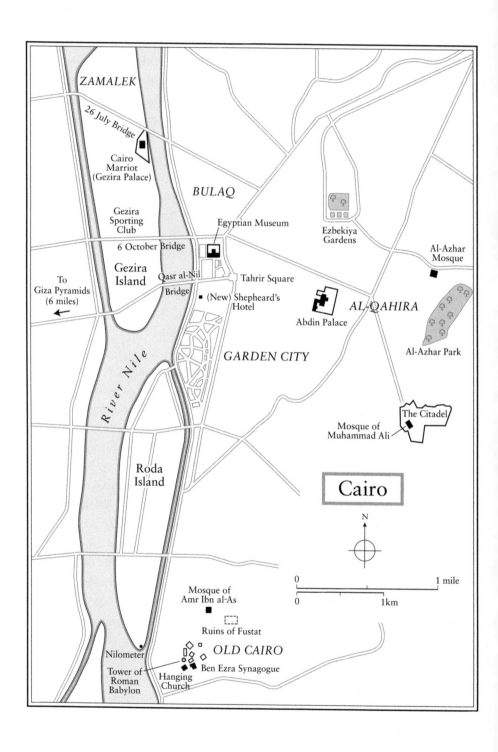

stand, impressive testaments to the Romans' military engineering. The reason for their preservation, ironically, is the use to which they were later put: when Egypt, along with the rest of the Roman Empire, converted to Christianity in the fourth century AD, the fortress of Babylon provided firm foundations for some of the Nile Valley's earliest churches. The northern round tower is today the Greek Orthodox church of St. George, while the semicircular bastions of the Water Gate support the famous fourth-century "Hanging Church" of the Virgin Mary. Other ancient centres of Christian worship in the vicinity include the fifth-century church of St. Sergius, now several feet below street level, where the Holy Family is said to have taken refuge during their sojourn in Egypt, and the church dedicated to St. Barbara, one of Egypt's early Christian martyrs. The surrounding streets of the Coptic enclave, pedestrianised and peaceful, preserve an atmosphere of antiquity and spirituality that can be difficult to find in the busier parts of Cairo. Christian women can walk here, unmolested, with their heads uncovered; shop-owners are content to stand in their doorways and have tourists come to them.

The close proximity of Fustat to Old Cairo—the site of the first Arab capital lies immediately to the north-east of the Christian quarter—is no accident. Today, we are accustomed to a narrative of religious conflict in the Middle East, but the Arab conquest of Egypt tells a very different story. Ever since the Council of Chalcedon in AD 451, when a doctrinal dispute about the nature of Christ caused a split between the Egyptian and Eastern Orthodox churches, the Copts had suffered discrimination and persecution by their Byzantine overlords. So when the Arab armies under Amr ibn al-As invaded Egypt in AD 639, Egypt's native (Christian) leaders cooperated with them, hoping they would be more benign. The Arab forces made rapid progress in conquering the country, starting with the battle of Heliopolis on the north-eastern approaches to Cairo (better known today for the international airport and presidential palace). The Byzantine army, having lost control of most of the Delta and Nile Valley, retreated to the fortress of Babylon to make its last stand. Amr's forces besieged the fortress for six months, from October 640 to April 641, until the Byzantine army finally capitulated. Thus Egypt became a province of the expanding Arab empire, ruled by a governor appointed by the caliph in Mecca. But there was no wholesale process of Islamicisation. The majority of the population remained Christian (at least until the tenth century) and retained their ancient language. For hundreds of years, Christians and Muslims, Arabs and Copts, lived peacefully side by side.

Christianity and Islam were not the only religions of the book to flourish in medieval Cairo. Judaism, too, played an important—though now largely forgotten—role in the story of Egypt's capital. That the contribution of Cairo's Jews to their city's culture and economy is known at all is due to a remarkable discovery made in an attic in the Coptic quarter. Just a street away from the Hanging Church, hidden behind high walls and trees, stands a pale yellow building with a decorative parapet and graceful, arched windows. The only outward clues to its identity are the guards by the entrance and the discreet Stars of David moulded on the window-surrounds. Through an open pane, it is just possible to catch sight of a seven-branched menora. For this is the synagogue of Ben Ezra, once home to a flourishing community of Jews, now a beautifully restored monument open to the public.

According to local tradition, the synagogue is situated on the site where the baby Moses was rescued from the reedy banks of the Nile. Scarcely less shrouded in myth and legend is the history of the building itself. The generally accepted version tells how a synagogue was built in Old Cairo, on the edge of Fustat, some time in the ninth century, only to be converted into a church. This church was destroyed on the orders of the caliph in 1012, then rebuilt and rededicated in 1025. In 1115, so the story goes, Rabbi Abraham Ben Ezra came to Cairo from Jerusalem and petitioned the Muslim authorities to restore the building to the Jewish community. On payment of twenty thousand dinars, his wish was granted and the building became a synagogue again. This complicated history helps to explain the mix of Christian and Jewish features, a pair of confessionals flanking the ark of the covenant. From the tenth to the nineteenth century, Ben Ezra synagogue was the principal place of worship for the Jews of Old Cairo.

It was not devotions that made Ben Ezra special, however, but its secondary role as a repository for old documents. Jewish tradition maintained that any document containing words written in Hebrew—divine words—was sacred and could not be thrown away. Every Jewish community therefore had a *genizah*, a repository for old documents, usually located in the attic of the local synagogue, out of harm's way. The Ben Ezra genizah is two stories high, at the far end of the building. Here, for generation upon generation—in fact, for more than eight hundred years—the Jews of Old Cairo deposited their written material of every kind, ranging from poetry and love letters to business contracts and legal deeds. Out of sight, out of mind: the documents piled up, unseen and forgotten.

Until, that is, the end of the nineteenth century, when a Jewish scholar from the University of Cambridge, Rabbi Solomon Schechter, climbed a ladder into the Ben Ezra genizah and saw what lay inside: over a quarter of a million fragments of paper dating back over one thousand years, forming the largest collection of early and medieval Jewish manuscripts ever discovered. The Cairo Genizah provides a unique time-capsule of Jewish culture and belief. At a stroke, it has transformed our understanding and appreciation of early Judaism, of biblical and rabbinic literature, of medieval Islamic history—and study of the collection still continues. The manuscripts record the lives of Jews and the non-Jews with whom they interacted in Old Cairo from the ninth century (the earliest dated document is a marriage certificate from 6 October 871) until the late nineteenth century (the latest dated document is a marriage contract from 1899). They include the earliest fragment of rabbinic literature ever found, and other texts belonging to a breakaway Jewish sect called the Followers of Zadok. Their charismatic leader was referred to as "the Only One" and "the Teacher of Righteousness," recalling another Jewish leader from Nazareth. Because the Ben Ezra synagogue belonged to the Palestinian Jews, its liturgical texts reflected Palestinian religious practice which differed from the Babylonian rite contained in Jewish prayer books of today.

Despite their religious idiosyncracies, the Jews of medieval Cairo were fully integrated into their local community. They were at the heart of the city's commercial life, maintaining business and cultural links across North Africa and the Middle East. They were also respected members of society, and some attained high-ranking government positions. The great twelfth-century philosopher Rabbi Moses Maimonides lived within walking distance of the Ben Ezra synagogue. Another member of the congregation was a man from southern Italy who had converted to Judaism in 1102 at the height of the Crusades, found his way to Old

Cairo, taken the Hebrew name Obadiah, and flourished as a poet and composer. He left behind, in the Ben Ezra genizah, the oldest piece of Jewish sheet music in existence, a hymn to Moses set to the Gregorian chant of twelfth-century Italy.

Twentieth-century Egypt has been less tolerant of religious difference, and far less kind to its Jewish population. Most left after the 1967 war with Israel, when anti-Semitic sentiment was rife. The Jews of Old Cairo have gone, and today only a tiny Jewish community clings on in Egypt's capital, in the northern suburb of Abbassia.

LIKE EVERY OTHER SETTLEMENT in Egypt, Fustat–Old Cairo was founded with proximity to the Nile in mind. The Roman fortress of Babylon-in-Egypt had been positioned to guard a key river crossing, and its impressive Water Gate reflects the importance of access to the Nile. Although the Muslim conquerors who wrested Egypt from Byzantine rule in the mid seventh century were from the Arabian peninsula—an area of desert wastes as far removed from the green Nile Valley as it is possible to imagine—they were well aware of the importance of the Nile to Egypt's continued prosperity. One of Amr ibn al-As' first acts was to centralise the irrigation system and order a series of new projects to increase agricultural production. (He also reopened the ancient canal linking the Nile to the Red Sea to facilitate the transport of grain from Egypt to the Hijaz. Having been the breadbasket of the Roman Empire, Egypt now became the granary of the caliphate.) The Nilometer on Roda Island, constructed in the ninth century, measured the productive capacity of the whole country for nearly a thousand years and remains the oldest Islamic monument in Cairo. The Arab writer al-Muqaddasi, who visited around AD 1000, described it as "a pond in the middle of which is a tall column whereon are the marks in cubits and fingers; in charge of it is a superintendent, and around it are doors that fit together tightly."[3]

In continuation of ancient Egyptian and Christian custom, Egypt's early Arab rulers celebrated the festival of the banks of the Nile, which was a spectacle to behold. An historian who visited Egypt in 942 was privileged to be in Cairo on "the Night of the Bath," which marked the baptism of Christ, when the eastern side of Roda Island and the facing bank of Fustat were lit up by thousands of blazing torches:

Muslims and Christians, by hundreds of thousands, crowded the Nile on boats, or in kiosks overlooking the river, or on the banks, all eager for pleasure . . . The sound of music was heard all about, with singing and dancing. It was a splendid night, the best in all Egypt for beauty and gaiety; the doors of the separate (city) quarters were left open, and most people bathed in the Nile, knowing well that it is a sure preservative and cure for all disease.[4]

But the Nile, as the Egyptians well knew, could bring curses as well as blessings. In 967, an exceptionally low inundation led to widespread famine, and the death of over six hundred thousand people in and around Fustat—a large proportion of the population. Those who did not die, fled. The stage was set for the next decisive moment in Cairo's history.

Sensing Egypt's weakness, on 1 July 969 a North African army raised by the Shiite Fatimids entered the Nile Valley and swiftly took possession of the country. They established their headquarters to the north of Fustat—according to legend, on an auspicious date when the planet Mars ("al-Qahir" in Arabic) was in the ascendant. Hence they named their new city al-Qahira (Cairo). Not coincidentally, it also meant "the victorious." Maintaining control through force of arms, the Fatimids turned Cairo into a great fortified city, the centre of an independent Shiite caliphate that rivalled the Sunni caliphate of the East and controlled a rival empire stretching from North Africa via Sicily and Egypt to Palestine and Yemen. Egyptian harbours were expanded to accommodate the Fatimid fleet, and arsenals, shipyards and customs houses were established on the banks of the Nile at Fustat, restoring its fortunes by transforming it into a commercial centre. As for the Fatimids' new imperial capital of al-Qahira, it was dominated by a huge palace complex, the centre of their rule, which is said to have been so massive and looming that it looked from a distance like a mountain. Other palaces were built outside the city walls, especially by the sides of canals and the Nile—like all their forebears, the Fatimids drew refreshment and inspiration from Egypt's great river. Within their walled city, the Fatimids' most lasting foundation was the great congregational mosque of al-Azhar, constructed between 970 and 972. As well as being one of the Muslim world's most impressive centres of worship, al-Azhar also developed a reputation for teaching and learning, and retains to this day the accolade of being the oldest surviving university in the world.

From its headquarters in Cairo, Islamic scholarship led the world in the tenth and eleventh centuries AD. The West, by contrast, was still emerging from the Dark Ages. But what the West lacked in education, it more than made up for in military might. The launch of the Crusades in the early twelfth century—ostensibly to protect Constantinople from the Turks and secure the Holy Land for Christendom, but in reality to win empires for the European powers—brought death and destruction to Muslim lands across the Middle East. Egypt was invaded in 1117, and fifty years later another Crusader army burned and destroyed Fustat. Al-Qahira was next in the firing line, and the Fatimid rulers took the step of appointing the renowned leader of Syrian troops stationed in Egypt to defend the city against the Crusaders. It was a brilliant tactical decision, but a terrible strategic error. The troop-leader, by the name of Salah al-Din al-Ayyubi, built a huge citadel on high ground to the east of al-Qahira, with impregnable walls and a commanding view over the city. It not only resisted Crusader attack, but also provided Salah al-Din (better known in the West as Saladin) with his own powerbase. He cast off Fatimid rule, recognised the Sunni caliph in Baghdad, but effectively ruled Egypt independently. A great victory against the forces of Christendom in 1179 cemented his reputation as a Muslim warrior-hero, and he set about restoring Egypt to its former glory. Once again, harnessing the bounty of the Nile was the key to renewed prosperity. The citadel itself was supplied with drinking water by an aqueduct that ran all the way from the river. Saladin ordered the Bahr Yusuf to be dredged, to improve crop yields in the Fayum; improved the irrigation system throughout the country; and beautified the mosque of the Nilometer on Roda Island, in honour of the inundation itself.

Throughout the Middle Ages—under both Saladin's Ayyubid dynasty and the Turkic-speaking slave dynasty of the Mamluks which followed—Cairo, like the rest of Egypt, drew its strength from the Nile, and the river's annual regime dominated the city's cultural and religious life. Cairo's river-wharfs bustled with trade from all corners of the Mediterranean and Middle East, leading one Arab commentator to boast that the city was "the storehouse of the Occident, the entrepôt of the Orient."[5] Ibn Battuta wrote that on the Nile there were "thirty-six thousand vessels belonging to the Sultan and his subjects, which sail upstream to Upper Egypt and downstream to Alexandria and Damietta, laden with goods and commodities of all kinds."[6] Commerce created great wealth, and Egypt's rulers displayed their power and prosperity by building lavish new mosques throughout the capital. From Ibn Tulun with its immense courtyard and Sultan Hassan with its soaring portal to al-Hakim with its pepper-pot minarets and al-Aqmar with masonry that shines in the moonlight, the medieval mosques of Islamic Cairo are one of Egypt's cultural treasures—built, like the pyramids and temples of the pharaohs, on the Nile's bounty.

But with a burgeoning population, Cairo also suffered more than anywhere else in Egypt from the effects of low Niles. A seven-year famine of biblical proportions raged from 1066 to 1072, to be surpassed in misery only by the effects of a poor inundation in 1201–2. On the latter occasion, the ensuing starvation caused such a high mortality rate that "a single property was said to have passed through the hands of forty heirs within the space of a month."[7] According to one of the more colourful histories of medieval Egypt, "Men waylaid women in the streets to seize their infants, and baby fricassee and haggis of children's heads were ordinary articles of diet."[8]

With life poised so precariously between agony and plenty, it is little wonder that the atmosphere in Cairo reached fever pitch each year in August when the annual inundation was due. In 1050 AD, the Persian traveller Naser-e Khosraw recorded that "From the day it begins its increase, criers are sent through the city to proclaim how many 'fingers' God has increased the Nile that day."[9] Nearly eight centuries later, the same custom was witnessed by the English visitor Edward Lane, who noted that "the rise of the Nile is proclaimed daily in the streets of Cairo by The Crier of the Nile."[10] When the river had risen between twenty and twenty-one feet, "the completion of the Nile" was proclaimed. The city's grandees and much of its population would assemble on Roda Island ready for the "Day of the Breaking of the River" the following morning. Before dawn, workmen would start to dismantle the dam at Old Cairo, and when the Governor of Cairo arrived, the final cut would be made, allowing the floodwaters to pour through the dry ditch that bisected the city and into the dust-bowl of Ezbekiya, turning it into a muddy lake. This was an occasion for great rejoicing, as Lane recorded:

the government supplies a great number of fireworks, chiefly rockets, to honour the festival, and to amuse the populace during the night preceding the day when the dam is cut, and during the operation itself, which is performed early in the morning. Many small tents for the sale of sweetmeats, fruits, and other eatables, and coffee, etc., are likewise pitched along the bank of the isle of Er-Rodah, opposite the entrance of the Canal . . .

When the dam has been cut away . . . and all the great officers whose presence is required have arrived, the Governor of the metropolis throws a purse of small gold coins to the labourers. A boat, on board of which is an officer of the late Walee, is then propelled against the narrow ridge of earth, and breaking the slight barrier, passes through it, and descends with the cataract thus formed.[11]

People would plunge into the canal as part of the festivities (in 1834 three people were drowned), so grateful were they that the spectre of famine had been banished for another year.

By the time Edward Lane visited Cairo in 1834, Egypt under Muhammad Ali was on the brink of a modernisation programme that would change the country, and the character of its capital, for ever. For some visitors, change could not come too soon. One nineteenth-century American tourist commented, "Cairo is a big place, and can stand a good deal of improving."[12] But for many Europeans, the allure of Egypt—of the Orient—needed no refining. An aristocratic British visitor to Cairo, in the same year as Lane, was entranced by the view from the Citadel, and moved to poetry by "the majestic river, as it winds its way down this beautiful valley, bearing verdure and fertility on its dimpled waters."[13] Cairo was, after Constantinople, the greatest political and economic centre in the Middle East; its bazaars were filled with wares from across North Africa and the Levant (including slaves); and the Islamic city, with its maze of narrow streets and decorated mosques, conjured up images of *The Arabian Nights* in the Western imagination. European residents were few, and lived in their own quarter, shut off from the rest of the city by great wooden doors which were closed at night, and at times of riot or plague (a great pestilence the year after Lane's visit carried off a third of the population of Cairo). If there was no space in the

European (or "Frank") Quarter, travellers would stay in Bulaq, Cairo's main port situated a mile to the north-west of the Islamic city. Here the viceroy and other wealthy Cairenes had their summer palaces on the banks of the Nile.

AS THE NINETEENTH CENTURY PROGRESSED and the trickle of European visitors turned into a flood, the demand for lodgings in the city offered an opportunity for entrepreneurs, and Cairo's first purpose-built hotels began to appear. At first, these were located in the Frank Quarter or Ezbekiya immediately to the west. Although it was dotted with rubbish dumps and with fetid marshes left over from the annual inundation, Ezbekiya was nonetheless an open space in an otherwise congested city, and its desirability in European eyes had been further enhanced by the fact that Napoleon had set up his headquarters here in 1798. In the 1820s, there were just four hotels in Cairo (two in the Frank Quarter—Hill's and the Hotel du Nil—and two closer to Ezbekiya—Levick's and the Orient). Twenty years later, they had been joined by a clutch of competitors, including the Hotel de l'Europe where Florence Nightingale stayed for three weeks in 1849—arriving just two days after Gustave Flaubert, who stayed a night at the Orient. The cutting of a canal around Ezbekiya meant that the area no longer flooded during the annual inundation. Secured by gates locked at night, it was transformed into an elegant tree-lined garden, with a fountain at the centre, making it even more attractive to Europeans. Cairo's arrival on the international tourist scene was marked in 1850 when Hill's, also known as the British Hotel, moved to new premises at the north-west corner of Ezbekiya and changed its name to Shepheard's; over the succeeding century, it would become the most famous hotel in Egypt, if not the world.

Where Muhammad Ali had encouraged European immigrants to bring Egypt into the modern world, his grandson Khedive Ismail went one stage further. In his youth, Ismail had studied in Paris, and a subsequent visit to the city for the Exposition Universale in 1867 awakened major ambitions for his own capital. Ismail had the fortune to be guided around Paris by none other than Baron Haussmann, the architect and town planner who had transformed the French capital in the mid nineteenth century with the laying-out of wide boulevards and squares.

Ismail was so impressed that he decided Cairo needed the same treatment, but instead of rebuilding the Islamic city, he set about creating an entirely new district on low-lying marshy land to the west. To encourage the creation of fine buildings in the Parisian style, the Khedive offered free land to any developer who would build on it, within a year and a half, a property worth at least 3,000 francs. So the fine edifices of what is now downtown Cairo started to appear. Ezbekiya was no longer a park on the western extremity of the city but its central hub, graced with an opera house modelled on La Scala Milan, further enhancing its popularity with European expatriates and visitors; and to coincide with the official opening of the Suez Canal in 1869, another grand hotel was built next to Shepheard's (known as the New Hotel, it would later change its name to the Grand Continental).

An extract from an article in *Belgravia* magazine of 1873, entitled "Wintering in Egypt" (other articles in the same volume include "Boarding and Day Schools," "College Scouts," and "The Philosophy of Grand Hotels"), conjures up the attractions of the Egyptian capital for well-heeled British visitors in the late nineteenth century:

> Cairo is, par excellence, the most perfect Arab city of the present day, and one in which its inhabitants have, perhaps, attained a higher degree of civilisation than in any other city in the East . . . Cairo, from its clear dry atmosphere and equable temperature, is now admitted to be one of the most desirable winter resorts for invalids in the world . . . At Cairo, the invalid or tourist can be constantly in the open air, either on foot, donkey-back, horse-back, or in a carriage . . . The complete change, too, from the habits and customs of Western Europe . . . is, I am convinced, of immense importance . . . Who could think of dyspepsia or hypochondriasis while beholding the lovely sunrises and glorious sunsets . . .[14]

Amelia Edwards, too, in her own inimitable style, had plenty to say about the delights of Cairo. When not describing the bazaars with their "manifold combinations of light and shade, colour, costume, and architectural detail,"[15] she was passing comment on the motley crowd in the dining-room at Shepheard's Hotel:

Anglo-Indians homeward or outward bound, European residents, or visitors established in Cairo for the winter . . . invalids in search of health; artists in search of subjects; sportsmen keen upon crocodiles; statesmen out for a holiday; special correspondents alert for gossip; collectors on the scent of papyri and mummies; men of science with only scientific ends in view; and the usual surplus of idlers who travel for the mere love of travel.[16]

Late nineteenth-century Cairo was not only the playground of Europe, but, with the construction of the Suez Canal by the French and the proclamation of a British Empire in India, a scene of intense rivalry between the great powers. Since Ezbekiya and downtown Cairo had been modelled in the French style, the British decided to lay out their own part of the capital, Garden City, in the English style—complete with winding roads to conjure up memories of Surrey lanes, and mansions with large gardens leading down to the Nile.

Between the British and the French, not to mention Khedive Ismail, Cairo was transformed over the space of barely fifty years from an old Islamic city of narrow streets and mosques into a thoroughly modern, cosmopolitan capital of grand public buildings, majestic avenues and pleasure palaces. But this was not the first building boom in the city's history, nor would it be its last.

Despite the rash of modern excrescences that jostle with elegant minarets on the skyline of Cairo, the Pyramids at Giza are still visible across large parts of the city, standing proud and immoveable as they have for 4,500 years. They are the sole remaining Wonder of the Ancient World, and an ever-present reminder of Egypt's past glories. They owe their location to the ancient capital of Memphis, whose vast royal necropolis spread out along the western escarpment of the desert for a distance of thirty or forty miles, from the northern edge of the Fayum in the south to Abu Rawash in the north. Earlier pyramids had been built at Dahshur and Saqqara, but it was the particular genius of the Fourth Dynasty king Khufu, followed by his son and grandson, to situate their monuments on the elevated Giza Plateau, so as to make them appear even larger and more impressive. The statistics associated with the Great Pyramid of Khufu are humbling: 2,300,000 blocks of stone, each weighing an average of two tons, set in place at a rate of one block every two minutes for ten hours a day over a period of at least twenty years; alignment to true north with an error of only one-twentieth of a degree; and a finished height of 481 feet, making it the tallest building in the world until the construction of the great European cathedrals.

According to the Arab proverb, "Man fears Time, but Time fears the Pyramids"; and it is difficult to see, short of a nuclear Armageddon, how anything could obliterate the pyramids from the landscape; they are as close to eternal as any man-made construction can be. Yet, as the scars on the faces of the three Giza pyramids show, men have certainly tried to dent their majesty, if not dismantle them entirely. Perhaps the greatest outrage perpetrated on the pyramids, at least in modern times, was carried out in the name of science. The culprit was one Richard Vyse (1784–1853), a member of the English landed gentry who enjoyed a colourful and varied career as an army officer, member of parliament and latterly amateur archaeologist. Having voted against Catholic emancipation and parliamentary reform, Vyse was nothing if not sure of his own mind. A visit to Egypt in 1835—the year after Edward Lane—prompted an interest in the monuments of Giza, and Vyse returned a year later determined to open up their hidden secrets. His methods were brutally effective. First, he set up a drilling rig on the back of the Sphinx and bored into it to try to find hidden passages—without success. Worse still, he used gunpowder to blast out entrances to the three relieving chambers inside the Great Pyramid; the ink inscriptions that came to light proved beyond doubt that the monument had been built for Khufu. Vyse established the ownership of the third pyramid in the same manner, by blasting away some of the granite casing blocks and revealing the entrance. In the course of his "excavations" by dynamite, Vyse caused irreparable damage to nearly every pyramid at Giza. To add insult to injury, Vyse sent Menkaura's sarcophagus back to England, but the ship carrying it sank and the precious artefact was lost.

Vyse was not the first to attack the wonders of Giza. The Sphinx had been mutilated on the orders of a Muslim sheikh in AD 1300, and the Mamluk army had used it for target practice. The builders of Cairo's Fatimid-era city walls could not resist a tempting source of ready-cut stone, and stripped away most of the pyramids' casing blocks to supply their own construction project. (The blocks, of fine white limestone, had originally been brought to Giza by barge, during the inundation, from the quarries of Tura across the other side of the Nile. Those same quarries remain open today, producing cement for Cairo's modern construction boom.) In the mid nineteenth century, Flinders Petrie reported seeing caravans of up to three hundred camels every day carrying stone away from the pyramids for the construction of Khedive Ismail's new Cairo.

Today, unbridled development poses an equal threat. An oil well is being dug on the Giza plateau, just a few hundred yards from the archaeological site, while a building boom threatens the Giza pyramids not with destruction, but with encirclement. To the east of the pyramids, the city of Giza is now just an extension of metropolitan Cairo; in front of the Sphinx, roads, streetlights, car parks, shops, fast-food outlets, and seating for the sound and light show surround the great statue, robbing it of dignity. To the west, Cairo's huge satellite settlement, known as 6 October City, is sprawling southwards along the Fayum Road, almost surrounding the Giza Plateau. Where just a few years ago there was nothing but desert, today apartment blocks, electricity pylons and the minarets of new mosques ring the horizon. Within a few years, if construction continues at the same pace, the pyramids will be left marooned, a small island of antiquity in a sea of indiscriminate, uncontrolled, substandard development.

The pace of Cairo's expansion is dizzying. Adjoining 6 October City to the east, New Cairo was born in the 1990s as part of the Mubarak regime's project to relieve pressure on the Nile Valley. It is an extraordinary phenomenon—an enormous new city of apartment blocks and villas, built on barren desert. Yet not all Egyptians are able to keep up with this rush towards modernity. Below billboards advertising the latest household cleaning product, children wander barefoot through dirty streets, past canals filled with rubbish, sewage and dead animals. Men on donkeys ride past glitzy showrooms for Mercedes-Benz and BMW.

Since Egypt's 2011 revolution, property developers have taken advantage of the lack of a functioning government to circumvent the usual planning process and indulge in an even greater orgy of speculative construction, hoping to make a big profit when economic stability returns. The result is that hundreds of blocks of flats—empty or half-finished— litter the outskirts and even the inner suburbs of Cairo; many are built on agricultural land, leading to the loss of precious productive capacity. Each block is identical to its neighbour, a basic concrete frame with infill panels of shoddily laid bricks; a minor earth tremor would send them tumbling to the ground like a pack of cards. And all this at a time when ordinary Egyptians are so hard up that they cannot afford the rent on the smallest of apartments.

As well as disfiguring the landscape, threatening Egypt's ancient monuments and swallowing up agricultural land, the trend of rapid urbanisation is having a profound effect on society in Cairo and throughout the Nile Valley. The close-knit relationships that have characterised Egypt's communities for millennia are giving way to the disconnectedness and anonymity of city life. One of the aspects of the 2011 revolution that brought Egyptians most joy was the rediscovery, among the placards and tear gas, of a sense of common purpose, shared identity and communal pride. They will need to hold on to those values if the exponential growth of Cairo is not to do irreparable damage to people and environment alike.

ALTHOUGH A NEW RING ROAD has been built around Cairo, the wide, nineteenth-century boulevard that runs in a straight line between Giza and the city centre (the old Pyramids Road) is far more colourful, with its cafés, "papyrus institutes" (tourist bazaars), and twenty-four-hour traffic congestion. It presents a typical cross-section of Cairo life, from young men on mopeds talking into their iPhones to old widows swathed in black, balancing bags of food on their heads. Donkey-carts and horse-drawn caleches do battle with cars and lorries; the only rule of the road is to use your horn continuously. The Pyramids Road is a vivid illustration of what happens in a fast-growing city without rules, regulations or a functioning transport infrastructure—it is a chaotic free-for-all. Just before the end of its eight-mile run, as it prepares to disgorge its cacophonous contents into the heart of downtown Cairo, the road crosses an island in the Nile. Gezira (its very name means "island") has stood in midstream for thousands of years. Transformed over the last one hundred from a low-lying swamp into a fashionable district of designer boutiques and parks, Gezira occupies a ringside seat in the midst of Egypt's capital. From Gezira's leafy eastern shore, central Cairo can be observed at close quarters, yet at a safe distance, on the other side of the Nile. There are few better places to take the heartbeat of the city and chart its changing face. Few better places, either, in this country heavy with history, to experience Egypt's past, present and future so vividly and in such a small space. A walk along the Nile on Gezira Island offers the perfect summation of Egypt's riverine story.

Until the second half of the nineteenth century, Gezira was suitable neither for agriculture nor settlement. Prone to flooding and accessible only by boat, it was a neglected if picturesque spot on the western edge of Egypt's rapidly expanding capital. Muhammad Ali built a garrison and a harem on the island (he evidently liked his troops and his women to be within easy reach but safely secluded); and in 1863 his grandson Ismail began construction of a new palace on Gezira, to add to his thirty other royal residences. It was conveniently situated on the eastern shore of the island, directly opposite the landing-stages of Bulaq where boats destined for Upper Egypt moored to take passengers and cargo on board. (Amelia Edwards dismissed Bulaq as "a desolate place by the river, where some two or three hundred Nile-boats lay moored for hire."[17]) Inspired by the architecture of the Alhambra in Spain, the Gezira Palace was designed by a German and completed by a Frenchman, exemplifying the prominent role played by Europeans and European taste in the nineteenth-century development of Cairo. Indeed, the first guests at Ismail's island retreat were not Egyptian but European royalty: the Prince and Princess of Wales (the future King Edward VII and Queen Alexandra) stayed there in the spring of 1869, followed a few months later by an even more illustrious royal, Empress Eugenie of France (wife of Napoleon III). The reason for her visit was the official opening that summer of Ismail's greatest project, the Suez Canal—which, not coincidentally, had been designed by the Empress's cousin, Ferdinand de Lesseps. Eugenie had been invited by Ismail as the guest of honour, and she graced the Gezira Palace with a four-day stay before all the assembled dignitaries decamped to Ismailiya for the opening ceremonies.

After so grand a birth, the subsequent history of the Gezira Palace was decidedly chequered. At first, the Egyptian royal court used it as a summer palace, the cooling breeze off the Nile offering a welcome respite from the stifling heat of the city. Ismail had the banks of the island reinforced to prevent flooding, and commissioned the head gardener of Paris to lay out a grand park around the palace where he and other members of the royal family could saunter at their leisure. Following Ismail's bankruptcy and abdication, the palace was transformed into a hotel, before being sold as a private residence in the slump that accompanied the aftermath of World War I. Under General Nasser's socialist regime, the building was confiscated by the state and finally relaunched as a hotel, the Cairo Marriott, in 1983. (A plaque—in English—records its reopening by Hosni Mubarak, in the presence of the Egyptian prime minister.) One building thus perfectly embodies the defining trends of nineteenth- and twentieth-century Egyptian history.

Today, the Marriott is a magnet for wealthy Cairenes as much as for European visitors. The elite of the Egyptian capital flock to the hotel's Garden Promenade Café to take lunch on the sunny terrace, under the gilded ironwork arcades (prefabricated in Dresden, shipped to Cairo and assembled on site by German workers). On a typical day, a late-middle-aged businessman of ample girth sits smoking a fat Cohiba. Younger aspiring plutocrats in designer suits talk loudly on their mobile phones. Once-glamorous women of a certain age with flowing hair (there are no headscarfs on show here, let alone hijabs), brightly painted nails, heavy gold jewellery and large sunglasses try not to show how much they are keen to be noticed. A spoiled rich kid in shades, with a medallion dangling at his chest, tilts back his chair, bored by the conversation at his table. If the Marriott's Egyptian clients harbour worries about the future, they don't show it. For some, it seems, Gezira is still a bastion of wealth and privilege.

Beyond the hotel grounds, the neighbourhood of Zamalek occupies the northern tip of Gezira. Scarred by the ugly concrete flyover of the 26 July Bridge, it nonetheless preserves an air of gentility rare in this heaving city. Zamalek is the place where expats congregate, where Egyptian women can still wear Western fashion in public without fear of abuse or attack, where the cars are more likely to be Porsche Cayennes than the old Peugeot 504s so characteristic of the rest of Cairo. It also seems to be the only city district where butcher's shops display their meat inside the shop window, rather than hanging outside in the open air.

Opposite Zamalek, on the other side of the Nile, the buildings strung out along the corniche signal Cairo's status as a capital city. First there is the Foreign Ministry building, an impressive and elegant skyscraper combining Western and Islamic architectural forms. Despite the parlous state of the Egyptian economy, the Foreign Ministry is beautifully maintained: testament, no doubt, to the billions of dollars of U.S. aid that have propped up successive Egyptian governments as a peace dividend from the Camp David agreement. Less fortunate is the nearby Ramses Hilton, once one of Cairo's smartest hotels, which now looks tired, dejected and down-at-heel. Foreign investment in Egypt has dwindled following the 2011 revolution, and the future for luxury tourism, in this part of the country at least, does not look rosy. Even more battered than the Hilton is the television station, scene of fierce battles during the uprising against Mubarak. Somehow, it still functions, limping on like the rest of Egypt's creaking infrastructure. At least it was spared the fate of the towerblock housing the headquarters of Mubarak's National Democratic Party. Once the nerve centre of Egyptian politics, this has been reduced to a burned-out shell—gutted by fire in an act of rage against thirty years of kleptocratic despotism.

Cowering at the foot of the blackened building, hemmed in between the busy flyovers of the 6 October Bridge and the building site of the erstwhile Nile Hilton (a concrete skeleton swathed in dirty sheets, awaiting rebirth as the Nile Ritz-Carlton), sits one of Cairo's most iconic buildings. With its glazed dome and distinctive terracotta paintwork, the Egyptian Museum is one of Egypt's most visited attractions. It is the greatest repository of ancient artefacts on earth, situated in one of the world's most vulnerable locations. The Egyptian Museum is the place, above all, where Egypt's past, present and future collide most spectacularly.

It was the French who first encouraged Egypt to look after its antiquities. In 1834, in the aftermath of the Napoleonic expedition and the subsequent publication of the *Description de l'Egypte*, none other than the great Jean-François Champollion persuaded the Egyptian ruler to found a conservation department and establish a national collection. Unfortunately, Muhammad Ali used the collection as a convenient repository from which to take gifts for visiting (European) dignitaries, and he eventually presented the whole lot to Archduke Maximilian of Austria in 1855. Three years later, at the urging of Napoleon III, another Frenchman by the name of Auguste Mariette was created Egypt's first Director of Antiquities; with an extraordinary energy, he set about excavating, conserving and curating Egypt's patrimony. In 1863, Mariette oversaw the building of a museum in Bulaq (opposite the Gezira Palace) to display recently discovered objects. Bringing Egyptian antiquities to wider public attention was not without risks, however, and in 1867 the Empress Eugenie requested the cream of the collection for herself. To his eternal credit, Mariette refused, devotion to science trumping patriotism to France. The collection grew steadily, outgrowing the Bulaq museum and moving to Giza in 1891.

By the end of the nineteenth century, it had become clear that Egypt needed a purpose-built national museum in the heart of the capital city with enough space to display the many thousands of objects being dug from the sands of time. An international competition was launched, and the winner was yet another Frenchman, Marcel Durgnon (who died before even the foundation stone could be laid). His design was for a grand, neo-classical, sandstone building in the best tradition of European national museums. It opened its doors in 1902 and has been one of Cairo's most recognisable landmarks ever since.

The task of arranging objects in the new museum and publishing its immense Catalogue Générale fell to Mariette's successor as Director of Antiquities, Gaston Maspero. He collected together many of the brightest minds of the day to embark on one of archaeology's greatest-ever feats of scholarship. The Catalogue Générale, or CG, remains to this day the best record of the artefacts in the Egyptian Museum: the hundred thousand on display as well as the equal number in storage in the basement. While Egyptologists have cause to remember Maspero, the museum itself pays homage to its founding genius, Mariette: in the garden to the front of the museum stands Mariette's tomb, a stone sarcophagus of pharaonic proportions together with a statue and the inscription "L'Egypte Reconnaissante"—"a grateful Egypt."

But the gratitude has suffered of late. Post-Mubarak Egypt is too preoccupied with its present and future to worry about its past. Since February 2011, the guards and tourist police have vanished from the museum's galleries, and there is only token security at the entrance and exit. Upstairs among the treasures of Tutankhamun, cases stand empty, their priceless contents stolen at the height of the revolution. Only half the lights are working, and the glass in the dome is black from decades of traffic fumes. Through open windows and broken windows, sunlight streams down on to fragile, 2,500-year-old wooden objects, stored in ninety-year-old glass cases with no temperature or humidity controls. Each case holds a king's ransom, yet is secured by nothing more than a small padlock and a piece of wire with a wax seal. The conditions in which Egypt's treasures are being stored is both sad and alarming. But Egyptians have other concerns on their mind: the back wall of the museum is covered in graffiti, angrily (and offensively) denouncing Mohamed Morsi.

Back on Gezira Island, the revolutionary fervour seems far away. Under the 6 October Bridge, minibus drivers and private chauffeurs wash and polish their vehicles while their clients are out to lunch. A well-tended public park with clipped hedges and a couple of neat band-stands recalls the British colonial presence; no doubt the band of the Royal Marines used to play popular tunes here on Sunday afternoons. The park, Cairo's answer to the Victoria Embankment, even has its equivalent of Cleopatra's Needle, a granite obelisk of Ramesses II. It is odd that a pharaonic monument should look so out of place on the banks of the Nile. Most incongruous of all, even during the rule of the Muslim Brotherhood, the Blue Nile floating restaurant—with dodgem cars in its forecourt—sported a banner over the entrance announcing its forthcoming New Year's Eve party on a "mind-blowing Moulin Rouge theme." Next to the Blue Nile, behind iron gates, is the last survivor of British rule, the Gezira Club. With its polo ground and croquet lawns, it was the hub of expatriate life in the early twentieth century. It remains a haven of tranquillity and civility in downtown Cairo. But as I approach to take a closer look, the custodian firmly and rather pointedly shuts the gates in my face. Social exclusivity in Cairo now has an indigenous character.

The expulsion of the British in 1952—commemorated by the Cairo Tower on Gezira—and the subsequent nationalisation of foreign inter-ests marked the end of the era of European influence on Egypt. It also marked the end of the Egyptian monarchy, in a tale as sorry as any from the annals of pharaonic history. The last man to wear the crown of Egypt, King Farouk, was a frequent visitor to Gezira. The southern tip of the island was a favourite spot for tea-parties on the royal yacht *Kassed Kheir*, or at the ornamental royal rest-house nearby—when the king was not partying at the Semiramis Hotel across the river. Farouk was born in 1920 at Cairo's Abdin Palace into a dynasty founded by his great-

great-grandfather Muhammad Ali, an Albanian volunteer in the Ottoman army. (Egypt's last dynasty of kings was, like many of its ancient forebears, foreign in origin.) Sadly for Farouk and for Egypt, his abilities did not match up to the expectations for his future. Despite a costly education by private tutors, he failed to gain entry to Eton because he had not studied Latin, and he also failed the entrance exam for the Royal Military Academy at Woolwich. Having spent his childhood largely surrounded by his mother and her ladies-in-waiting, his four sisters and their English nanny, Farouk was uncomfortable in men's company and entirely unprepared for the burdens of high office. Yet, at the age of sixteen, following the sudden death of his father, Farouk found himself king.

He was forced to rely, to an unhealthy extent, on the guidance of Sir Miles Lampson, British High Commissioner (and susbequently ambassador) to Egypt. There was no doubt that Lampson called the shots, a fact that irritated and eventually poisoned the king against the British. Though Farouk was popular with ordinary Egyptians—the rector of al-Azhar called him "the first King of Egypt who has direct contact with the people"[18]—he was sidelined by his own ministers and belittled by Lampson, who continued to call him "the boy." As one of the king's biographers commented, "He was surrounded with all the appearances of absolute monarchy; he was given the deference one gave to a god. Yet he knew his power to be a fiction and the devotion of his entourage to be largely a form of theatre."[19]

Throughout World War II, Farouk was forced to do the British bidding—from dismissing a government because of its alleged pro-Axis sympathies, to accepting the stationing of over a million British soldiers in Egypt, the manning of thirty airfields and landing strips around Cairo by the RAF and the harbouring of a vast armada of British warships in Egypt's ports. The Egyptian capital was a vital communications link between Britain, India and the Far East. In February 1942, with Rommel advancing through North Africa, Lampson ordered six hundred British troops, tanks and armoured cars to surround Farouk's palace, before arriving in a Rolls-Royce and presenting the king with a stark choice: recall to power the pro-Allied Wafd party or abdicate. Farouk had little option but to comply. Humiliated and disgraced in the eyes of his own people, he abandoned all efforts to rule (though not to frustrate

British interests) and fell into a lifestyle of escapism and debauchery. He made nightly visits to Cairo's casinos, dressed in his field marshal's uniform, and his 1948 divorce from the popular Queen Farida eroded any remaining sympathy amongst the Egyptian public.

Thereafter, political tensions between pro- and anti-British parties rocked Egypt, culminating in riots in the streets of Cairo on 27 January 1952 ("black Saturday"), just eleven days after the birth of Farouk's son and heir. To regain control, the king attempted to tighten his grip over the army, but this merely provoked a mutiny among junior officers on 23 July. The leader of the Free Officers' Movement, Gamal Abdel Nasser, called for Farouk to abdicate. This time, there was no exit clause. Indeed, Farouk seems to have welcomed his fate; he is reported to have told the officers, "You have done what I always intended to do myself."[20] On 26 July 1952, at six o'clock in the evening, King Farouk boarded his royal yacht and sailed down the Nile, bound for exile. His possessions were confiscated and auctioned off by the military government (a special room at Sotheby's was set aside for Farouk's large collection of pornography), and his second wife was granted an annulment. Alone, obese and a figure of ridicule, Farouk choked to death in a Rome restaurant on 18 March 1965 at the age of forty-four. His remains were eventually laid to rest in Cairo's al-Rifai mosque, the ancestral burial-place of Muhammad Ali's dynasty.

"Torn between East and West, old and new, the mosque and the nightclub,"[21] King Farouk embodied the tensions that beset his country at large during the second half of the twentieth century. The coup of 1952 that toppled him did not resolve these tensions, but merely added a new element of dictatorship, leaving the Egyptian people increasingly cynical about their rulers. To Egypt's—and the world's—surprise, that cynicism and long-suppressed frustration boiled over on 25 January 2011, unleashing a popular revolution that toppled Mubarak and set the seal on the Arab Spring.

The epicentre of the uprising was Tahrir Square, a massive open space in front of the Egyptian Museum, which links directly with Gezira via the Qasr el-Nil Bridge (a venerable structure built in 1872 to connect the island to the rest of the city). Tahrir Square is today the political heart of Cairo, and a historically resonant location in more ways than one. Previously known as Khedive Ismail Square, it was first developed by the viceroy of Egypt, Said Pasha, in the 1850s as the site of a royal palace, the Qasr el-Nil ("fortress of the Nile"). Said's successor Ismail improved the area further by cutting the Ismailiya Canal which entered the Nile just north of the palace. (The mouth of the canal was plugged in 1912 and an Anglican cathedral built; this in turn was demolished in 1976 to make way for the 6 October Bridge.) Between the palace and the river, a large set of barracks housed British troops during the occupation of Egypt, which was razed to the ground when the British left. (One of the onlookers who went to the square to witness the lowering of the British flag was Umm Sety.) Following the 1952 coup, Khedive Ismail Square was renamed Tahrir ("Liberation") Square, and the corniche, once the preserve of a few British officials and titled Egyptians, was opened up to the masses, giving back to the Egyptian people access to their river.

But the euphoria of liberation did not last long. The site of the barracks on the west side of the square was developed as a hotel (the former Nile Hilton), the first of a new generation of international establishments intended for use by Western tourists and wealthy Cairenes. In the 1990s, the hotel ballroom was a popular venue for Egyptian wedding parties, while the ground-floor bar was a noted gay pickup joint. On the south side of Tahrir Square, an equally prominent building attracted even more resentment, tinged with fear. The giant, Soviet-style edifice known as the Mugamma contained various government departments including the hated Ministry of the Interior. Here Egyptians (and foreign visitors) had to queue for hours to have their identities checked, papers stamped and all the other casual indignities that a dictatorship obsessed with bureaucracy and control heaps upon its citizens.

Bounded by government buildings redolent of corruption and cronyism, advertising hoardings promising inaccessible luxuries, a hotel for the wealthy and the stately Egyptian Museum as a reminder of the country's glorious past, it is little wonder that Tahrir Square became the focus of dissent against the Mubarak regime. For eleven days in late January and early February 2011, the huge granite, marble and sandstone monument in the centre of the square—originally the pedestal for a statue of Khedive Ismail—became a platform for protestors, a focal point for their revolution. Battles with Mubarak's hired thugs were fought in the square itself and in the surrounding streets. Some of the fiercest clashes took place on the Qasr el-Nil Bridge, which runs into the south side of the square from Gezira Island. Here, in 1970, millions of Egyptians had gathered to watch Nasser's funeral cortège cross the Nile into central Cairo. Now, their children and grandchildren were fighting on the very same bridge to overthrow the power of the generals.

Eighteen months after the Arab Spring, Tahrir Square is still occupied by demonstrators, although their numbers have dwindled. A calm of sorts has returned to the Qasr el-Nil Bridge. There is very little activity on the river below, except for a solitary police-boat, patrolling this notorious flashpoint at a particularly anxious time for Egypt. Groups of lads with trendy hairstyles sit on the parapet, while burkha-clad women walk by. Caleche-drivers rest their horses, fruit-sellers set up their stalls and a teenager takes a photo of his friend next to one of the great bronze lions that guard the bridge. Their stone pedestals are covered in political graffiti, unthinkable two years earlier. Egyptians, especially in Cairo, have discovered free expression with a vengeance, and every wall and hoarding is covered with political slogans. Those in Arabic are short and to the point—"It's your constitution, not ours" and "Morsi is a murderer" compete with "God is great"—but one, in English, reflects the high-minded ideals behind the revolution—"You will not kill our idea."

SO OUR JOURNEY down the Nile comes to an end, on this island in the river's stream. To our right, westwards, lie the Pyramids and Sphinx, emblems of Egypt's glorious past. To our left, eastwards, sprawls Tahrir Square, cradle of a revolution that has ushered in a chaotic present and an uncertain future. And next to us is the one constant, the eternal friend upon which every generation of Egyptians can depend, the Nile.

Postscript

In July 2013, the escalating confrontation between Mohamed Morsi's government and its opponents, and the long-running (eighty-five-year) struggle for national dominance between the Muslim Brotherhood and the military, culminated in Egypt's first democratically elected president being forcibly removed from office by the army. The generals retook the reins of power, reversing many of the gains of the Arab Spring. The schism between the religious and secular visions of Egypt's future is profound and will not easily be bridged. The country is more divided than at any time in its recent history. Its immediate future looks bleak, its ultimate destiny deeply uncertain.

Amid the chaos and confusion, the dependability of the Nile will be a vital reassurance for the Egyptian people as they navigate turbulent and uncharted waters; and we can be certain that Egypt's eternal river will continue to witness many more momentous events that will reverberate throughout the Nile Valley, the Middle East and the wider world.

Timeline

DATE	PERIOD	RULER	PEOPLE & EVENTS
700,000–10,000 BC	Lower/Middle/Upper Palaeolithic		Earliest humans in the Nile Valley
10,000–5000 BC	Late Palaeolithic		Fishermen of el-Hosh Formation of Birket Qarun, c. 7000 BC
5000–2950 BC	Predynastic Period		Earliest agriculture, Fayum, c. 5000 BC Badarian culture, fifth millennium BC
2950–2575 BC	Early Dynastic Period	Khasekhemwy	
2575–2125 BC	Old Kingdom	Khufu	Construction of Great Pyramid, 2545 BC
2125–2010 BC	First Intermediate Period	Intef II	Civil war Heqanakht
2010–1630 BC	Middle Kingdom		
1630–1539 BC	Second Intermediate Period		
1539–1069 BC	New Kingdom		Foundation of Luxor Temple, 1539 BC

DATE	PERIOD	RULER	PEOPLE & EVENTS
1539–1069 BC	Eighteenth Dynasty	Hatshepsut Amenhotep III Akhenaten	Senenmut Foundation of Akhetaten, 1349 BC
	Nineteenth Dynasty	Seti I	
	Twentieth Dynasty	Ramesses III	Strikes in Thebes, 1157 BC Tomb robberies begin at Thebes, 1114 BC
1069–664 BC	Third Intermediate Period		Jews resident on Elephantine, eighth to fourth centuries BC
664–332 BC	Late Period		Princess Nitiqret travels to Karnak, 656 BC Persian conquest of Egypt, 525 BC Herodotus visits Egypt, fifth century BC
332–309 BC	Macedonian Dynasty	Alexander	
309–30 BC	Ptolemaic Period		Foundation of Karanis, c. 270 BC Construction of Edfu Temple, 237–70 BC Egypt's last native pharaoh is defeated, 186 BC
30 BC–AD 395	Roman Period	Augustus	Colossi of Memnon "sing," 27 BC–AD 202 Strabo visits Egypt, 25–24 BC
		Hadrian	Hadrian's visit to Egypt, AD 130 Birth of St. Antony, AD 251

DATE	PERIOD	RULER	PEOPLE & EVENTS
30 BC– AD 395	Roman Period	Diocletian	Diocletian visits Luxor, AD 298 Gnostic Gospels written, fourth century AD
		Theodosius	Egypt forcibly Christianised, AD 379 Closure of Egypt's temples, AD 392 Last hieroglyphic inscription carved, AD 394
AD 395– 639	Byzantine Rule		Arab invasion of Egypt, 639
AD 639– 969	Islamic governors		Arab conquest of Egypt completed, 641
AD 969– 1171	Fatimid Dynasty (caliphs)		al-Muqaddasi visits Egypt, c. 1000 Naser-e Khosraw visits Cairo, eleventh century
		Saladin	Crusader invasion of Egypt, 1117
AD 1171– 1250	Ayyubid Dynasty (sultans)		Death of al-Qenawi, Qena, 1196
			Death of Abu el-Haggag, Luxor, 1243
AD 1250– 1517	Mamluk Dynasty (sultans)		
AD 1517– 1914	Ottoman Rule		An anonymous Venetian visits Luxor, 1589 Richard Pococke travels up the Nile, 1737–8 Napoleonic expedition to Egypt, 1798

DATE	PERIOD	RULER	PEOPLE & EVENTS
AD 1517–1914	Ottoman Rule	Muhammad Ali	Belzoni visits Egypt, 1815–19 Champollion deciphers hieroglyphics, 1822 Luxor obelisk taken to Paris, 1831 Edward Lane visits Egypt, 1834 David Roberts visits Egypt, 1838
		Ismail	Lucie Duff Gordon lives at Luxor, 1862–9 Opening of the Suez Canal, 1869 Thomas Cook's first Nile tour, 1870 Amelia Edwards visits Egypt, 1873–4 Opening of first hotel in Luxor, 1877
		Abbas Hilmi II	Petrie's first excavation in Egypt, 1893 Construction of Aswan Dam, 1899–1902 Opening of the Cataract Hotel, Aswan, 1900 Opening of the Egyptian Museum, Cairo, 1902 Completion of Esna Barrage, 1906 Opening of the Winter Palace, Luxor, 1907
AD 1914–1922	British Protectorate		

DATE	PERIOD	RULER	PEOPLE & EVENTS
AD 1922–1952	Independent Kingdom	Fuad I	Discovery of Tutankhamun's tomb, 1922
		Farouk	
AD 1952–2011	Republic (military rule)	Gamal Nasser	Burial of Aga Khan at Aswan, 1959 Completion of Aswan High Dam, 1971
		Anwar Sadat	Temples of Philae reopened on new site, 1980
		Hosni Mubarak	Arab Spring, 2011
AD 2011–2013	Republic (elected government)	Mohamed Morsi	Death of Pope Shenouda III, 2012
AD 2013–	Republic (transitional government)		

Notes

PREFACE

1. LUCIE DUFF GORDON, *Letters from Egypt*, VIRAGO, LONDON, 1997 (FIRST PUBLISHED IN 1865), pp. 67–8.

2. Herodotus (tr. A. D. Godley), *The Persian Wars*, Books 1–2, Harvard University Press, Cambridge MA and London, 1926, Book II:5; a more accurate translation of the Greek is "Egypt . . . is land acquired by the Egyptians, given them by the river."

3. Amelia Edwards, *A Thousand Miles up the Nile*, Century, London, 1982 (first published in 1877), pp. 360–1.

4. MS, personal communication, December 2012.

ONE The Nile

1. Samuel Cox, quoted in Deborah Manley and Sahar Abdel-Hakim (eds), *Traveling Through Egypt from 450 BC to the Twentieth Century*, The American University in Cairo Press, Cairo and New York, 2004, p. 9.

2. Strabo (tr. Horace Leonard Jones), *Geography*, Book 17, Harvard University Press, Cambridge MA and London, 1949, 1.4.

3. Edwards, *A Thousand Miles*, p. 92.

4. Ibid., p. 167.

5. al-Muqaddasi (tr. B. A. Collins), *The Best Divisions for Knowledge of the Regions*, Garnet Publishing, Reading, 1994, p. 177 (Arabic text p. 193).

6. Richard Madden, *Travels in Turkey, Egypt, Nubia and Palestine*, Henry Colburn, London, 1892, vol. 1, p. 387.

7. Strabo, *Geography*, 1.4.

8. Abd al-Latif al-Baghdadi (tr. K.H. Zand, J. A. and I. E. Videan), *The Eastern Key: Kitab al-Ifada wa'l-I'tibar*, George Allen & Unwin, London, 1964, p. 23 (Arabic text p. 5, left).

9. Pliny (tr. H. Rackham), *Natural History*, Book 5, Harvard University Press/Heinemann, Cambridge MA/London, 1961, p. 58.

10. Giovanni Belzoni, quoted in Brian Fagan, *The Rape of the Nile: Tomb Robbers, Tourists, and Archaeologists in Egypt*, Charles Scribner's Sons, New York, 1975, p. 204.

11. Edward Lane, *An Account of the Manners and Customs of the Modern Egyptians*

(Written in Egypt During the Years 1833–1835), Darf, London, 1986 (first published in 1836), p. 342.

12. John Mason Cook, quoted in Manley and Abdel-Hakim, *Traveling Through Egypt*, p. 107.

13. A. H. Sayce, *Reminiscences*, Macmillan, London, 1923, p. 178.

14. Tomb inscription of Ineni, Thebes (author's own translation).

15. Stela of Merka from Saqqara (author's own translation).

16. Causeway of Unas, Saqqara (author's own translation).

17. Edwards, *A Thousand Miles*, p. 91.

18. Ibid., p. xi.

19. Ibid., p. 37.

20. Ibid., preface to the 1st edition.

21. Thomas Cook & Son, *Programme of Cook's International Tickets to Egypt, Season 1887–88*, Thomas Cook & Son, London, 1887, p. 3. (The full, gloriously Victorian title of this illuminating little publication is *Programme of Cook's International Tickets to Egypt including The Nile to the Second Cataract, Philae, Luxor, Thebes, Assouan, Aboo Simbel, &c., &c. Also particulars of arrangements for Steamers and Dahabeahs. With maps and plans of steamers. Under the special and exclusive contracts and arrangements of Thos. Cook & Son, sole owners of the only First Class Tourist Steamers specially built for the Nile [Price Sixpence, Post Free]*.)

22. Ibid., p. 4.

23. Ibid., p. 4.

24. Ibid., p. 4.

25. Ibid., p. 4.

26. Ibid., p. 8.

27. Ibid., p. 9.

28. Ibid., p. 13.

29. Edwards, *A Thousand Miles*, p. 83.

30. Ibid., p. 90.

31. Ibid., p. 36.

32. Sayce, *Reminiscences*, p. 175.

33. Ibid., p. 176.

34. Ibid., p. 232.

35. Ibid., p. 235.

36. Ibid., p. 229.

37. Ibid., p. 278.

38. Ibid., p. 289.

39. Ibid., p. 338.

40. Thomas Cook & Son, *Programme*, p. 4.

TWO   Aswan

1. Herodotus, *The Persian Wars*, Book II:28.

2. *Great Hymn to the Aten*, Amarna (author's own translation).

3. John Hanning Speke, quoted in Christopher Ondaatje, "Search for the Source of the Nile," in Robin Hanbury-Tenison (ed.), *The Seventy Great Journeys in History*, Thames & Hudson, London, 2006, pp. 196–7.

4. Herodotus, *The Persian Wars*, Book II:28.

5. Isambard Kingdom Brunel, quoted in Isambard Brunel, *The Life of Isambard Kingdom Brunel, Civil Engineer*, Nonsuch Publishing, Stroud, 2006 (first published in 1870), p. 378.

6. Ibid., p. 378.

7. Edwards, *A Thousand Miles*, p. 194.

8. Ibid., p. 392.

9. Ibid., p. 184.

10. MS, personal communication, September 2010.

11. Tomb inscription of Harkhuf, Aswan (author's own translation).

12. William Willcocks, *Sixty Years in the East*, William Blackwood & Sons, Edinburgh and London, 1935, p. 144.

13. Ibid., p. 155.

14. Sayce, *Reminiscences*, p. 290.

15. Winston Churchill, quoted in N.A.F. Smith, *The Centenary of the Aswan Dam 1902–2002*, Thomas Telford Publishing/The Institution of Civil Engineers, London, 2002, p. 54.

16. Lord Cromer, quoted in Smith, *Centenary*, p. 34.

17. Sayce, *Reminiscences*, p. 291.

18. Ibid., p. 338.

19. Ibid., p. 292.

20. MS, personal communication, September 2010.

21. Madden, *Travels*, vol. 2, pp. 115–16.

22. Ancient inscription, quoted in Fagan, *The Rape of the Nile*, p. 31.

23. I. Philae II 201, published in Jitse Dijkstra, *Philae and the End of Ancient Egyptian Religion*, Peeters, Leuven, Paris and Dudley, 2008, p. 339.

24. Edwards, *A Thousand Miles*, p. 207.

25. William Garstin, quoted in Osman Rostem, *The Salvage of Philae*, Institut Français d'Archéologie Orientale, Cairo, 1955, p. 5.

26. William Willcocks, quoted in Rostem, *Philae*, p. 14.

27. William Matthew Flinders Petrie, *Seventy Years in Archaeology*, Sampson Low, Marston & Co., London, 1931, p. 154.

28. Rose Macaulay, *Pleasure of Ruins*, Thames & Hudson, London, 1966 (first published in 1953), p. 328.

29. Rostem, *Philae*, pp. 12–13.

30. Ibid., p. 14.

31. Agatha Christie, *Death on the Nile*, HarperCollins, London, 2001 (first published in 1937), pp. 52–3.

32. W. E. Kingsford, *Assouan as a Health Resort*, Simpkin, Marshall, Hamilton, Kent & Co., London, 1899, p. 46.

33. Sadruddin Aga Khan, quoted in Anne Edwards, *Throne of Gold: The Lives of the Aga Khans*, HarperCollins, London, 1995, p. 222.

THREE The Deep South

1. Winifred Blackman, *The Fellahin of Upper Egypt*, The American University in Cairo Press, Cairo, 2000 (first published in 1927), p. 280.

2. *Admonitions of Ipuwer*: 2,12 (tr. Miriam Lichtheim, *Ancient Egyptian Literature*, vol. 2, University of California Press, Berkeley, 1976, p. 151).

3. *Dispute of a Man with His Ba*: 79 (tr. Lichtheim, *Literature*, p. 165).

4. Sayce, *Reminiscences*, p. 240.

5. Ibid.

6. Edwards, *A Thousand Miles*, p. 190.

7. Ibid., pp. 406–7.

8. Ibid., p. 125.

9. Ibid., p. 159.

10. Ibid., p. 162.

11. Stela of Qedes from Gebelein (author's own translation).

12. Ibid.

13. MS, personal communication, September 2010.

FOUR Luxor

1. Edwards, *A Thousand Miles*, p. 148.

2. Ibid., p. 134.

3. Ibid., p. 135.

4. Dominique Vivant Denon (ed. Bernard Bailly), *Les Monuments de la Haute Egypte*, Comité Vivant Denon, Université pour Tous de Bourgogne, Chalon-sur-Saône, 2003 (first written down in the late eighteenth/early nineteenth century), p. 20 (author's own translation).

5. Ibid., p. 58 (author's own translation).

6. Jean Baptiste Apollinaire Lebas, *L'obélisque de Luxor. Histoire de sa translation à Paris*, Carilian-Goeury et Vr Dalmont, Paris, 1839, p. 11 (author's own translation).

7. Jean-François Champollion, quoted in Lebas, *L'obélisque*, p. 13 (author's own translation).

8. Baron d'Haussez, writing to Charles X of France on 25 November 1829, quoted in Lebas, *L'obélisque*, p. 15 (author's own translation).

9. Lebas, *L'obélisque*, p. 18 (author's own translation).

10. Ibid., p. 20 (author's own translation).

11. Ibid., p. 69 (author's own translation).

12. Ibid., p. 161 (author's own translation).

13. Edwards, *A Thousand Miles*, p. 139.

14. Ibid., p. 139.

15. Ibid., p. 141.

16. Stela of Amenhotep III from Kom el-Hetan (author's own translation).

17. Stela of Suti and Hor (author's own translation).

18. Statue of Amenhotep III from Luxor Temple (author's own translation).

19. David Roberts (memoir, 8), quoted in Krystyna Matyjaszkiewicz, "Roberts, David (1796–1864)," *Oxford Dictionary of National Biography*, vol. 47, Oxford University Press, Oxford, 2004, p. 146.

20. David Roberts (last will and testament), quoted in Matyjaszkiewicz, "Roberts," p. 149.

21. David Roberts (record book 1.108), quoted in Matyjaszkiewicz, "Roberts," p. 148.

22. David Roberts, quoted in Helen Guiterman, *David Roberts R.A. 1796–1864*, private publication, London, 1978, p. 8.

23. David Roberts, quoted in Guiterman, *David Roberts*, p. 9.

24. David Roberts, quoted in Guiterman, *David Roberts*, p. 10.

25. David Roberts, quoted in Guiterman, *David Roberts*, p. 8.

26. David Roberts (eastern journal, 28 January 1839), quoted in Matyjaszkiewicz, "Roberts," p. 148.

27. W. E. Nickolls Dunn and George Vigers Worthington, *Luxor as a Health Resort*, H. K. Lewis, London, 1914, p. 9.

28. Sayce, *Reminiscences*, p. 211.

29. Lucie Duff Gordon, *Letters*, p. xiii.

30. Ibid., p. 36.

31. Ibid., p. xi.
32. Ibid., p. 102.
33. Ibid., p. 144.
34. Edwards, *A Thousand Miles*, p. 454.
35. Ibid., p. 454.
36. Ibid., p. 455.
37. Ibid., p. 455.
38. Ibid., pp. 456–7.
39. Pierre Loti, *Egypt*, T. Werner Laurie, London, 1910, p. 180.
40. Nickolls Dunn and Worthington, *Luxor*, p. 10.
41. Ibid., p. 10.
42. Ibid., p. 10.
43. Ibid., p. 10.
44. Ibid., p. 13.
45. Edwards, *A Thousand Miles*, p. 151.
46. Ibid., p. 148.
47. Ibid., p. 143 footnote.
48. Nitocris Adoption Stela, line 17 (author's own translation).
49. Ibid., line 16 (author's own translation).

FIVE Western Thebes

1. Ancient graffito, quoted in Nicholas Reeves and Richard Wilkinson, *The Complete Valley of the Kings: Tombs and Treasures of Egypt's Greatest Pharaohs*, Thames & Hudson, London, 1996, p. 50.
2. Statue inscription of Senenmut from Thebes (author's own translation).
3. Turin Strike Papyrus: recto 2, lines 15–17 (author's own translation).
4. Giovanni Belzoni, quoted in Brian Fagan, *The Rape of the Nile*, p. 161.
5. Ancient graffito, quoted in André and Étienne Bernand, *Les inscriptions grecques et latines du colosse de Memnon*, Institut Français d'Archéologie Orientale, Cairo, 1960, p. 33.
6. Ancient graffito, quoted in Bernand, *Les inscriptions*, p. 54.
7. Ancient graffito, quoted in Bernand, *Les inscriptions*, p. 37.
8. Ancient graffito, quoted in Bernand, *Les inscriptions*, p. 81.
9. Diodorus Siculus (tr. C. H. Oldfather), *The Library of History of Diodorus of Sicily*, Book I, Harvard University Press/Heinemann, Cambridge MA/London, 1968, 47.
10. Percy Bysshe Shelley, "Ozymandias of Egypt," in BBC, *The Nation's Favourite Poems*, BBC Worldwide, London, 1996, p. 58.
11. Ancient graffito, quoted in Reeves and Wilkinson, *Valley of the Kings*, p. 50.
12. Strabo, *Geography*, 1.46.
13. Ancient graffito, quoted in Reeves and Wilkinson, *Valley of the Kings*, p. 51.
14. Claude Sicard, quoted in Reeves and Wilkinson, *Valley of the Kings*, p. 52.
15. William Browne, quoted in Reeves and Wilkinson, *Valley of the Kings*, p. 53.
16. Vivant Denon, quoted in Reeves and Wilkinson, *Valley of the Kings*, p. 55.
17. Papyrus Amherst, p. 2, lines 3–7 (author's own translation).
18. Late Ramesside Letters, no. 28 (tr. Vivian Davies and Renée Friedman, *Egypt*, British Museum Press, London, 1998, p. 149).
19. Walter Scott, quoted in Stanley Mayes, *The Great Belzoni*, Putnam, London, 1959, p. 11.
20. Sadler's Wells playbill, quoted in Fagan, *The Rape of the Nile*, p. 101.
21. Giovanni Battista Belzoni, *Narrative of the Operations and Recent Discoveries*

within the Pyramids, Temples, Tombs, and Excavations, in Egypt and Nubia, 2nd edition, John Murray, London, 1821, p. 37.

22. Ibid., p. 39.

23. Giovanni Belzoni, quoted in Mayes, *Belzoni,* p. 210.

24. Charles Dickens, quoted in Mayes, *Belzoni,* p. 12.

25. Theodore Davis *et al., The Tombs of Harmhabi and Touatânkhamanou,* Constable & Co., London, 1912, p. 3.

SIX Qift and Qena

1. William Matthew Flinders Petrie, *Koptos,* Quaritch, London, 1896, p. 1.

2. John Wortham, *British Egyptology 1549–1906,* David & Charles, Newton Abbot, 1971, p. 79.

3. Petrie, *Seventy Years,* p. 19.

4. Ibid., p. 150.

5. Ibid., p. 150.

6. Ibid., p. 21.

7. Ibid., p. 155.

8. Petrie, *Koptos,* p. 1.

9. Petrie, *Seventy Years,* p. 148.

10. Petrie, *Koptos,* p. 2.

11. Petrie, *Seventy Years,* p. 151.

12. Musée des Beaux-Arts de Lyon, *Coptos. L'Egypte antique aux portes du désert,* Réunion des musées nationaux, Paris, 2000, p. 26.

13. Sharon Herbert and Andrea Berlin, "Excavations at Coptos (Qift) in Upper Egypt, 1987–1992," *Journal of Roman Archaeology,* Portsmouth RI, 2003, p. 14.

14. Petrie, *Koptos,* p. 7.

15. Ibid., plate IX (bottom).

16. Strabo, *Geography,* 1.46.

17. Petrie, *Seventy Years,* p. 151.

18. Hans Winkler, *Rock Carvings of Southern Upper Egypt,* vol. 1, Egypt Exploration Society, Oxford, 1938, p. 6.

19. Ivory label of Den (author's own translation).

20. Tomb inscription of Mahu, Amarna (author's own translation).

21. Sayce, *Reminiscences,* p. 235.

22. Ibid., p. 235.

23. Ibid., p. 236.

24. Jean-François Champollion, quoted in Fagan, *The Rape of the Nile,* p. 258.

25. A member of Champollion's expedition, quoted in Fagan, *The Rape of the Nile,* p. 259.

26. Edwards, *A Thousand Miles,* p. 124.

SEVEN Abydos

1. Dorothy Eady, quoted in Jonathan Cott (in collaboration with Hanny El Zeini), *The Search for Omm Sety: A Story of Eternal Love,* Rider, London, 1988, p. 174.

2. William Matthew Flinders Petrie, *Royal Tombs of the First Dynasty,* vol. I, Quaritch, London, 1900, p. 4.

3. Petrie, *Seventy Years,* pp. 172–3.

4. Ibid., p. 172.

5. "une bête puante"—Gaston Maspero, quoted in Petrie, *Seventy Years,* p. 173.

6. Petrie, *Royal Tombs*, p. 2.
7. Petrie, *Seventy Years*, p. 178.
8. Ibid., p. 185.
9. Canon H. D. and N. Rawnsley, *The Resurrection of Oldest Egypt*, Beaver Press, Laleham, 1904, pp. 8 and 15.
10. Stela of Ikhernofret (author's own translation).
11. *Gospel of Thomas*, quoted in Elaine Pagels, *The Gnostic Gospels*, Weidenfeld & Nicolson, London, 1980, p. xv.
12. *Secret Book of John*, quoted in Pagels, *Gospels*, p. xvi.
13. *Gospel of Philip*, quoted in Pagels, *Gospels*, p. xv.
14. *Thunder, Perfect Mind*, quoted in Pagels, *Gospels*, p. xvii.
15. Strabo, *Geography*, 1.42.
16. Dorothy Eady, quoted in Cott, *Omm Sety*, p. 61.
17. Dorothy Eady, quoted in Cott, *Omm Sety*, p. 174.

EIGHT Middle Egypt

1. Isambard Kingdom Brunel, quoted in Brunel, *The Life*, p. 378.
2. Edwards, *A Thousand Miles*, p. 97.
3. Béatrix Midant-Reynes (tr. Ian Shaw), *The Prehistory of Egypt: From the First Egyptians to the First Pharaohs*, Blackwell, Oxford, 2000, p. 152.
4. Boundary stela of Akhenaten, Amarna (author's own translation).
5. *Great Hymn to the Aten*, Amarna (author's own translation).
6. Ibid. (author's own translation).
7. Tomb inscription of Petosiris, Tuna el-Gebel (tr. Miriam Lichtheim, *Ancient Egyptian Literature*, vol. 3, University of California Press, Berkeley, 1980, p. 46).
8. Ibid.
9. Aurelius Victor, quoted in Anthony Birley, *Hadrian: The Restless Emperor*, Routledge, London and New York, 1997, p. 248.
10. Birley, *Hadrian*, p. 3.
11. Hadrian, quoted in Birley, *Hadrian*, p. 256.
12. Inscription on the Pincio obelisk, Rome, quoted in Birley, *Hadrian*, p. 256.
13. Ibid., p. 255.
14. Hadrian, quoted in Royston Lambert, *Beloved and God; The Story of Hadrian and Antinous*, Weidenfeld & Nicolson, London, 1984, p. 142.
15. Clement of Alexandria, quoted in Lambert, *Beloved and God*, p. 7.
16. Saint Jerome, quoted in Lambert, *Beloved and God*, p. 7.

NINE The Fayum

1. Strabo, *Geography*, 1.35.
2. Ibid.
3. Willeke Wendrich and René Cappers, "Egypt's earliest granaries: evidence from the Fayum," *Egyptian Archaeology* 27 (2005), p. 12.
4. Ibid., p. 15.
5. Heqanakht papers (tr. Richard Parkinson, *Voices from Ancient Egypt: An Anthology of Middle Kingdom Writings*, University of Oklahoma Press, Norman OK, 1991, p. 103).
6. Ibid., p. 107.
7. Gertrude Caton-Thompson, *Mixed Memoirs*, The Paradigm Press, Gateshead, 1983, p. 56.

8. Ibid., p. 91.

9. Ibid., p. 110.

10. Papyrus UCL 32795 from Gurob, quoted in Ian Shaw, "Gurob: The key to unlocking a royal harem?," *Current World Archaeology* 23 (June/July 2007), p. 18.

11. Sel. Pap. II, 416, quoted in Alan Bowman, *Egypt after the Pharaohs*, Oxford University Press, Oxford, 1990, p. 172.

12. Flinders Petrie, quoted in Susan Walker and Morris Bierbrier, *Ancient Faces. Mummy Portraits from Roman Egypt*, British Museum Press, London, 1997, pp. 37–8.

TEN Cairo

1. al-Muqaddasi, *The Best Divisions*, p. 181 (Arabic text p. 197); the Arabic text refers to Fustat (Old Cairo), rather than the later city.

2. Edwards, *A Thousand Miles*, pp. 66–7.

3. al-Muqaddasi, *The Best Divisions*, p. 189 (Arabic text p. 206).

4. Ma'sudi, quoted in Stanley Lane-Poole, *A History of Egypt in the Middle Ages*, Frank Cass & Co., London, 1968, p. 86.

5. al-Muqaddasi, *The Best Divisions*, p. 181 (Arabic text p. 197).

6. Ibn Battuta (tr. H.A.R. Gibb), *The Travels of Ibn Battuta*, Cambridge University Press, Cambridge, 1958, p. 42.

7. Afaf Lutfi al-Sayyid Marsot, *A History of Egypt from the Arab Conquest to the Present*, 2nd edition, Cambridge University Press, Cambridge, 2007, p. 28.

8. Lane-Poole, *Egypt in the Middle Ages*, p. 216.

9. Naser-e Khosraw (tr. W. M. Thackston, Jr.), *Naser-e Khosraw's Book of Travels*, Bibliotheca Persia/The Persian Heritage Fund, New York, 1986, p. 41.

10. Lane, *Manners and Customs*, p. 496.

11. Ibid., p. 501.

12. Anonymous, quoted in Fagan, *The Rape of the Nile*, p. 122.

13. William Fitzmaurice, quoted in Manley and Abdel-Hakim, *Traveling Through Egypt*, p. 50.

14. J. Lewis-Farley, "Wintering in Egypt," *Belgravia: A London Magazine*, vol. 20, no. 77 (March 1873), p. 70.

15. Edwards, *A Thousand Miles*, p. 3.

16. Ibid., p. 1.

17. Edwards, *A Thousand Miles*, p. 11.

18. Sheikh al-Mangi, quoted in Philip Mansel, *Sultans in Splendour: The Last Years of the Ottoman World*, André Deutsch, London, 1988, p. 168.

19. Adel Sabit, *A King Betrayed: The Ill-Fated Reign of Farouk of Egypt*, Quartet Books, London and New York, 1989, pp. 6–7.

20. King Farouk, quoted in Mansel, *Sultans*, p. 179.

21. Mansel, *Sultans*, p. 173.

Further Reading

HISTORY OF EGYPT

Alston, Richard, *Soldier and Society in Roman Egypt*, Routledge, London and New York, 1995

Bowman, Alan, *Egypt After the Pharaohs*, Oxford University Press, Oxford, 1990

Cook, Steven, *The Struggle for Egypt from Nasser to Tahrir Square*, Oxford University Press, Oxford, 2012

Glickman, Mark, *Sacred Treasure: The Cairo Genizah*, Jewish Lights Publishing, Woodstcock VT, 2011

Mansel, Philip, *Sultans in Splendour: The Last Years of the Ottoman World*, André Deutsch, London, 1988 (Chapter 11, "The Fall of the Throne of Egypt")

Marsot, Afaf Lutfi al-Sayyid, *A History of Egypt from the Arab Conquest to the Present*, 2nd edition, Cambridge University Press, Cambridge, 2007

Wilkinson, Toby, *The Rise and Fall of Ancient Egypt: The History of a Civilisation from 3000 BC to Cleopatra*, Bloomsbury, London, 2010

HISTORICAL ACCOUNTS OF NILE TRAVEL

Duff Gordon, Lucie, *Letters from Egypt*, Virago, London, 1997

Edwards, Amelia, *A Thousand Miles up the Nile*, Century, London, 1982

Lane, Edward William, *An Account of the Manners and Customs of the Modern Egyptians (Written in Egypt During the Years 1833–1835)*, Darf, London, 1986

TRAVEL AND TRAVELLERS IN EGYPT

Fagan, Brian, *The Rape of the Nile: Tomb Robbers, Tourists, and Archaeologists in Egypt*, Charles Scribner's Sons, New York, 1975

Humphreys, Andrew, *Grand Hotels of Egypt in the Golden Age of Travel*, The American University in Cairo Press, Cairo and New York, 2011

Manley, Deborah and Sahar Abdel-Hakim (eds), *Traveling Through Egypt from 450 BC to the Twentieth Century*, The American University in Cairo Press, Cairo and New York, 2004

Reeves, Nicholas, *Ancient Egypt: The Great Discoveries*, Thames & Hudson, London, 2000

Sattin, Anthony, *The Pharaoh's Shadow: Travels in Ancient and Modern Egypt*, Victor Gollancz, London, 2000

INDIVIDUAL SITES

Gurob Harem Palace Project (www.gurob.org.uk)

Kemp, Barry, *The City of Akhenaten and Nefertiti: Amarna and Its People*, Thames & Hudson, London, 2012

O'Connor, David, *Abydos: Egypt's First Pharaohs and the Cult of Osiris*, Thames & Hudson, London, 2009

Reeves, Nicholas, and Richard Wilkinson, *The Complete Valley of the Kings: Tombs and Treasures of Egypt's Greatest Pharaohs*, Thames & Hudson, London, 1996

Soueif, Ahdaf, *Cairo: My City, Our Revolution*, Bloomsbury, London, 2012

Wendrich, Willeke, "Egypt's earliest granaries: evidence from the Fayum," *Egyptian Archaeology* 27 (2005), pp. 12–15

Acknowledgements

My list of thank-yous is short, but no less sincere: to my fellow travellers on the Nile, before and after the Arab Spring, for their company and curiosity; to the crew and staff of the dahabiya *Afandina*, for their friendly and attentive service; to Medhat Saad, doyen of guides and irrepressible commentator on Egyptian politics, ancient and modern; to Dr. Ben Outhwaite, Head of the Genizah Research Unit, Cambridge University Library, for information about the Cairo genizah collection; to my agent and editors, for their invaluable support and expert judgement; to Michael Bailey, as always; and, last but by no means least, to the people of Egypt, for their exceptional hospitality, their good humour in the face of adversity and their resilience. May their hopes and dreams for a better future be fulfilled.

Index

A NOTE ON THE TYPE

This book was set in Adobe Garamond. Designed for the Adobe
Corporation by Robert Slimbach, the fonts are based on types first
cut by Claude Garamond (c. 1480–1561). Garamond was a pupil of
Geoffroy Tory and is believed to have followed the Venetian mod-
els, although he introduced a number of important differences,
and it is to him that we owe the letter we now know as "old style."
He gave to his letters a certain elegance and feeling of movement
that won their creator an immediate reputation and the patronage
of Francis I of France.

Composed by North Market Street Graphics,
Lancaster, Pennsylvania

Printed and bound by Berryville Graphics,
Berryville, Virginia

Designed by Cassandra J. Pappas